S0-ADE-985

DATE DUE

WITHDRAWN

Columbia College Library
600 South Michigan
Chicago IL 60605

WITHDRAWN

NORTHERN INDIA

WHITE STAR PUBLISHERS

NORTHERN INDIA

Text by
Marilia Albanese

Editorial coordination
Valeria Manferto
De Fabianis
Laura Accomazzo

Graphic design
Clara Zanotti

Translation
C.T.M., Milan

The publisher would like to thank the following people and institutions for their kind cooperation in the realization of this book: Consul General of the Consulate of India in Milan, Mr. Om Prakash; Archaeological Survey of India, Dehli; Mistral Tour of Turin; Giorgio Boccalari.

CONTENTS

1 left Khajuraho is the paradise of the beautiful surasundari, heavenly nymphs and initiates in erotic cults who are sent to tempt ascetics. The site has many temples designed in nagara architecture, typical of northern India.

1 right Detail of a relief of Stupa 2 at Sanchi, Madhya Pradesh.

2-3 India has been the source of many religious and philosophic visions: one of the most recent is the monotheist and aniconic Sikh religion that has the Golden Temple at Amritsar as its holiest site.

4 top Painting is used to express the extensive Indian mythology with certain themes being particularly popular. This is the case with the cycle based on Krishna, the heroic and erotic god whose incarnation is colored dark blue. This image comes from the Raj Mahal, Orchha.

© 2004 White Star S.p.A.
Via Candido Sassone, 22/24
13100 Vercelli, Italy
www.whitestar.it

All rights reserved. No part of this publication may be reproduced, stored in a retrieval system or transmitted in any form or by any means, electronic, mechanical, photocopying, recording or otherwise, without written permission from the publisher. White Star Publishers® is a registered trademark property of White Star S.p.A.

ISBN: 978-88-544-0041-2

REPRINTS:
2 3 4 5 6   11 10 09 08 07

Color separation: Fotomec, Turin

Printed in Indonesia

CHINA

PAKISTAN

NEPAL

BANGLADESH

Arabian Sea

Bay
of Bengal

SRINAGAR
MARTAND

AMRITSAR

DELHI
BIKANER
FATEHPUR
SIKRI
MATHURA
JAISALMER
AGRA
JODHPUR
JAIPUR
LUCKNOW
GUALIOR
JAUNPUR
PATNA
PANDUA
RANAKPUR
DATIA
Ganges
GAUR
BUNDI
ORCHHA
BENARES
Ganges
Mount Abu
DEOGARH
SASARAM
BODHGAYA
UDAIPUR
CHITTORGARH
KHAJURAHO
MODHERA
UDAIPUR
AHMEDABAD
SANCHI
BISHNUPUR
Mount
Girnar
DHAR
CALCUTTA
JUNAGARH
DABHOI
MANDU
Narbada
PALITANA
Mahanadi
Gir Forest
RATNAGIRI
AJANTA
NASIK
ELLORA
BHUBANESHVARA
AURANGABAD
KONARAK
DAULATABAD
PURI
KANHERI
BOMBAY
Godavari
ELEPHANTA
KARLA
BHAJA
BEDSA

HYDERABAD

GOA

MANGALORE
MADRAS

BANGALORE

COCHIN

MADURAI

N

TRIVANDRUM

A

PREFACE

B

Indian art is a metaphor of the sacred. The task of the artist is to evoke a vision of the Divine following expressive and codified rules that have been used for a thousand years.

The Indian temple is a complex convergence of mathematical, geometrical and astronomic calculations. It represents the supreme synthesis of various artistic disciplines – architecture, sculpture, painting and dance – each making their own contribution to the expression of the ultimate Truth.

The precise and evocative symbolism underlying Indian architecture aims at the transfiguration of matter and aspires to unification with the Divine. The purpose of the construction ritual is for the architect-priest to rearrange the polarities of everyday life in order to achieve the holy Unity that pervades every phenomenon.

Although sacred constructions are also for the benefit of the less spiritual (for whom simpler, immediate and exterior forms of communication are provided), "he who knows" can read the ineffable essence of the eternal Principle in the forms of the stone and journey with the artist on his path of ascesis as he passes through the labyrinthine depths of the psyche in order to elevate himself to the heavenly dimension of the spirit. From the multiple to the One, from the periphery to the center, from the exoteric to the esoteric, the Indian temple is the map of the meeting between man and God.

A composite and complex universe, India expresses its artistic wealth in an incredible number of monuments; in an attempt to classify them both geographcial and thematic criteria have been used: Buddhist, Jainist, Hindu, Indo-Moslem and colonial art.

This guide has a two-fold purpose: first, to provide ready reference to India's most important artistic sites in each of the country's major northern states, and second, to offer an opportunity for study of the various cultural settings that produced these architectural works of art.

Following an overview of the main historical events and dynasties of Indian civilization: the Hindu religious world, Buddhist thought, Jain asceticism, erotic rituals, the epic of chivalry of the *Rajput*, the advent of Islam in India and the substance of the Sikh religion.

The chapter dedicated to Haryana concentrates exclusively on Indo-Moslem art and its three pivotal architectural forms: the mosque, the mausoleum and

A - The enigmatic smile of the Hindu gods evokes the concept of maya, an illusory perception of existence that is dual and relative.

B - Marble decoration of the Diwan-i-khas (Hall of Private Audience) of the Red Fort, Agra.

C - The mountain simbolizes the spiritual ascent of man towards the Divine but also his descent into the depths of the Self, paradoxical journeys which ultimately converge. Shatrunjaya is one of the mountains holy to the Jainists.

C

connected with each area described, the first chapter introduces the reader to the symbolism of the Hindu temple. It makes suggestions for a more esoteric understanding of the temple's structural elements as well as providing a technical description. The following seven chapters deal with the largest northern states: Madhya Pradesh, Orissa, Gujarat, Bengal, Ladakh, Haryana and Rajasthan. With additional information being provided in boxes, the most impressive sites in each of these states have been linked to the salient events in the history

the fort. The last chapter concludes the discourse on Indo-Moslem art with a selection of sites classified by location, mentioning again those already described in Madhya Pradesh, Gujarat and Bengal, and adding others in Uttar Pradesh and Kashmir. Maps, plans, reconstructions of the sites and diagrams illustrate the text while the bibliography suggests further reading for those who wish to study certain topics in more depth.

The glossary lists original language terms with their original gender (mosque, for example, is *masjid*

[masculine]). A simplified transliteration has been used for Urdu and Persian terms while for Sanskrit, which requires an official transcription with diacritic signs, a less complex system has been adopted to facilitate reading: for example, "c" in *Devanagari*, the Sanskrit alphabet, is always pronounced and has been rendered as "ch" as in "church"; the palatal and lingual "s" has been transcribed as "sh" as in "sheep"; the vocalic "r" becomes "ri" as in ring and the letter "g" is always hard, as in "game".

CHRONOLOGICAL TABLE

SATAVAHANA

MAURYAN EMPIRE
UNDER ASHOKA

KUSHANA EMPIRE
UNDER KANISHKA

✦ **3000 BC:** peoples originally from Baluchistan and Iran settle in the Afghan-Baluchistan regions.

✦ **2500-2000 BC:** the apogee of the flowering and expansion of the Indus valley civilization in Sind, the Punjab and Gujarat.

✦ **1500-1000 BC:** immigration of Aryan tribes, whose origin is still unknown, in the north-west and central north of India.

✦ **1000-600 BC:** the Aryans settled throughout northern India as far as the Bay of Bengal.

✦ **6th century BC:** Mahariva, founder of Jainism, and Buddha were born although the dates are debated

✦ **5th-4th century BC:** disputes over commercial control of the Ganges were fought between kingdoms under the dominion of absolute monarchs and confederations controlled by aristocratic oligarchies (the best known is Shakya with its capital

Kapilavastu on the Nepalese border, the birthplace of Buddha). The kingdoms were victorious with Kosala and Magadha predominant. Kosala annexed the ancient kingdom of Kashi, better known today as the holy city of Benares. Magadha, which was later to become the cradle of various pan-Indian empires, became a major power during the Sishunaga dynasty and in particular under king Ajatashatru who built the city of Pataliputra (the future Patna) on the river Son. The Sishunaga dynasty ended in 425 when it was supplanted by the low caste Nanda dynasty, in tun overthrown by Chandragupta, the founder of the Mauryan empire, in about 322.

✦ **327 BC:** expedition of Alexander the Great to the Punjab and Sind, satrapy of the Persian empire: Alexander descended via the passes of the Hindu Kush and the valley of

Kabul and reached Taxila in 326. Here he won a battle against Porus on the river Chenab, then pushed on to Bias where he was forced to turn back when his army refused to go further.

✦ **320 BC:** foundation of the Mauryan empire by Chandragupta Maurya who married a daughter of Nicator, the Seleucid king of Babylon, from whose ambassador, Megastenes, we have learned much about Pataliputra. The empire stretched from the Indus to Bengal and from the Himalayas to the Vindhya mountains. The empire was extended under Chandragupta's successor, Bindusara, when Deccan was conquered.

✦ **264-226 BC:** the kingdom of Ashoka and propagation of Buddhism; much information has reached us from Buddhist sources and the edicts proclaimed by Ashoka himself, cut in stone and translated into the different languages of the empire.

✦ **185 BC:** end of the Mauryan empire and a new dynasty, the Hindu Shunga, that moved the capital to Vidisha. After a 112 year reign over Magadha and the surrounding areas, Vasudeva, a minister of the Shunga rulers, founded the dynasty of Kanva which lasted 45 years until destroyed by the southern kingdom of Andhra.

✦ **183-130 BC:** expedition of Demetrius, the Indo-Greek king of Bactria, Sogdiana, Parthia and Baluchistan in the north-west and central northern areas of India. He left his brother Apollodotus as viceroy in the Indus valley and Menander as governor of the Punjab. Demetrius reigned until 130 BC at Sakala, a splendid and prosperous Indo-Greek city mentioned in Buddhist chronicles. The Greeks, with their high quality coinage, gave

rise to Indian monetization and their art made a notable contribution to the formation of the Gandhara school.

✦ **140 BC:** invasions by nomads from central Asia; first came the Pallava or Parthians followed by the Shaka or Scythians. They descended into India occupying the Punjab, Sind, Gujarat and western Deccan.

✦ **78-226 AD:** the Kushan people of Turkish-Mongol lineage arrived from Afghanistan. Kanishka was the greatest of the leaders and is variously dated from 78 to 225 AD. He moved the capital to Purushapura (now Peshawar in Pakistan) so that the center of gravity of the Kushan empire was moved towards India. Maximum splendor was enjoyed over a period of 98 years.

✦ **320 AD:** an obscure character named Gupta founded a dynasty of the same name in Magadha and, with his nephew, Chandragupta I, the Gupta era began in 320. His successor, Samudragupta, (335-375) attacked the kingdom of the Naga to the north-west and also pushed south but was stopped at the river Krishna by a coalition led by the Pallava kings. Chandragupta II Vikramaditya (375-415) married the daughter of the king of the Vakatakas of Deccan so extending his empire from Bengal to the Indus and from the forts of Nepal to the river Narmada. His son Kumaragupta I (415-455) consolidated the power of the empire and confronted the first wave of Huns. The danger from these invaders was momentarily quelled under Skandagupta (455-470) but his empire was exhausted.

✦ **497 AD:** the Gupta empire came to an end

under Budhagupta.

✦ **500-528 AD:** the Huns streamed over the north-west of India. Toromana and his son Mihirakula grabbed huge areas of land and destroyed the Buddhist culture. They were finally defeated by a coalition led by Yashodharman, the heir of the Gupta dynasty, in 528.

✦ **606-647 AD:** Harsha created an empire, with capital Kanauj, which stretched from Thaneswar in the Punjab as far as Bengal.

✦ **700-1100 AD:** local dynasties precariously balanced against one another.

✦ **1192 AD:** first Moslem arrivals and defeat of Indian coalition led by King Prithviraj III of the Chauhan dynasty which had dominated Rajputana (today Rajasthan) as far as Delhi from the 10-12th centuries.

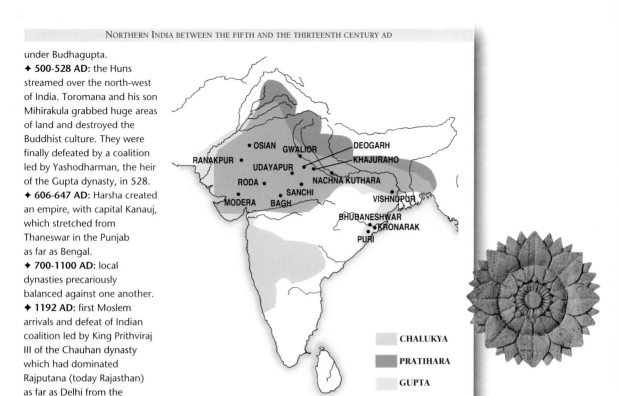

CHALUKYA

PRATIHARA

GUPTA

✦ **12th-15th century:** period of the Muslim sultanates and regional Hindu kingdoms.

✦ **15th-18th century:** Mogul empire.

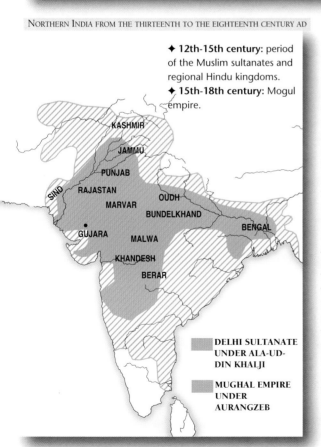

DELHI SULTANATE UNDER ALA-UD-DIN KHALJI

MUGHAL EMPIRE UNDER AURANGZEB

THE PRINCIPAL DYNASTIES OF NORTHERN INDIA AND THEIR MONUMENTS UP UNTIL THE ARRIVAL OF THE MOSLEMS

MAURYA: 320-185 BC
SHUNGA: 185-72 BC
CHEDI: 180-100 BC (caves of Khandagiri and Udayagiri)
SATAVAHANA OR ANDHRA: 220 BC-250 AD (portals at Sanchi)
INDO-GREEK: 182 BC-200 AD
KUSHANA: 78-200 AD (art of the Gandhara and Mathura)
ISHVAKU: 175-250
GUPTA: 320-497 (temples at Nachna Kuthara, Bhumara, Ahicchatra, Bhitargaon, Sirpur and Deogarh and Temple 17 at Sanchi)
WESTERN GANGA: 450-985
MAITRAKA: 475-766 (temples at Roda)
VARDHANA: 500-648 (temples at Gwalior fort)
KARKOTA: 600-850 (temple at Martand)
EASTERN GANGA: 750-1250 (temples at Bhubaneswar, Konarak)
PALA: 770-1175 (universities of Nalanda and Vikramashila)
SENA: 1175-1205
RASHTRAKUTA: 757-973 (Kailasanatha temple at Ellora)
GURJARA-PRATIHARA: 740-1036 (Osian, Jagat, Abaneri, Teli ka Mandir temples at Gwalior)
NOLAMBA: 800-1150
UTPALA: 855-939
CHEDI: 895-1150 (temples at Chandrehi, Sohagpur and Gurgi)
CHALUKYA OR SOLANKI: 941-1197 (temples at Modhera, Mount Abu, Mount Girnar, Dabhoi)
PARAMARA: 949-1088 (Udayeswar temple at Udaipur)
CHANDELLA: 950-1203 (temples at Khajuraho)
GAHADAVALA: 1080-1184
KACHHAVAHA: 10th century (Gwalior)
KACHHAPAGATHA: 11th century (Sas Bahu temple at Gwalior)
TOMARA: foundation of Delhi in 736 (Man Mandir at Gwalior)
CHAHAUN: 12th century-1192

THE INDUS VALLEY CIVILIZATION

A - The temple is seen as a manifestation of the god in stone, a representation of the universe and also a demonstration of the religious commitment of the temple patron and architect. It is therefore a representation of the sacred. This sculpture is to be found in the temple of Konarak, Orissa.

B - This wheel is one of the main elements of the so-called Surya's Carriage, in the Sun Temple of Konarak, Orissa.

C - Every aspect of existence must be shown on the walls of the temple. The natural world is displayed winding around volutes and the holiness of the tree, the symbol of life, is heavily emphasized. This relief comes from the Temple of Surya, Konarak, Orissa.

The principal aim of traditional art is to give form to the religious vision while at the same time aspiring to transcend that form. Architecture is a sacred form of expression, an allusion to the divine activity which freely delimits itself in time and space to reveal the universe. It is through this delimitation that existence comes into being: for this reason, the artistic creativity implies discipline and sacrifice, the only virtues able to liberate art from the will of the ego and make of it the deepest expression of the Self. A work of art is less the realization of the

the expression of the metaphysical contents of the Hindu culture: the Indian temple is a *darshana* (a sacred vision) in which every tiny detail represents a part of the Divine and must therefore follow precise religious and symbolic dictates. The nearby presence of water is fundamental, better still if in front of or to the left of the building. Before starting construction, the land must be ploughed by twelve bulls pulling twelve ploughs; this act has a cosmic nature alluding to the path of the sun through the twelve signs of the zodiac. Once the land has been seeded and the crops are ripe,

THE ALTAR OF FIRE

India's most ancient archaeological sites are situated along the course of the river Indus and show the existence of an advanced civilization that, because of its position, the archaeologists named "the Indus Valley civilization." Already established before 2800 BC, the Indus valley civilization reached its apogee around 2500 BC with the large twin cities of Mohenjo-Daro and Harappa, now in Pakistan, and of Kalibangan and Lothal in Gujarat. Around 2000-1900 BC, the civilization began to decline due to natural

C

genius of a single artist than the embodiment of a burst of song from a divine choir filtered through the individual sensibility.

Spiritual preparation is thus essential prior ro creation. Such preparation includes ascetic practices, the study of holy texts, meditation and interiorization and visualization of the truth to be transmitted. In nearly all cases, the architect is a Brahman, a member of the highest caste in Hindu society, the caste of priests responsible for the passing on of knowledge. The function of the artist is imbued with a certain holiness as it invites the divinity to "incarnate" itself in the stone. The temple is therefore an *avatar* (descent to earth) and tangible apparition of the sacred, evoked by the faith of the patrons and by the esoteric knowledge of the executors. All architectural operations aim at the transfiguration of the profane – the materials used and the process of construction – into the sacred, in which the temple built according to the rules becomes the mystical cosmic body of the Divine.

Architecture is, therefore, essentially

cows and calves are allowed to graze there so that they can purify the soil with their auspicious presence. As a symbol of provident and benevolent nature, the cow is particularly holy and its five products – milk, butter, *ghee* (clarified butter), urine and dung – are basic elements in ritual and everyday life: milk and butter in offerings, dried dung as fuel and urine to disinfect and exorcise the environment.

Complicated mathematical divisions centered more on the remainders in the calculations than the answers govern the dimensions of the construction and ensure its positiveness. It is the remainder that produces existence: if nothing remains, nothing can be produced. When the universe has ended its cycle and, suspended in an inert cosmic night, it waits to create itself once more, it is not by chance that the god Vishnu, the providential face of the Divine and Lord of the preservation of life, sleeps on the primordial serpent named Sesha (Remainder), symbol of the vital energy of nature left over from the previous cycle waiting to be activated in a new dawn of being.

and climatic causes and to internal socio-economic processes, although the arrival of the Aryans hastened its end. The provenance of this nomadic tribe is controversial and still under debate. They settled over a period of centuries but left too few articles in their wake to allow us to reconstruct their development with certainty. They seemed to flow into India from around 1800 BC (although many doubts surround that date) until the 3rd century AD but no significant traces of their places of worship have been found. On the other hand, this is perhaps not surprising given that they were a nomadic tribe. What is known about the Aryans has been discovered from literature: the four "Veda," texts centering on the sacrificial liturgy, form the basis of the social, philosophic, and religious development of India. The *vastuvidya* (science of architecture) is also dealt with in the "Shulvasutra," part of the works of the "Vedanga," six supplements to the "Veda." The "Shulvasutra" were probably written between 500 and 200 BC. They state the measurements to be carried out in the construction of the Altar of Fire, fulcrum of the ritual prescribed by the "Veda," and contain wide knowledge of geometry.

The altar is the most ancient element of

sacred Hindu architecture and its symbolism inspires the construction of the temple. According to the Vedic conception, the existence of the cosmos is ensured by the interaction of innumerable forces and man is able to catalyze the positive energy or exorcise the negative energy by means of ritual. This consisted of the sacrifice of animals in the past but in the presentation

A

A - The worship of trees dates back to antiquity and evidence has been found of it in the earliest of archaeological finds. Buddha's enlightenment occurred under a tree, here celebrated in an ornamental motif from Sanchi.

B - The Great Goddess is the oldest Indian deity and was worshipped by the Indus valley civilization in the 3rd millennium BC. She is the Lady of life and death and is represented by Shakti, the kinetic energy of the Divine. This image comes from temple of Deogarh.

C - The universe reappears cyclically thanks to the "remainder" of the karma of its creatures. The serpent on which Vishnu, Lord of Providence, sleeps is called Shesha (Remainder). This image is from the temple of Deogarh.

D - The oldest temples still standing were built in brick and decorated in terracotta, like this one at Deogarh. The lunette shows how skilled the artists were in placing figures in small spaces.

E - The Indus valley civilization inspired the idea of the vahanas (animal mounts of the classical gods). In the 5th century temple of Deogarh, Vishnu comes down from heaven on Garuda, the man-vulture.

C

B

of offerings in temples in more recent times.

Once the ritual area has been bounded by a plough or a palisade, the pole to which the sacrificial animals are tied is raised. The pole symbolizes the center of the cosmos, the *axis mundi* around which the universes are harmoniously structured: it is therefore a representation of the presence of the Divine in the sense of order of the Whole. Symbolising the connection between earth and heaven, it is fitted with rungs and climbed by the officiant and patron in a ritual allusion to the passage from the profane to the sacred, made possible by understanding and the exact execution of the rite. The memory of this initiatory rite, that has today lost its meaning, lives on in the folklore of the climbing of the greasy pole in which the prizes to be claimed by those competitors successfully reaching the top hark back to the spiritual treasure of understanding that liberates and saves.

The sacrificial stake is also linked to the symbolism of the tree that is so important in Indian culture. The tree is a symbol of life and fertility and, rooted in the ground and stretching up to heaven, it indicates the spiritual path to be followed. Sacred events, such as divine apparition or attainment of a transcendental state, often take place

beneath its foliage. Since the most ancient of times, India has believed trees to be the homes of guardian spirits, the *yakshas*, and their companions, the *yakshinis*, and it is no coincidence that Buddha received enlightenment at the foot of a *pipal* tree. At the back of the temple area, the sacrificial pole has survived as an isolated column overlooking the entrance to the sanctuary and is now used to fly the temple banner. Around the pole there will be one or more altars of different shape and used for different purposes: the circular *garhaputya* is positioned to the west and connected to the physical world; the square *ahavaniya* is situated to the east and refers to the blue orb of the sky; the half-moon *dakshinagni* faces south and is associated with the atmosphere between earth and heaven.

The shape of the circle evokes the undivided unity of the First Principle and its projection as an active, fecundating Heaven; it is favored by nomads as it refers to the ceaseless movement at the base of existence. The blue vaults of the sky are boundless so that the center is only symbolic and may be positioned any and everywhere: the *templum* is simply a bounded area chosen for "contemplation" of the heavens. When a nomadic tribe settles, the circle becomes a symbol of the future which, at the macrocosmic level, finds its place in the continuous cycle of conservation and destruction of the universe while, at a microcosmic level, it represents the *samsara*, the rebirth of man in the ceaseless flow of existence in accordance with the law of *karma*. This "act" is understood to be cause and effect of all actions: in the universe, as the sum of all actions of all living beings, *karma*, determines the development of phenomena; in man, representing all actions, *karma* imprisons the soul in the circle of births and deaths where present existence, nourished by desire and ignorance, is conditioned by past lives and itself conditions future life. In this context, the circle connotes the link to be broken and the limit to be transcended.

The square is preferred by settled populations. It is connected with the earth and symbolizes eternal Being, universal Law, the divine as opposed to the mundane, the sacred as opposed to the profane. Hindu architecture tends to superimpose shapes and to transform the first into the second process apparently "squaring the circle" as it metamorphoses into the square representing existence governed by the canons of the First Principle.

Construction of the Altar of Fire – and later the temple – aimed at restoration of the perfection preceding the manifestation of the world and the reconstruction of the One from the multiplicity of fragments to which it was reduced. This architectural liturgy is inspired by the Rigveda, the most important of the four "Veda," and in

D

E

particular by the myth of the sacrifice of the *Purusha*, the giant paradigm of man used by the gods as a sacrificial victim. The entire universe and the human species organized in castes originate from this giant's partial dismemberment. On a microcosmic level, the liturgy celebrates the divine macrocosmic rite of the passage from the One to the multiple but it is in this event that the root of cosmic pain and individual suffering lies. The apparition of the world flows from polarity and opposition so that existence is a conflict between life and death while man experiences separation from the Principle, from God, as privation and alienation.

It is for this reason that sacrifice and the construction of the holy site are concluded with the reconstitution of the ineffable Unity that incorporates and transcends opposites and that brings the soul back to its Lord. In the construction of the Altar of Fire from the outside inwards, the assembling of a ritual number of bricks in accordance with a codified procedure evokes the recomposition. The empty space left at the center of the altar, called the *umbilicus*, is the symbol of emptiness and the inscrutable Absolute.

The solid returns to the void and

emerges again: emanation and absorption repeats incessantly. This is how, along with the resolution of the multiplicity into the One, construction also evokes the imposition of divine order on the amorphous, chaotic mass of primordial matter. According to myth when some indefinable forces obstructed the universe the gods hurled themselves down upon it, immobilising the universe, each blocking a portion. The disordered fluctuation of primitive chaos was stabilized as the ordered cosmos thanks to the intervention of the luminous and divine beings, the *devas*, which gave form to existence.

The emblem of disorder and the devilish appearance of matter is an *asura*, a demon represented as a human figure, its face squashed in the *vastupurushamandala*, the square grill making up the plan of the temple. The *asura*, subdued by the *sthapati*, the priest-architect leading the workers, is renamed the *vastupurusha*, the "giant of existence," the archetype of the construction. Again, the physical act of building has transformation as its aim: in a symbolic "rotation," the demon with the squashed face – symbol of passivity but also the power of plasticity and thus shape – becomes the *Purusha*, the perfect man, his face turned toward the sky: the divine essence that pervades matter infuses it with sacred shape.

The *Purusha* pervades the *vastupurushamandala* like a vital essence; the *prana*, or "breath" that animates the macro and microcosm, runs through vital points of the temple plan. These "nerve centers" are called *marmans*, vital but vulnerable points that must not be obstructed by being incorporated in walls, pillars or doorways. If that were the case, potentially lethal falls in energy levels of the bodies of builder and patron would take place. The analogy between the temple, a mystical body composed of five cosmic elements, and the psycho-physical human body is very strong. The square plinth connected to the earth refers to the body between the feet and the knees; the walls, connected with the water element, evoke the portion between the knees and the loins; the covering of the inner sanctum, correlated to fire and the triangle, the part between the loins and heart; the *kalasha*, the vase of water that completes the inner sanctum, alludes to the element air and the body between the heart and the eye sockets; the pinnacle, symbol of ether and space, equates to the area of the eyebrows and the top of the head. The temple is the body of God and his worshippers.

13

THE TRACING OF THE TEMPLE GROUND PLAN

The process of transmutation and consecration is particularly evident in the tracing of the ground plan of the temple. A pole is erected at the center of the chosen site making an ideal axis around which the building is constructed, almost as though it were a spiral turned to stone, the symbol of expansion and ascent. A double length cord is tied to the stake and used like a pair of compasses to trace a circle. At particular moments of the sun's passage, the

A

shadow of the pole will mark the cardinal points east and west on the circumference; the two points are joined by a straight line, then the two cardinal points are in turn used as center points to draw other circles that have as their radius the diameter of the first circle (i.e. the east-west line). The intersections of these two larger circles coincide with the north and south points between which another straight line is drawn to form a cross symbolising the expansion of the First Principle towards the four main directions.

Using the tangent points of the north-south line with the circle as centers for the compass and the distance between the two points as radius, two more circles are drawn. The intersections of the four circles based on the cardinal points mark the four corners of a square. This gives the "squaring" of the circle, an

B

allusion to the passage from the profane to the sacred. The earth is transfigured and consecrated: fixed by the four cardinal points, representing tangents with the sky, it is transformed into the bride of the heavens. Considering the point occupied by the pole and the cross created from it as the initial element, the first type of temple ground plan is created – the *manduka* – based on a module of 4 central squares divided into a grid of 64 squares. If we start from the square superimposed on the first circle and place 8 further squares around it, the second fundamental type of temple ground plan is obtained – the *paramashayin* – based on a module of 9 squares and divided into a grid of 81 squares.

Although both cases symbolize the passage from the concealed to the manifest by means of the passage from the One to the multiple based on the directions of space, the two ground plans represent different levels of understanding and spiritual illumination.

The origin of the *manduka*, based on 4 squares, lies in the *bindu*, the "point." Symbol of the mystery of existence, the point is free of dimensions and therefore invisible but it is, however, what gives dimension to the visible. It therefore contains the infinitely large in the infinitely small; it is the origin of space and creates boundaries by forming lines and other geometric forms; it is also the principle of time which is built on the theory of instants. It is the seed from which the universe-macrocosm flows and the drop of sperm from which the man-microcosm is born; it is the vibration that divided the original nucleus in a sort of "big bang" and the tremor of desire that cracks the unity of the

cosmic Awareness introducing the splitting of subject/object; it is the unification of opposite poles, of male and female, and of the devotee and his God. Because of its adimensional actuality, the *bindu* symbolizes true Being; that is, what cannot be measured by human means or defined by space-time categories. The ground plan based on the point is thus considered ideal for a priestly environment as the Brahmans, holders of spiritual power, occupy the highest level of Hindu society and able to grasp the subtle, esoteric meaning of the symbol in a macrocosmic context.

The ground plan based on the 9 squares – the *paramashayin* – has its origin in the square, a symbol relating to the Absolute in its manifest and therefore "coarser" form. As the square is a balanced shape with symmetrical lines, it evokes condensation, solidity and stability; it refers to the element earth and to human space. This ground plan is more suitable for a warrior environment where temporal power is exercised. A warrior occupies the second hierarchic level in Hindu society and is expected to be capable of understanding the significance of symbols only in their more obvious, microcosmic dimension.

The two ground plans form the basis for a further series of grids on which different types of temples are set.

If the ground plan evokes the passage from the One to the multiple, and therefore the manifestation, there will also be the inverse route, i.e. the resolution of the cosmic plurality into the divine Unity. This is symbolized by the recomposition of the polarities: space and time, sun and moon, male and female.

The 4 boxes of the *manduka* ground plan, laid on the cross given by the cardinal points marked by the sun, refer to the temporal dimension but also educes space as a result of which terrestrial space and heavenly time are overlaid and fused in the same symbolic operation. In the other ground plan, the eight squares that surround a central square are connected to the four principal compass directions and to the four intermediate directions in space; however, as these are connected with the course of the sun, the two dimensions of time and space are once again represented united.

If time and space are unified in the temple ground plan, the sun and moon are also subjected to the same process. The frame of twelve squares that surrounds the four central ones of the *manduka* refers to the

A - One of the strongest Hindu symbols is the linga-yoni, *seen here in an inner sanctum at Khajuraho. It is a stylized representation of the male and female sex organs which refers to the cosmic polarities and their union.*

B - *Innumerable mythical beings crowd the temple walls at Konarak temple where two* nagas *(part cobra, part human dispensers of material and spiritual treasures) refer to the subterranean and aquatic worlds.*

C - *The* vastupurushamandala, *the* mandala *(design) of the "giant of existence" on which the temple stands represents a figure crushed to the ground – the* asura *or demon of chaos – conquered by the gods representing order.*

base (indicating that it does not rest on nor arise from any point in space or time in the world of the profane), the *linga* represents the cosmic egg from which the heavens, the earth and all that lives between the two spilled when it was broken. The Center of the earth, it is venerated as an instrument of procreation but also as an emblem of the dominion of the passions, ascetic cipher of essentiality and concentration. In its representation as a source of existence, the *linga* either sits below a container dripping water or is placed in a basin, alluding to the birth of the universe from cosmic waters and the spark that was struck in their womb. Indeed, the *linga* is also a symbol of fire and light. The circular plinth that the *linga* is placed on is the *yoni*, genital symbol of the Goddess inherited from ancient traditions. The *lingayoni* correspond to the couple of Shiva-Shakti, the great God and his female Energy, the static and dynamic, the union of the principles of fire and water. The exterior, abounding in images and detail, evokes *Prakriti* or "Nature" in the various forms of the universe in the unending play of the future, while the interior of the inner sanctum, almost always bare, is related to the *Purusha*, the spiritual Principle, pure Being and Awareness.

D - *As forms of the Absolute, the gods manifest themselves on Earth as avatars (descents in human form) often accompanied by their wives. At Deogarh, the Dashavatara temple (the Ten Descents) celebrates just that.*

E - *Each* pada *(section) of the grid is animated by a divine presence, as shown in the drawing by Stella Kramrish: the area of the inner*

sanctum is dedicated to Brahma, a fundamental aspect of the Divine in the guise of the Lord of the Origin.

twelve houses of the zodiac and therefore to the sun. The final frame of 28 squares is dedicated to the 28 *nakshatra*, the houses of the moon. The 8 squares in the *paramashayin* surrounding the central square are connected not only to the principal directions in space but also to the sun, moon, the 5 planets (Mercury, Venus, Mars, Jupiter and Saturn) and Rahu, the demon of the eclipse with the role of sun in the center. The frame of 16 squares in the next ring is related to the lunar fractions while the 32 squares of the outer ring of the grid include the 28 lunar houses and 4 squares related either to the cardinal (solar) regions or to the solstices and equinoxes; thus, the sun and moon are once more involved.

The union of male and female in certain temples is clearly explained by a particular type of icon found in the inner sanctum: the *linga-yoni*. The *linga*, an aniconic and phallic representation of the god Shiva, has a wide range of symbolic interpretations: it is the visible form of the cosmic axis around which all worlds revolve and, when the stone is clearly rounded at the top and

ROGA	AHI	MUKHYA	BHALLATA	SOMA	BHUJAGA	ADITI	DITI	AGNI
PAPA-YAKSHMAN	RUDRA						APA	PARJANYA
SHOSHA		RAJA YAKSHMAN	PRTH IVIDH	ARA		APA VATSA		JAYANTA
ASURA		M I				A R Y		INDRA
VARUNA		T R	BRAH M	A		A M A		SURYA
KUSUMA-DANTA		A				N		SATYA
SUGRIVA		INDRA	V I V A S V	A N	SAVITR			BHRSHA
DAU-VARIKA	JAYA						SAVITRA	ANTAR-IKSHA
PITARAH	MRGA	BHRNGA-RAJA	GAN-DHARVA	YAMA	BRHAT-KSHATA	VITATHA	PUSHAN	ANILA

THE CAVE AND THE MOUNTAIN

The rules of architecture are contained in a series of texts of which the most important are: "The Compendium of Measurements" from the "Manasara," an anonymous text of the 6th-7th century; "The Architect of the Universe" from the 11th century "Samaraganasutradhara" by Bhojadeva; "The Supreme Law of Vishnu" from the "Vishnudharmottara," an appendix to the 5th-7th century "Garudapurana;" the "Mayamata;" "The Jewel of Architecture" from the "Shilparatna" of uncertain date; various "Vastushastras" and "Shilpashastras" or "Treatises on Architecture." Interpretation of the symbolism of

A - Aesthetic requirements eclipse the need for realism. This is equally true for representation of the male body and particularly the Jains who, if reality were important, would be shown emaciated.

the rules is handed down orally or hidden in esoteric passages.

Many elements contributed to the formation of the temple structure: the mobile wooden tabernacles that held the simulacrum of the divinity which travelled in the retinue of the nomad community may be one of the oldest prototypes. Of the others, the current *rathas*, the processional carriages on which idols are placed during religious festivals, are wooden models of the temple the idols belong to; in many cases the *rathas* appear as real stone constructions. Once a nomadic tribe has settled, construction of the house of god may be inspired by the house of the elders, the focus of village life. In Aihole in Karnataka, the 5th

century temple of Lad Khan is a stone copy of the entrance verandah, the screened windows and the wooden roof beams of a common residence used for meetings of the council of village elders. A sort of spire-cum-niche holding an image of the God is placed on the roof to distinguish the temple from the other buildings and as a sign of its holiness. The oldest surviving evidence is in the form of rock carvings, for example the caves of Udayagiri in Orissa which date back to the 2nd-1st centuries BC. Without doubt, the caves were one of the first places to be used for worship and later inspired the construction of the inner *sanctum* of the temple. Uterus of the mother earth and theater for the appearance of the divine to man, the cave is the womb of

nature as provider where Heaven placed the divine embryo so that it would be cared for and nurtured. The darkness of the cave is reminiscent of the primordial gloom and of the emptiness from which came light and the fullness of the manifest being. In the context of the microcosm and the analogy of the human body, the cave (and therefore the inner *sanctum* of the temple) symbolizes the heart cavity, the place where the Divine abides. The *murti* (formal manifestation) of the divinity is located in the *garbha-griha* (the womb or chamber of the embryo), just as the image of the god resides in the heart of the devotee. The cave is included in the bowels of the mountain, a cosmogonic symbol and place of initiation, ascent and pilgrimage which, in the temple, is represented by the

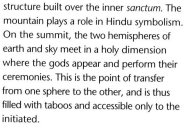

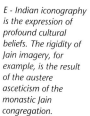

B - Cracks in the rock are enlarged by inserting wooden staves that are then soaked with water. The heavy work is continued using picks and scalpels labors that, however, guarantee spiritual benefits.

C, D - One of the oldest holy places in India is the cave which is considered the womb of the Earth Goddess. Rock architecture was still used reletively recently as seen in this 15th century Gwalior site.

D

E - Indian iconography is the expression of profound cultural beliefs. The rigidity of Jain imagery, for example, is the result of the austere asceticism of the monastic Jain congregation.

structure built over the inner *sanctum*. The mountain plays a role in Hindu symbolism. On the summit, the two hemispheres of earth and sky meet in a holy dimension where the gods appear and perform their ceremonies. This is the point of transfer from one sphere to the other, and is thus filled with taboos and accessible only to the initiated.

Hindu cosmology views the world as a giant *mandala*, a cosmogram depicting divine order. In the center stands Mount Meru, the axis which connects the world to the sphere of the heavens on one hand, and to the sphere of the underworld on the other. Mount Meru (or Sumeru), the "Mountain of the Lotus," the "Peak of the Jewel," is the cornerstone of this mystical geography. It stands in the center of seven

island continents arranged concentrically around it, each surrounded by seven seas; consisting respectively of salt water, the juice of sugar-cane, an alcoholic drink, clarified butter, curdled milk, fresh water and ordinary milk. At the foot of Mount Meru stands the Jambudvipa, the "Continent of the Rose Apple," the land of India, holy because of its direct contact with the divine mountain. Emanating from this axis are the four cardinal points and the four intermediaries which together divide the universe into a series of quadrants, each governed by a deity. The *dikpala* or *lokpala* are the custodians of the eight quadrants: Kubera, the god of riches, governs north; Varuna, lord of the oceans, west; Indra, king of the gods,

east; Yama, lord of the dead, south; Vayu or the host of the Marut are found to the north-west; Soma, god of the moon, or Ishana, "Sovereign, lord" (this is a name of Shiva or Agni) to the north-east; Nirrti, the black goddess of destruction, or Surya, god of the Sun, to the south-west; and Agni, god of fire, to the south-east. To these gods are also added Brahma, regent of the zenith, and the serpent Ananta, Vishnu's pallet, or Vishnu himself, regent of the nadir. Each custodian god is seated on the back of a male elephant. The heavens of the eight *lokpala* are located on the slopes and summit of Mount Meru. The Vaikuntha of Vishnu is the golden and bejewelled citadel of Brahma situated on the highest peak. The heavenly river Ganges flows around the citadel and divides into four terrestrial water-courses

E

that descend the mountain towards the four cardinal points. In the profane world of the multiple, the terrestrial mountain recounts the genesis of the manifestation. The potentialities of the Divine are realized on its slopes, the multiple states of existence made manifest in pyramidal succession, from the finest to the coarsest. This reflects the triangle in which the sides, representing the polarities generating multiplicity, emanate from the tip, representing the One. Multiplicity is implicit in the power of the One: it emanates from and returns to the One, as shown in the base of the triangle linking the sides and taking them back to the tip.

THE NAGARA TEMPLE AND ITS STRUCTURES

For the sake of convenience, it is usual to classify Hindu architecture according to geographical criteria but also by the type of covering built over the inner sanctum. Geographical division gives the *nagara* style which was generally developed in the north, the *dravida* style that developed in the south, and the *vesara* style from the center of the country, a fusion of the other two. The second type of categorization gives temples with three types of covering, the curvilinear, the pyramidal or prismatic, and the cylindrical or barrel vault. Indian texts refer to square and rectangular coverings for the *nagara* style, hexagonal and octagonal coverings for the *dravida* style, and circular, oval and apsidal coverings for the *vesara* style. However, these divisions do not do justice to the great variety of styles that characterize Hindu architecture.

Nothing remains of the first timber constructions but the use of wood influenced later styles of carved stone, clearly derived from carpentry techniques.

One of the oldest temples is Stupa 17 in Sanchi near Bhopal in the region of Madhya Pradesh. This temple was built in the 4th or 5th centuries during the era of the Gupta dynasty. The temple has an inner sanctum with a flat covering preceded by a porch with decorated columns over a stepped plinth. This typology was developed during the late Gupta period (5th-6th centuries) in which smaller temples were built in brick joined by pegs and given flat roofs made with stones with overhanging edges. The temples of Ahicchatra and Bhitargaon in Uttar Pradesh, Shiva in Bhumara, Parvati in Nachna Kuthara and Sirpur in Madhya Pradesh are significant examples.

It is however with the Vishnuite temple of the 5th century Dashavatara, at Deogarh in the province of Jhansi in Uttar Pradesh, that the first attempt at a pyramidal covering, the *shikhara*, is seen.

A - Indian artists tend to emphasize a fundamental characteristic of an animal: with the lion, it's muscular tension before it pounces.

B - Decorations showing elephants are shown at the base of a temple, almost as if wanting to suggest that they support and provide stability for the construction.

A

The temple is a cubic structure built on a plinth with axial steps. It has three false doors decorated with splendid terracotta panels and the entrance is adorned with an elaborate frame.

During the 7th-8th centuries, this covering grew in height. The temple complexes at Bhubaneswar in Orissa (8th-13th centuries) and Khajuraho in Madhya Pradesh (10th-13th centuries) are the

B

perfect examples of the *nagara* style.

The noblest material for building a temple, and the one that bestows the greatest spiritual merit on the patron, is stone. The stone is extracted from quarries by boring holes and inserting wooden wedges; the wedges are soaked in water which then expand and crack the rock. This technique is still used to increase the size of caves and to create the shape and dimension of environment required. Construction of a temple is often based on the assembly of prepared pieces which are joined together with locking pins so that the use of mortar is avoided. Preferred design features were the architrave and the 'false' arch in which the stone or ashlar overhang at every layer of bricks in order to provide support for the one above. To give the effect of a vault, the architect used a series of smaller overhanging cornices and closed the remaining space at the end with slabs. Although the Moslems brought the technique of the pointed arch to India in the 13th century, the Hindus continued to use the 'false' arch and the vault with successive overhangs.

The basic structures of the *nagara* temple are:
• The *adhisthana*, the plinth, a tall platform with one or more flights of steps leading up it.
• The *ardhamandapa*, a hypostyle entrance porch.
• The *mandapa*, a hypostyle room with pyramidal covering.
• The *antarala*, a hall, the space that joins the *mandapa* to the inner sanctum.
• The *garbha-griha*, the square inner sanctum that houses the *murti* of the divinity: this stands on the *pitha*, the pedestal which is placed on the spot where a jar is buried containing symbolic objects, for example nine jewels which refer to the planets. The jar symbolizes the fertile womb of *Prakriti*, Nature, and the pedestal used for the *murti* refers to Mount Meru.
• The *shikhara*, the ogival structure that stands over the inner sanctum, is perhaps influenced by the ancient Vedic altar covering made from bamboo

C - The monstrous serpent of the waters of ancestral memory appears in a fight with a hero in the ornamental motif of Stupa 3 at Sanchi.

pointed at the top; it is achieved by cutting successive horizontal moldings to create a dome effect. The *shikhara* evokes Mount Meru as well as the idea of a sacrificial flame rising towards heaven.

To smooth the angles of the *shikhara* and to counterbalance the horizontal dimension of the moldings, the corners are accented with *angashikharas* or *urushringas*, miniature repetitions of the *shikhara* that have the precise function of emphasizing the ogive and accentuating the vertical dimension. Consequently, the horizontal plane, which alludes to the various existential planes and forms, and the vertical plane, which evokes the essential ontological unity enclosing manifestation, are harmonized in a single, compact upward movement. The convergence of

centrifugal and centripetal forces exercises strong tension on the surrounding space and transforms the building into a spiral of cosmic and divine energy.

The series of curved lines and succession of planes of the *shikhara* are joined and compose the *pattika*, the drum that connects the *shikhara* to the *amalaka*, the *amalaka*, a sort of segmented, cushion-like element copied from the fruit of the gooseberry bush. On the *amalaka*, we find the *kalasha* or *kumbha*, a vase-shaped element, also placed on the roof of the *mandapa*, which contains water used for consecration of the temple; the symbolism attaches to the primigenial fluid of chaos and to the cosmic waters, the womb of life and to which life

eventually returns. Like rivers such as the Ganges, they hold the ashes of the dead. The symbol of divinity kept in the inner sanctum or the temple flag nearly always stands over the *kumbha*.

The indentations in the walls suggests to the spectator performing the *pradakshina*, the sacred circling of the temple, that the temple is actually breathing in its expansions and contractions. This is the reproduction of the *spanda*, the primordial vibration of the One that determines the emanation and expansion of the universe, its synchronized, ceaseless and mysterious division and recomposition.

The *alamkara* (decoration) of the temple, is an integral part of its design, not just an additional feature. Its purpose is to

attract the attention of the devotee with its beauty and to convey its underlying symbolism to the spiritually mature.

The decoration is arranged in accordance with precise criteria: *makara* (aquatic monsters, grotesque animals and elephants) are often shown along the plinth of the temple whose function it is to support the building; gods and mythical beings are depicted on the walls of the *mandapa* and the inner sanctum framed by plants swollen with the sap of life; anthropomorphic representations are rare on the sides of the *shikhara* and in general there are only *vyalas* (gryphons) or similar mythical creatures supporting the *amalaka* and looking out towards the four cardinal points. The prevalence of geometric decorations on the covering of

A

B

A - Gods and demons respectively represent positive and negative tensions: their struggle has the purpose of restoring the balance of forces. Here Durga is killing the buffalo demon in the temple of Rishabdeo.

B - The humped bull is a symbol of the generating forces of nature. It was turned into Nandi, the vahana of Shiva who is among other things a yogin master and therefore an ascetic able to dominate all natural impulses.

C

the inner sanctum relates to the world of ethereal forms.

The Hindu architect does not face the problem of having to match the building to the natural environment as nature is included in the design of the temple: it pulses in the animal forms and tangle of tropical plants, leaves and flowers.

Another important feature is the white plasterwork used to cover statues and decorative elements whose features are then usually painted. White is the symbol of purification and spiritualization and the color associated with *sattva*, one of the three *gunas* or "qualities" that makes up the *Prakriti*, the eternal primordial substance. *Sattva* is the creator of what is stable, pure, luminous and joyous; *rajas* causes what is dynamic, passionate or sad; *tamas* is the root of what is inert, slow or dim. Their supremacy also determines the castes: the Brahmans are dominated by *sattva*, the warriors by *rajas* and the other two castes – traders and servants – by *tamas*.

The colors associated with the *gunas* are, respectively, white, red and black. The temple is, therefore, the divine made tangible on earth and a passage from the One to the multiple. The *bindu*, the point on the pinnacle over the *kumbha*, symbolizes the seed of existence that contains all the pluralities of the manifestation. This evolves from slender forms represented by the *shikhara* with geometric, abstract decorations to larger shapes depicted on the walls of the *mandapa* and inner sanctum in which the *bindu* is manifested

D

E

C - There is a symbolic aspect to every Indian decoration: the lion is the emblem of courage and refers to warriors and rulers. It is also the preferred vahana of the warrior goddess. The image comes from Bhubaneswar temple.

D - The similarity of the color of the elephant (this one is at Sanchi) to the color of monsoon clouds means the elephant is considered a beneficent bringer of rain. The elephant is also the vahana of Indra, the ancient king of the gods, and therefore the earthly mount of the king.

E - The heraldic symmetry of two riders on lions stands out in the kalpavalli, the plant that grants wishes and which winds around the jambs of the gateways at Sanchi.

in the divine image, the *murti*.

The symbolism of the temple architecture can be read either from top to plinth or vice versa: the descent of the deity and genesis of the universe or, alternatively, the ascent of man and dissolution of the cosmos. The temple includes forms from the basest to the most sublime, the One and the multiple, the immanent and the transcendent: all originates with *bindu* and all returns there.

Besides vertical interpretation, there is also the horizontal; this view contrasts the external walls covered with statues and ornaments with the bareness of the inner sanctum. Once removed from the plane of phenomena with its kaleidoscopic and distracting images, the attention moves to within one's own being, to the silence of one's own heart for contemplation of the One as directed by the *murti* in the bare and dark inner sanctum. The outside of the temple is the form, the inside is the essence; the cell is the body and the *murti* is the spirit.

This contrast between what is external, illuminated, multiform and temporal with what is internal, dark, unitary and atemporal is the cipher that represents the path to which the mystical fruition of the Hindu temple leads.

21

SANCHI

MADHYA PRADESH, HEART OF INDIA

MAP OF SANCHI
THE SANCHI SITE
CONTAINS OVER FIFTY
MONUMENTS AS
NUMBERED BY
MARSHALL. MOST OF
THEM STAND AT THE
TOP OF THE HILL.

A STUPA 1 OR "GREAT STUPA"
B STUPA
C STUPA 3 OR "LITTLE STUPA"
D TEMPLES
E MONASTERIES
F TEMPLE 45
G TEMPLE 17
H TEMPLE 18

SANCHI,
THE HILL OF STUPAS

Madhya Pradesh, located in the center of India, has one of the country's richest artistic heritages: Buddhist, Hindu and Jain temples and Moslem mosques offer a wide historical overview of the developments in Indian civilization.

India's best preserved stupa complex stands at Sanchi, 43 miles from the state capital Bhopal. The site is located on an idyllic isolated rise at the confluence of

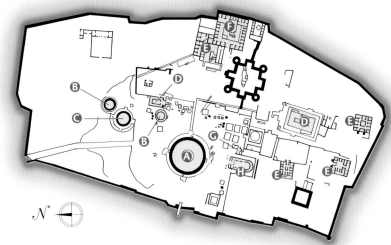

A

B

two rivers and near the prosperous trading city of Vidisha.

The many votive inscriptions show the extent to which the splendor of Sanchi is due to the rich community of local merchants.

Inhabited since the 3rd century BC until the 12th century AD, Sanchi played no part in the life of Buddha but was instead connected with Mahendra, son of the emperor Ashoka, supporter and defender of Buddhism and responsible for taking the teachings of the Enlightened One to Sri Lanka. Queen Devi, mother of Mahendra, was born to a family of rich merchants in Vidisha and it therefore seems very probable that the construction of the Great Stupa, Stupa 1, can be dated to the reign of Ashoka, 273-236 BC.

Third king of the bellicose Mauryan dynasty, Ashoka devoted his youth to territorial expansion until he dominated almost all of India. During the conquest of Kalinga, a kingdom overlapping present day Orissa, Ashoka suffered a profound crisis of conscience. From that moment, he based his policies on the moral concepts derived from the teachings of Buddha and made large donations to the monastic communities. The golden centuries of

Buddhism began with Ashoka: stupas were built everywhere, monastic communities spread and universities flourished. Despite the splendor of the Mauryan dynasty ending with the death of Ashoka and the first pan-Indian empire disintegrating into a myriad of local states, the spread of Buddhism continued without pause, particularly in cities and in merchant communities.

Consequently, Sanchi's busy existence continued under the successive dynasties. After a period of stasis building work began again during the pan-Indian imperial dynasty of the Guptas in the 5th century. Influenced by the classical school of Mathura, a holy site 90 miles from Delhi, the local artists engaged upon the image of Buddha and installed four statues of him at the base of the Great Stupa in front of the entrances. The Guptas were also responsible for the construction of Temple 17, one of the oldest Hindu sanctuaries in existence.

During the reign of Harsha, from one of the cadet branches of the Gupta dynasty and the last of the great Indian emperors, other temples and monasteries were built in the 7th century although the quality of the

C

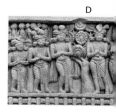

D

E

A - Stupa 1, is enclosed by a balustrade that is made to simulate a wood plant and opens towards the cardinal points of the compass through 1st century AD toranas. These magnificent gateways have triple architraves.

B - Stupa 2 near to the top of the hill, has no torana but a balustrade decorated with medallions decorated with floral patterns and animals, like this elephant leaving his stall.

C - The decorative tiles inserted in the narrative panels offer a wide range of images; one of them is a group of horses guided by a single rider in a tangle of plants and flowers.

D - This photo depicts a detail of the North Gate way of the Great Stupa.

E - The architrave of the torana to Stupa 3 is supported by yakshas, pot-bellied spirits of the trees which later became part of the retinue of Kubera, god of riches, dear to the merchant community that patronized Sanchi.

statues was not high.

Sanchi's decline began in the 13th century brought about by the collapse of the great Indian empires that had promoted the expansion of trade and urban settlements and so benefited the merchant class in which Buddhism had found its greatest lay supporters. Indeed, it was along the caravan trade routes that the monasteries were built as another of their functions was to take in and welcome travellers.

When the Moslem hordes burst into India, razed the monastic universities of Taxila, Nalanda and Vikramashila to the ground and destroyed the monasteries in Gandhara, Kashmir and Bihar, the trade routes were made unsafe and Buddhism began to disappear throughout the country.

Sanchi fell into oblivion and it was only in 1818 that General Taylor discovered the site by chance. In 1822, Captain Johnson, the political agent in Bhopal, opened the Great Stupa in search of treasure but caused it to collapse. The stupa did contain treasures but, being a reliquary, the treasures were spiritual, i.e. the remains of the great Buddhist masters. This was reported by Alexander Cunningham, the first superintendent of the

Archaeological Survey of India, and by Captain Maisey who found urns in Stupas 2 and 3.

Local farmers had also greatly contributed to the destruction of Sanchi by carting away materials to be used for their own building purposes and even dismantling one of the most beautiful and famous of Ashoka's columns to use its materials for squeezing sugar-cane juice.

Total disaster was averted in 1881 by Major Cole who began to protect the site from intrusion and to clear the monuments of the suffocating vegetation. He strengthened the Great Stupa to prevent its total collapse, rebuilt its western and southern *toranas* and also the *toranas* of Stupa 3. Sir John Marshal, superintendent of the Archaeological Department from 1912-19, continued the work of clearing the jungle, restored the south-western part of the Great *Stupa*, the balustrade and the topmost sections of the construction, restored *stupa* no.3 and a series of temples and built a small museum where finds were displayed. In 1936, Mohammad Hamid opened up the rest of the huge monastery standing at the foot of the hill.

A

A - The spiral at the top of the architraves symbolically refers to the continual process of emanation and dissolution of the universe and to the expansion and contraction of awareness.

B - The statues of Buddha at the base of the great stupa were produced at a later date. Up until the 2nd-3rd centuries AD, the Enlightened One was always shown by symbols and never as a man.

Today Sanchi is one of the best preserved sites in India and its monuments, over fifty as numbered by Marshall, stand in two groups at the top of the hill and at the bottom on the western slope. The hilltop section is an irregular rectangle measuring 1200 feet north-south by 628 feet east-west and bounded by an 11th-12th century wall. A path near the western *torana* of the Great Stupa leads to Monastery 51 and Stupa 2 and joins up with the old road.

The most significant element of Buddhist architecture is the stupa, a reliquary derived from ancient funerary tumuli. Legend has it that, after cremation, the remains of Buddha's body were divided between the largest warrior clans that had been present at the funeral and that the first ten stupa in India were erected over these holy relics. The principal stupa at Sanchi is 119' wide and 53'6" high excluding the pillar with the three parasols.

C - The pradakshinapatha, *the walkway that the faithful follow, keeping the place of worship to their right as a sign of veneration, is* situated between the balustrade and the stupa. *The steps lead to another ambulatory on top of the plinth.*

D

E

It incorporates a smaller construction attributed to Ashoka and made from fired brick cemented with mud. During the 2nd century, it was rebuilt and enlarged by building a new wall around it from local sandstone covered in a thick coat of plaster. A terrace was added with a double flight of steps, balustrades, a covered walkway for the *pradakshina* and a *harmika* in the form of a reliquary.

There is a precise cosmic symbolism to this structure: the high circular plinth, called the *medhi*, represents the earth; the domed body of the structure, the *anda*, represents the sky, the square balustrade that rises over the construction, the *harmika*, refers to the mythical cosmic mountain at the center of the universe; the dominion of the ultimate Truth, the ethereal world, is symbolized by the central pillar, the *chattravali*, around which the stupa winds, 'compressing itself' like a three dimensional spiral. The *chattravali* is structured as three parasols, or *chattra*, typical elements of regal ceremonial which celebrate the three jewels of Buddhism: the Buddha himself, the *Sangha* and the

D - *The story of the generous prince Vessantara is illustrated on the first architrave of the northern* torana. *Vessantara was the previous incarnation of Buddha as narrated in the "Jataka," a collection of tales chronicling the past lives of the Enlightened One.*

E - Yakshas *also appear on the western* torana *in the Great Stupa. Together they hold up the architrave while facing the four cardinal points; their large turbans and heavy jewels emphasize their splendor.*

B

C

F - According to
tradition, the origin of
the stupa dates from
the death of Buddha
when the dynastic
rulers built tumuli to
contain the ashes
from his cremation.

G - As an object of
devotion, miniature
stupa often appear in
the tiles of the torana
to celebrate nirvana,
the ineffable state of
extinction of sorrow
realized by Buddha on
his death.

Dharma – the Enlightened One, the
Community and the Doctrine.

As a cosmic mountain, the axis of the
universe and the *umbilicus* of the world, the
stupa symbolizes the totality of existence
and therefore Buddha himself.

A stone enclosure, the *vedika*, around
the *stupa* delimits the perimeter of the
space used for the central rite of Buddhist
devotion, *pradakshina*, in which the
devotee circles the object of worship
clockwise. The *vedika* stretches to the four
cardinal points where overhanging
structures end in huge gateways, the
toranas, built in the 1st and 2nd centuries,
surmounted by a triple architrave. The
original wooden versions of both the *vedika*
and the *torana* can be seen: the balustrade
is made from fixed joint laths that
reproduce a stockade and the gateway
with slightly curved architraves reproduce
the design of structures previously made
from canes and curved staves.

If one examines the ground plan of the
stupa, the shape of the *mandala* at the base
of all holy Indian architecture, whether
Hindu or Buddhist, is evident. The plan is
laid over a geometric tracing where the
point, the circle and other shapes
symbolize determined cosmic events,
divine presences and states of awareness
that justify the term 'psycho-cosmogram'
given to the *mandala*.

The heart of the *stupa* is represented
by the reliquary which corresponds
to the central point in the drawing
of the *mandala*. The reliquary may or
may not be enclosed in a special chamber.
The point is the symbol of the origin
of time and space, the source from
which existence irradiates and to where
it returns, the holiest of holies. The process
of emanation from the One to the multiple
and of cosmic expansion is symbolized
by the circle; in the *stupa* this is
represented by the bell-shaped structure
made from concentric circles of bricks
alternating with loose stones, and topped
by a final layer of stones.

The *toranas* at the four cardinal points
are arranged as if on the arms of a cross
which has the center of the *mandala* as its
midpoint. The cross stretches towards the
periphery symbolising the concepts of

H - The architrave of
the northern
gateway of the Great
Stupa is supported by
groups of four
elephants. These
animals refer to the
birth of the Buddha
which was announced
to his mother in a
dream by an
elephant.

cosmogonic and doctrinal irradiation in the sense that the message of the Buddha, whose 'stone' body is actually the stupa itself, spreads equally towards all regions of the universe. The *toranas* also evoke the initiatory symbolism of the doorway, a place of communication between the profane and the sacred worlds, a cipher of spiritual transformation that occurs when entering the temple perimeter.

There are no pictures of Siddhartha (Buddha as a young man) on the gateways of Sanchi. The followers of the Hinayana considered him not as a god but as the master of supreme enlightenment and thus there was no sense in depicting him, either because Buddha's human form had already been extinguished on his attainment of *nirvana*, or because it was the master's message that was

D

B

A - The minute details that the craftsmen of Vidisha engraved on the toranas at Sanchi are like a picture album of the clothes, hairstyles and jewellery of the period.

B - A dvarapala (guardian of the door) protecting the western torana. The figure is not supposed to be aggressive; his spiritual stature not his weapons lends him authority.

C - This is a wonderful example of the attention paid to detail at Sanchi: the caparisoned elephants wait to rise while the riders open their parasols.

D - The architrave panels refer to the important moments in the life of Buddha: the bodhi tree celebrates his enlightenment and the goddess sprinkled with elephants, Maya, is a symbol of his birth.

C

D

important, not his historical figure.

Buddha's presence in the bas-reliefs is evidenced by symbols connected with particular events: the horse refers to Siddhartha's departure from his family home, the tree symbolizes the moment of enlightenment, the throne and the parasol emphasize his prominence among the members of the monastic communities, the wheel signifies diffusion of his doctrine, the stupa is the celebration of his attainment of *nirvana* (the state of extinction of the incessant and agonizing earthly existence), and the feet indicate the presence of the Enlightened One.

The creative urge of the artists however found ample material for expression in the "Jataka," the writings of the previous lives of

the Buddha, the most famous of which is the "Vessantarajataka" in which he appears as a generous prince. Many others record his adventures in the guise of animals and so the bas-reliefs on the *torana* at Sanchi show gazelles, elephants and monkeys in the wild with extraordinary realism and skill. After the formal and hieratic representations influenced by Persian art, Indian artists learned to represent the natural world with skill and fluidity.

The first images of the Buddha date from the 2nd-3rd century AD. They were created by the Indian school of Mathura and by the Gandhara school influenced by Greek art. It is probable that images of Jain saints and *yakshas* (tree spirits) carved as supports for the western gateway at

E - The decorations on the western torana show lovely shalabanjikas and yakshis (tree nymphs) from the abacus on the upright to the spiral volute on the first architrave.

F, G - One of the most common images on the torana is the tree of the bodhi, the pipal tree that Buddha was sitting under when he achieved enlightenment. Decorated with festoons, it is the destination of religious processions as shown on the two panels on the upright of the western torana. The third scene (F) comes from the "Mahakapi Jataka" in which the incarnation of Buddha as the king of the monkeys sacrifices his life for them.

E

Sanchi, were the Indian models for the anthropomorphisation of the Buddha while the Hellenist Gandhara school, in the north-west, found ideological justification in using the figure of the Greek philosopher as their basis. Supporting evidence for this theory is that the former was the incarnation of the *dharma* (the Buddhist doctrine) and the other the incarnation of Logos (the controlling principle of the universe in Greek philosophy).

The doors consist of two pillars topped by four lions, elephants and *yakshas* supporting three curved architraves. The architraves end in spirals and are separated by square blocks and processions of cavalry mounted on elephants and horses. Extending from the uppermost part of the capital to the spiral scroll of the first architrave, charming *shalabajikas* (*yakshis*

F

or tree nymphs) decorate the whole. The final architrave is raised above the others by the 'wheel of law' flanked by two fan-carriers and two *triratnas* (symbols of the triple jewel). An oft-repeated image is the *kalpavalli*, the 'plant that grants all desires': a vine that winds from the molding to the balustrade offering jewels, flowers and other delights.

The painted decorations of the architraves were worked on by ivory and wood carvers, metal engravers and jewellers. They are based on the "Jataka" and salient episodes from the life of Siddhartha – the most powerful of which is the temptation by the demon Mara – as well as various Buddhist themes. The northern *torana* is the best preserved.

G

A

The nearby Stupa 3 is much smaller and simpler. It was built at the same time as the larger stupa but is preceded by a single portal like the others of the 1st century AD. Although of a lesser artistic value, this stupa has great religious importance as it contains two sarcophagi in the reliquary chamber with the remains of Shariputra and Maugdalyayana, famous disciples of the Buddha.

Stupa 2 stands on an artificial terrace 1040 feet below the summit of the hill. It is similar to Stupa 3 but without *toranas* although its balustrade is decorated with simple, archaic scenes and by splendid images of flowers and animals. The reliquary chamber is strangely off-center and houses the remains of at least three generations of illustrious Buddhist masters.

There are many other stupa all around

B - Stupa 3 is a smaller and simpler version of the Great Stupa. Both are from the 2nd century BC and have only one portal. This stupa is less important for its design than it is for the reliquaries it contains.

D, E - Only the central structure and tower remain of Temple 45, which seems to have been built in the 10th century. It stands in a monastery complex where the oldest parts

date from the 7th-8th centuries. A lovely statue of Buddha in a meditative pose sits under the porch that once bordered the courtyard of the monastery.

C

D

B

A, C - The decoration on the jamb of the only torana of stupa no. 3 is what is called the "column of Ashoka." Ashoka was the emperor responsible for spreading Buddhism throughout India. Supported by four lions (which celebrate the warrior class Buddha and Ashoka were born into), the wheel is the symbol of the Dharma (doctrine) and therefore an object of veneration. The motif is repeated on a panel in the architrave.

in different states of preservation: they are built in brick or stone depending on their size, on square or round ground plans and were erected by the votive gifts of pilgrims.

Among the most important finds, like other similar relics elsewhere in India, Ashoka's sandstone column reveals the influence of Persepolis. It is made from a single block, with a bell-shaped capital (preserved in the museum) decorated with lotus petals and a circular plinth with four lions at its base. The lion refers to the warrior class into which both Buddha and Ashoka were born.

The many temples in different states of preservation help to reconstruct the genesis of holy Indian architecture. Temple

17 is extremely important from this viewpoint. It is a typical example of 5th century Gupta architecture with a hall preceded by a colonnaded porch and topped by a flat roof. Temple 18 from the 7th century has an apse and an intact and impressive colonnaded porch. Temple 45, with a tower, has been rebuilt several times.

Of the *viharas*, the largest and most legible is Monastery 51; this structure is almost square, measuring 108' by 106'3", and is divided into twenty two cells around a wide porticoed courtyard. The central cell is larger than the others and preceded by an antechamber; it probably housed an image of the Buddha and was used as a chapel.

H - Although it is architecturally modest, Stupa 2 has interesting medallions at the intersections of the beams of the balustrade. Elephants, peacocks and horses are set against a background of flowers with great freshness and spirit.

I - Enclosed by a large balustrade and without any toranas, Stupa 2 contains the remains of many important Buddhist masters.

F

G

H

I

F - Temple 17 is a typical example of 5th century Gupta architecture. It is a simple flat-roofed structure with a hall and a porch with finely decorated columns.

G - Monastery 51 stands on the western side of Sanchi hill. This nearly square structure comprises 22 cells around a large, porticoed courtyard. The central cell, larger than the others and with an ante-chamber, probably contained an image of the Buddha.

KHAJURAHO, THE PARADISE OF THE SURASUNDARIS

One of the most famous sites of the *nagara* style of Hindu architecture is to be found at Khajuraho, 109 miles from Jhansi. Of the 85 temples built there between 950-1050, about twenty remain. They were discovered in the jungle in 1840 by the British but restoration work began only in the early part of the 20th century.

The temples were built by the Chandella kings, formerly known as *Chandrateyas*, descendants of Chandrama, god of the

A - Khajuraho's most impressive temple is Kandariyamahadeva which stands in the western group. It was built by the Chandella dynasty between 1017-1029 in honor of the god Shiva.

B, E - Kandariyamahadeva temple is adorned with more than 650 statues and is considered the masterpiece of the Chandella artists. Beautiful surasundari

(heavenly nymphs), experts at love-making, decorate the niches in the outside walls. The niches are separated by architectural elements and friezes.

C, D - This close-up of the mahamandapa at Kandariyamahadeva temple illustrates the attractive chamber in the center of the temple in which four slender pillars support the domed ceiling. This room leads into the cell (D) that is decorated with wonderfully carved jambs and architraves. In the background there stands the marble linga, aniconic and phallic symbol of Shiva.

moon. The dynasty reached its peak with Dhanga (950-1008) and continued until 1202 when the Moslems began their first incursions into India and undermined the dynasty's power. This was a prelude to annexation by the sultanate of Delhi in 1310.

The temples of Khajuraho are a splendid synthesis of architecture and sculpture, usually in sandstone. They are spread across an open area with no enclosing walls and stand on large platforms often also supporting four small corner temples. They are characterized by a high plinth with elaborate moldings which emphasizes the vertical sweep.

The ground plan of the more elaborate temples like Kandariyamahadeva and Vishvanatha is based on the shape of a cross with the major axis being east-west and with a double transept. The *ardhamandapa* (entrance porch facing east) is decorated with a *torana* and runs into the hypostyle *mandapa* onto which the *mahamandapa* opens; the *mahamandapa* is an ornamented area with four central pillars that support a domed ceiling whose transept is formed by two balconied sections. The *antarala* (hall) is positioned before the *garbha-griha* (inner sanctum) which one enters via a *chandrashila* (a half-moon step). The *pradakshinapatha* (ambulatory which surrounds the inner sanctum) extends on

F - Near Kandariyamahadeva stands the small chapel of Mahadeva with a statue of a sardula (sort of gryphon) and kneeling figure.

three sides with an equal number of overhanging balconies so creating a second transept. Single statues or groups of statues stand in niches in the external walls delimited by architectural elements and separated by embellishments. The ogival *shikhara* (covering) is enlivened by a series of miniatures of itself, *angashikharas* or *urushringas*, which wrap around the main structure. Placed on the *shikhara* is the *amalaka* (the flat, grooved cushion resembling the fruit of the myrobalan) itself topped by the *kalasha* (the pinnacle in the shape of a water vase). The incredible profusion of decoration transforms the temple into a work of sculpture: festive processions, military parades, groups of ascetics and warriors, gods and their attendants, lovers, heavenly nymphs – *surasundaris* (the most beautiful) or *alasakanyas* (reclining girls) – mythical animals such as *shardulas* and *vyalas* (gryphons), intertwining plants and

F

1000 years ago. The processions of elephants and horsemen and the scenes of battle, hunting, dancing and love are all remarkable.

The temple of Vishvanatha built in 1002 and dedicated to Shiva shares the double transept plan of Kandariyamahadeva. Three female figures decorate the building, a nymph playing a flute with her back to the spectator, a nymph cradling a baby and another with a parrot on her wrist. The Nandi pavilion opposite the main entrance contains one of the most beautiful and largest figures of Shiva's spouse. To the south-west of Visvanatha is the small temple of Parvati dedicated to the best-known manifestation of Shiva's bride.

G

H

I

geometrical motifs follow one after the other in a palpitating tangle of life.

The site of Khajuraho is divided into two sections, the most important being the western area with the following temples: Varaha, Lakshmana, Kandariyamahadeva, Mahadeva, Devi Jagadamba, Chitragupta, Parvati, Vishvanatha and the temple of the Sixty Four Yogis.

The most magnificent temple is the Kandariyamahadeva with its 101-foot *shikhara*. It was perhaps built between 1017-1029 and is dedicated to Shiva. The temple is divided into *ardhamandapa, mandapa, antarala, garbha-griha* and *pradakshinapatha* but originally had four other sanctuaries at the corners of the platform. The *torana* at the entrance to the *ardhamandapa*, the

ceilings of the *mandapa* and the columns and cornice of the door to the *garbha-griha* (where a marble *linga* stands) are decorated with elegant engravings. Also decorated with 650 statues, this temple is considered the masterpiece of the Chandella artists.

The ruins of the temples of Mahadeva and Devi Jagadamba (1002-1017) stand on the same platform as Kandariyamahadeva. Devi Jagadamba temple was not originally dedicated to Kali, goddess of the world and one of the forms of Shiva's consort, as it is today, but to Vishnu as shown by the image engraved on the entrance.

Not far from Devi Jagadamba temple stands the temple of Chitragupta dedicated to Surya, god of the sun, whose figure has stood in the tabernacle since it was erected

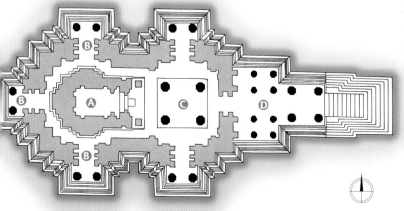

MAP OF
KANDARIYAMAHADEVA
TEMPLE

A INNER SANCTUM OR
    GARBHA-GRIHA

C AMBULATORY OR
    PRADAKSHINAPATHA

D CENTRAL ROOM WITH
    FOUR COLUMNS OR
    MAHAMANDAPA

E ENTRANCE PORCH OR
    ARDHAMANDAPA

G, H - The Vishvanatha temple, in the form of a cross and with a double transept, is split into an ardhamandapa

(entrance porch), mandapa (hypostyle room), mahamandapa (large room), garbha-griha (inner sanctum) and antarala (hall). The succession of rooms that increase in height is visible in the picture H.

I - This image shows the Vishranatha with the White Temple of Parvati alongside.

MAP OF LAKSHMANA TEMPLE

A ARDHAMANDAPA
B MANDAPA
C MAHAMANDAPA
D ANTARALA
E GARBHAGRIHA
F PRADAKSHINA PATHA

A - Lakshmana temple was built in 954 and dedicated to Vishnu. It stands on a platform with four corner sanctuaries and is decorated with a parade of warriors and erotic scenes.

A

B

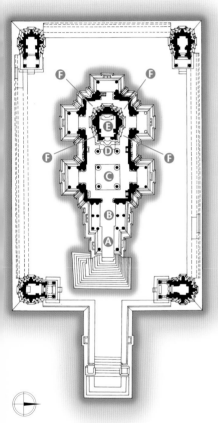

C

D

The temple of Lakshmana was begun by Lakshmanavarman and finished in 954 by his son Dhanga. Four corner sanctuaries frame the central construction built to house the image of Vishnu-Vaikuntha with three heads, the center one human and the other two (both *avatars* of the god) of a lion and a boar.

The friezes, the statuary groups, the lovers and other decorative elements are magnificently carved.

E - One of the characteristics of the god Shiva, as shown in the temple of Lakshmana, is his association with snakes, a symbol of rebirth and time.

F

G

E

H

F, H - The interior of the temple is sculpted: the principal deities are represented in hypostyle niches while geometric, floral and architectural friezes frame the other gods. The plinths with complex moldings (as shown in picture H) are one of the elements that help to emphasize the vertical sweep of Chandella constructions.

G - The picture shows the chandrashila *(half-moon step) in front of the inner sanctum and the statue of the three-headed Vishnu-Vaikuntha in Lakshmana temple.*

B, D - The temples at Khajuraho show a close relationship between architecture and sinuous, sensual sculpture. The temple of Lankshmana comprises the four traditional areas – porch, two hypostyle rooms and inner sanctum with hall – and is crowned like all temples at Khajuraho with an ogival shikhara.

C - A steep flight of steps leads to the main entrance of Lakshmana temple. The temple is embellished with a torana *consisting of a festoon of (mythical aquatic monsters) and is screened by a wide overhang.*

A

An enormous representation of Varaha, the 'boar,' stands near the 1st small temple of Varaha. It was in the guise of a boar that Vishnu saved the Earth goddess held prisoner in the depths of the ocean.

The temple of the Chaunsath Yogini is unique in its structure and in its material; it was built in granite around the end of the 11th century. The temple is dedicated to the '64 yogis,' the divine ascetics with esoteric powers that assist Devi, one of the forms of Shiva's bride. The wide courtyard is surrounded by 64 bare cells that form a wing to the Goddess's small sanctuary.

Various temples make up the eastern and southern sections of the site: those of Brahma, Vamana, Javari, Duladeo and Chaturbhuja, of which the latter two boast

B

C

D

excellent statuary groups.

Jain temples stand to the south of Khajuraho. The Jains were an ascetic group founded by Mahariva, also known as Jina (the Victor), in the 6th century BC. The most important is the Parsvanatha temple enclosed by a wall and topped by a *shikhara* of perfect proportions ringed by *urushringas*. Its rich decorations divided into three friezes do not include erotic motifs like those of Khajuraho, due to the ascetic doctrine of Jainism. The Ghantai temple, built in 1148, is given that name for the chain pattern of sculpted bells on the pillars; it is also famous for its ceiling decoration.

Many examples of the rich sculptural style of the Chandella dynasty have been collected in the Museum of Khajuraho and the vast range of Hindu deities and holy characters to be found in Buddhism and Jainism demonstrates the openness and farsightedness of the local sovereigns.

Another wonderful example of *nagara* architecture is found about 45 miles from Sanchi at Udaipur. This is the temple of Udayeswar, also known as Nilakantheswar,

E

the "Lord of the blue throat:" Shiva who burned his throat when breathing in a terrible miasma threatening to destroy the universe. Built by Udayaditya of the Paramara dynasty in 1059, the temple is composed of a *mandapa* with three entrance porches, a hall and an inner sanctum. The well-proportioned *shikhara* has seven storys and its slender ogival shape is emphasized by three vertical bands interrupting the horizontal lines of the friezes. A splendid dancing Shiva dominates the decorative tablet on the elaborate *shukanasa* (overhanging projection of the *shikhara* towards the roof of the *mandapa*). Three other temples dedicated to Shiva by the leaders of the Chedi dynasty (895-1150) can be seen in Madhya Pradesh – at Chanderi, Sohagpur and Gurgi – which have many stylistic affinities with the temples at Khajuraho.

F

A - This statue of the chaturbhuja *(four-armed) Vishnu sits inside the temple of the southern group. The shell, disk and club are the principal symbols of the god who shows the palm of his fourth hand in the* abhayamudra, *the gesture that invites devotees to approach without fear.*

G
H

I - Another Jain temple is dedicated to Shantinatha, the 16th Tirthankara. It contains a statue of Adinatha, the 1st Tirthankara, represented completely naked, like all the others, as a sign of complete poverty.

B - The Varaha Pavilion stands next to Lakshmana temple. It contains the image of the "boar," one of the forms that Vishnu assumed in his providential descents to earth.

C, E - Duladeo temple is one of the eastern group at Khajuraho. It is ascribed to the 11th century and boasts a well-proportioned shikhara with smaller shikharas at the corners. The walls below are decorated with attractive groups and single statues.

D - Chaturbhuja temple is south of the Archaeological Museum. It has no mahamandapa and lacks any emphasis of the vertical plane.

F - Parshvanatha temple stands out among those in the eastern group at Khajuraho. Unlike the others, it is enclosed by a wall and topped by a perfectly proportioned shikhara.

G - The wall decoration of Parshvanatha is remarkable. Statues of the main mythological characters decorate the parts of the temple that protrude, while grill and mythical animal motifs predominate in the indented sections. Although the temple is Jain, the iconography is a transformation of the Hindu pantheon.

H - Parshvanatha temple is dedicated to the Tirthankara of the same name, the last but one of the twenty-four "ford makers" or enlightened characters that spread the Jain doctrine. The icon in the inner sanctum is made from black marble.

I

EROTICISM, ON THE CUSP
BETWEEN SACRED AND PROFANE

A - Alasakanya (reclining girls) are explicit forms of the Indian ideal of feminine beauty. Here, one raises her arm to paint the red dot on her forehead as she looks at herself in the mirror.

B - The profusion of erotic scenes, often obscene, that adorns the temples of Khajuraho has long intrigued scholars. No agreement has yet been reached on a satisfactory interpretation.

C - The visual representation of maithuna is perhaps connected with magical-shamanic beliefs that considered sex as a means of increasing fertility and of warding off evil. Images of loving couples are old and celebrate the union of male with female, indispensable to life.

D - The groups of lovers invalidate the thesis that the maithuna (sexual union) represents the relationship between God and the soul and the hypothesis that the scenes are a kind of education inspired by the "Kamasutra," the famous "Treatise on the Art of Loving." The idea that they were influenced by Tantrism is also improbable; it is true that this school of belief includes sexual practices but the secrecy that has always surrounded their rites contrasts with the explicit images of Khajuraho.

B

C

A

The temples of Khajuraho are known above all for the profusion of erotic scenes that adorn them. The *surasundaris* (beautiful nymphs shown reclining and also called *alasakanyas*) are the pictorial definition of voluptuousness with the soft curvature of their arms and legs, their full bodies, heavy breasts and rounded ankles. The deep meaning of their existence is however hidden behind their immobile faces. And if the presence of the divine girls is intriguing, what is to be made of the complicated *maithuna* (representations of sexual union) that often involve several people and sometimes animals?

Among the many attempts made to justify the eroticism that often borders on obscenity, the least convincing is the one that sees the *maithuna* as an allegory of the relationship between God and souls. Neither does recourse to the "Kamasutra" (Treatise on the Art of Loving) written by Vatsyayana between the 3rd-5th century AD seem plausible. Not even the "Kamasutra" describes the orgiastic unions or the episodes with animals shown on the walls, and the few mentions made are in disapproving terms.

The influence of Tantrism – a current of thought that sees the most powerful primordial impulse in the *eros* and uses it as a means of asceticism, including using the *maithuna* as a cardinal element in rituals – does not seem sufficient to explain the iconographic scenes at Khajuraho where it seems possible the Tantric sect of Kapalika was pre-eminent. One of the characteristics of Tantrism is in fact secrecy, so much so that the texts are written in a deliberately ambiguous manner and the rites are known only to initiates. The open pictorial description of sexual practices would seem to be in contrast with Tantric customs unless the theory that says that the crudely erotic scenes hide a subtle meaning understood only by adepts is valid.

It also seems tortuous reasoning that beginning of spring: Holi, a festival that has been celebrated in India from time immemorial to the present day, includes just these traits.

On the other hand, *mithuna* (pictures showing an amorous couple though not during lovemaking) are part of an ancient tradition and appear on the first Buddhist constructions. It was, however, in the 10th century that the *maithuna* (sexual union) motif was widely used in the decoration of holy buildings, either due to the influence of Tantrism or perhaps following the transformation of

alchemy and magic – as a tool to obtain strength and health, if not longevity or immortality.

Whatever the explanation may be, the main erotic motif at Khajuraho is that of the ascetic with either the courtesan or the expert girl initiate; this celebrates the power acquired by the ascetic from chastity and then liberated through sex, so resetting the balance that extreme asceticism would have risked compromising. There are many myths of ascetics made over-powerful and arrogant by chastity to whom the gods, scared of

D

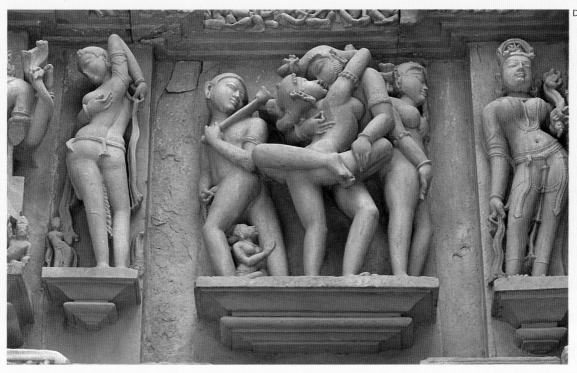

the most extreme scenes were included by the constructors of the temple just to ridicule Tantric practices.

The popular tradition sees the *maithuna* as a sort of charm to ward off the evil eye and thunderbolts or as a means to test the spirituality of the devotees who were supposed to remain impassive before the carnal scenes.

One of the most credible explanations put forward is by D. Desai who sees an ancient magic-shamanic heritage in the eroticism and obscenity of Khajuraho in which the sexual rites foster fertility while at the same time acting as protection against evil and negative forces. The positive and protective aspect of the obscenity can be seen in the carnival festivals at the end of winter and the

the temple into a royal court. This was how the *rajas* lived, surrounded by courtesans and dedicated to every pleasure, and how the god in his temple was attended to by the *devadasis* (handmaidens of the gods) who were dancers and experts in erotic love. Both court and temple protocols included sexual practices in which ritual union of the sovereign or the priest with the *devadasis* was aimed at fostering the fertility of the kingdom and the favors of the gods.

There is no doubt that degeneracy was indulged in, particularly when Tantrism was adopted by the nobles and kings, not as a path to spiritual elevation, but for reasons of pleasure and, above all - given the relationship of sex with

losing their sway, send *surasundaris*, skilful temptresses who nearly always succeed in their purpose.

As has been shown, there are diverse interpretations of the erotic scenes: ancient orgiastic rites of fertility; the magical and protective function of sex and obscenity, above all where the orgy scenes appear on the weakest parts of the temple, for example, the walls of intersection between the various parts of the building, the celebration of ascetic and sexual power; 'publicity' for the *devadasis* and the temple; hidden meanings for initiates behind the gross forms of sexuality; and representation of the force of existence, particularly in temples dedicated to the sun where the erotic ritual reproduced the solar function of dispensing life.

GWALIOR

ORCHHA

DATIA

THE RAJA FORTS: GWALIOR, ORCHHA AND DATIA

C

B - Tirthankaras are characterized by long earlobes deformed by heavy ear-rings used before renunciation of the world, "beauty folds" on the neck, staring eyes and the particular shape of the breastbone.

E

I n ancient times, the use of durable materials was reserved for temples, the houses of the gods. In civil constructions, stone was only used for the base of fortifications, terraces on which wood and brick dwellings stood, and for city gateways.

Remains of civil Hindu architecture do not therefore date back to before the 12th century; to this era belong parts of the fort of Uparkot at Junagadh in the state of Gujarat where Dabhoi, about 19 miles from Baroda, is also found. Dabhoi

A - The climb to Gwalior Fort flanks rocky walls where innumerable statues of Tirthankaras, the Jain prophets, were sculpted towards the 15th century.

A

D

B

is noted for its city walls and particularly for its splendid 13th century gates: Hira, the 'Diamond' Gate that faces east and which is framed by two finely sculpted wings each housing a temple, the well-preserved and attractive Baroda gate to the west, Nandod gate facing south and Moti, or the Pearl Gate, facing north.

Gwalior, one of the oldest and loveliest forts in Madhya Pradesh, appears to have been founded in the 3rd century AD. After being part of the Pratihara and Kachhavaha dominion, it became dependent on the Chandella dynasty of Khajuraho with the Kachhapagatha clan at the start of the 11th century. Next came the Paramara dynasty which reigned from 1128-1232 at which time Gwalior fell into the hands of the sultan of Delhi. With the decline in power of the sultanate, a new dynasty, the Tomara, took possession of the area in the 14th century. It was under their sovereign, *raja*

F

C - The pillar reproducing the ancient sacrificial stake and the cosmic mountain symbolizes the concept of the axis mundi, the element that regulates the world and represented to Jains by the doctrine.

D - When the Tirthankara is shown seated, the legs are in the padmasana (lotus position) and the hands rest one on top of the other face up in the dhyanamudra (gesture of meditation).

E - The images of the Tirthankaras stand in niches preceded by verandahs and arranged on different levels connected by steps. Wooden structures were used to complete the site but have since disappeared.

Man Singh (1486-1516) that Gwalior attained its maximum splendor. It was conquered by the Moguls but regained its independence in 1732 with the Scindia clan, members of the Maratha people. Mahadji Scindia, the last of the clan, was obliged to hand over the fort to the British in 1780 but it was returned to the Scindia who then retained it until 1948.

The difficult climb to the fort winds through a gorge containing caves once inhabited by Jain ascetics and flanked by 15th century sculptures of the Tirthankaras, the prophets that revealed the saving doctrine of Jainism. After passing a series of fortifications, the visitor reaches Urvahi, the main entrance.

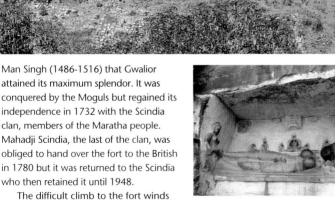

F - The Jain community divided into two strands: one dresses in white clothes, the other, the digambara (clothes of heaven), wears nothing.

The latter sect show the Tirthankara standing naked and fully frontal. A shapely body with powerful shoulders fits the Indian ideal of masculine beauty.

G - The reclining female figure alludes to the birth of a Tirthankara, probably Parshvanatha or Mahariva, respectively the 23rd and 24th prophets.

H - Panels showing animals – bulls with humps, winged lions and elephants – appear in the decoration at the base of the statues or to fill in space on the rock walls.

A

B

The huge pool of water inside the fort, the Suraj kund, next to a temple dedicated to Surya, the sun god, is believed to be the place where the divine hermit Gwalipa, after whom the fort is named, cured King Suraj Sen, founder of the fort, of leprosy.

Just beyond the Teli ka Mandir (the Temple of the Caste of Oil Sellers), there is an interesting construction: a huge cubic structure with a tall rectangular inner sanctum and porch dedicated in the 11th century by the Pratihara dynasty to *Shakti*, the divine female Energy. The covering of the construction has recently been rebuilt and there is an unusual, oblong double *shikhara* which stands over the sanctum. The *shikhara* has two large *chaitya* windows of which the one on the first level is blind and which vaguely resembles the *khakhara* style of window in certain temples in Orissa in the shape of half a watermelon.

C

D

A, B - Il Suraj Kund is the mythical pool in which the divine hermit Gwalipa, after whom the fort is named, is supposed to have cured king Suraj Sen, founder of the fort, of leprosy. On the banks, a kiosk (B) and a small temple dedicated to the monkey god Hanuman (A) reveal the Islamic influence.

C - The Teli ka Mandir (Temple of the Oil-Sellers) is a massive cubic construction from the 11th century with a high oblong inner sanctum fronted by a porch with a modern covering.

E

F - The entrance to the Temple of the Oil-Sellers is decorated with delicate statues: the female figures are long-limbed and sinuous as seen on the upright.

G - The scene depicted on this panel would seem to be a dance lesson in which the master is correcting the dancers.

F

G

D, E - The soberly decorated Teli ka Mandir is dedicated to Shakti, the divine female energy. The niches in the sides are framed by delicate cornices and crowned by horseshoe shaped arches (D) and reproductions of shikharas (E).

Two other temples worthy of note at Gwalior Fort are the Sas Bahu group (Sister-in-law and Daughter-in-law), two buildings from the second half of the 11th century constructed by Mahapala of the Kachhapagatha dynasty. The larger is composed of a two-floor porch and a three-floor central section with a twelve corner ground plan. There is no *shikhara* but the covering of the porch is a beautiful example of a *samvarana* (a pyramid of bell-shaped layers topped by a lotus flower). The smaller temple is an open pavilion also covered in the *samvarana* style and resembling the *mandapa* of Khajuraho.

D - The Temple of the Bahu (daughter-in-law) comprises a two-floor porch and a three-floor central section. A pyramidal roof made from bell-shaped sections is topped by an upturned lotus.

A - The Sas Bahu Mandir comprises two elegant temples known as the temples of the Daughter-in-law and Sister-in-law. They were built in the second half of the 11th century in honor of the god Vishnu. The Temple of the Daughter-in-law is shown here.

B, F - The Sas Mandir (Temple of the Sister-in-law) is an open pavilion and resembles the *mandapa* of Khajuraho and is also covered by a pyramid made from bell-shaped elements. The interior has finely sculpted columns and is unusually light.

C, E - At the end of the porch, a sculpted doorway leads into the central chamber of the Bahu Mandir. This is a monumental three-floor hypostyle area with twelve sides. Tympanum reinforcement beams (E) are inserted among the pillars to support the heavy domed ceiling (C).

G

H

H - In this picture one can see Gwalior Pal, one of the entrances to the fort.

I, L - One of Man Mandir's most remarkable features is the floral and animal decorations in blue, yellow and green enamelled tiles. The favorite floral images are the stylized tree of life (I), lotus buds and bouquets of flowers held up by makaras (aquatic monsters) with a proboscis and a fish's tail (L).

MAP OF MAN MANDIR
THE PALACE HAS TWO MAIN COURTYARDS (A) AROUND WHICH THE VARIOUS SECTIONS OF THE PALACE ARE ARRANGED. THERE ARE OTHER SMALL KIOSKS (B) IN THE ZANANA (THE AREA RESERVED FOR THE WOMEN).

G - Gwalior Fort is one of the oldest examples of Hindu palace architecture to survive unspoiled. It is built with two floors above and two below ground, the latter contain the serdab, the cool and shaded apartments used during the hot season.

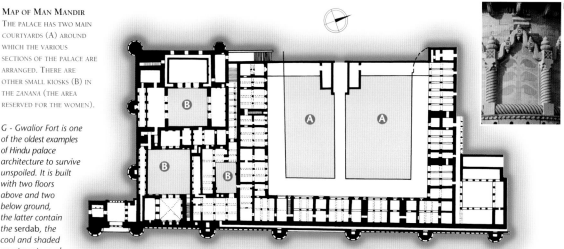

I

J

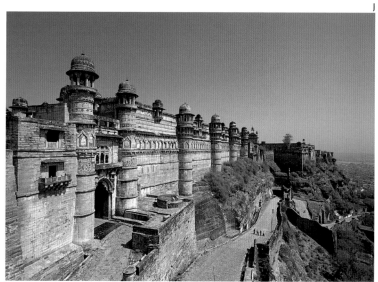

J - Man Mandir is the palace built by Man Singh of the Tomara dynasty (1486-1516). The eastern facade includes six circular towers topped by chattri (small domed kiosks supported on slender columns).

K - The zanana (an area of the palace reserved for use by women) is protected from the sight of the outside world by galleries, fretted screen towers and colored panels showing elephants and other animals.

K

L

One of the oldest unspoiled examples of Hindu palatial architecture is the splendid Man Mandir built by Man Singh from the Tomara dynasty (1486-1516). The magnificent Hathi Pol (Gate of the Elephants) opens in the eastern side of the building decorated with six circular towers crowned by chattris (domed kiosks topped by slender columns). The walls are adorned with marquetry, animals and embellishments in colored enamelled ceramic tiles. Although small, the palace has two main courtyards overlooked by two floors of apartments. The zanana (the section reserved for the women) faces onto the courtyards from a screened gallery protected by a large sloping roof, and continues on the terrace above in a series of chattris.

A

B

C

D

E

Two underground floors house the *serdab* (the cool, shaded summer apartments). The interior is decorated with mullions, balustrades, carved architraves, bands and panels ornamented with floral and geometric patterns.

At the foot of the fort stands the Gujari Mahal, the palace built by *raja* Man Singh for his favorite wife. It now houses a museum and is interesting for the statues connected with the worship of the *Shaktis* and their attendants, the *Yogins*.

Another noteworthy monument at Gwalior, clearly influenced by the Mogul style of the Moslem court at Delhi, is the 16th century Tomb of Muhammad Ghaus which contains the cenotaph of one of the spiritual teachers of the emperor Akbar. The tomb is crowned with an elegant dome flanked by *chattris* and decorated with *jali* (marble tracery in the walls). Next to it stands the tomb of the great 16th century musician, Tansen, in the shadow of a tamarind tree whose leaves are said to sweeten the voices of singers.

A - This detail from the so-called "Music Room" resembles marquetry. The oldest palaces were, in fact, built from wood.

B, C - Delicate tracery executed in soft sandstone surrounds the door openings in a series of ever different geometric and floral patterns.

*D, G - Animal-shaped projections under the porch support overhangs that simulate tiles.
A monster with a long proboscis squeezes an elephant in its jaws (D) and a makara rolls over on itself (G).*

G

F

F - The decorations of the palace show the abilty of the craftsmen: depicted here is a colored elephant from the external decoration.

H - The influence of Islamic architecture can be seen in the 16th century tomb of Muhammad Ghaus at Gwalior fort, crowned by an elegant cupola flanked by chattri and adorned with fretted marble walls.

I - Close to Man Mandir at Gwalior Fort stand the ruins of other palaces. The picture shows the entrance to the Karan Mandir topped by slender chattris.

E - The principal sections of Man Mandir are decorated with pilasters, projections and friezes at the height of the architraves. They face onto the courtyards with a series of porches protected by large overhangs.

H

I

ORCCHA, THE KINGDOM OF RAMA

A - The Ramji Mandir
was built as a palace
but soon after
converted into a
temple. The cupolas
show the influence
of Islamic design
although the upturned
lotus and water vase
pinnacles are Hindu.

Orchha, founded on an island
in the river Betwa by *raja* Rudra
Pratap (1501-1531) was the political
and cultural center of Bundelkand
for a couple of centuries. Bundelkand
is a wide region between northern
Madhya Pradesh and south-western
Uttar Pradesh. Its monuments are
located in a beautiful natural setting
and are among the most impressive

A

B

C

D

of the *Rajput* constructions.
The palace of Ramji Mandir was
built by Pratap Singh and his son
Bharti Chand (1531-1554).
The palace was later converted to
a temple by *raja* Madhukar (1554-
1591) and linked with a local legend:
the wife of the sovereign was a
worshipper of Rama, one of the
principal incarnations of the god
Vishnu, and had taken a holy statue
to Orchha after Rama had advised
her in a vision to build a palace
worthy of him where the statue
should remain forever.

B - The cross-shaped
Chaturbhuja is
actually a temple
but it was designed
to look like a large
palace with a
monumental
entrance, towers,
buttresses, shikhara
and a central cupola
with chattris.

E

F

Whilst awaiting the completion of a magnificent temple, the Chaturbhuja, the queen had kept the statue in her palace but, once the inner sanctum built for the statue had been finished, it refused to leave the royal apartments. Consequently, the palace was converted into a temple, the Ramji Mandir, and is still venerated by the devotees of Rama. An effigy of Vishnu was placed in the incredibly luminous and spacious Chaturbhuja making it a unique temple. It was built between 1558-1573 for the fervently devoted band of Vishnu worshippers in the shape of a cross. The exterior looks like a large, multi-floor palace with a huge entrance, towers and buttresses. It is capped by a long, slender, almost pinnacle-like *shikhara* and by a central dome with *chattris*.

G, H - The Royal chattris, a combination of small shikharas and domes with large overhangs, rise above the wings of enclosure walls several storys high with a central section topped by a slim-spired shikhara.

G

H

C - Imposing sandstone cenotaphs known as "royal chattris" were built on the banks of the river Betwa where the rulers of Orchha were cremated.

D - A detail of Orchha founded in 1500 on an island in the river Betwa. Ramji Mandir on the left is a temple dedicated to Rama that is still used today; the Chaturbhuja temple is on the right. Both were built in the 16th century.

E - This view shows Phul Bagh (the Park of Flowers) where rulers relaxed during the hot season with fountains and canals and in the cool of underground apartments.

F - The water vases on the chattris of the Phul Bagh (the Islamic inspired small tower and kiosk) refer to the cosmic waters from which the universe originates.

A - The Raja Mahal (Royal Palace) at Orchha was built by raja Madhukar (1554-1591). It is a compact building enclosed by walls and arranged around a number of courtyards.

A

B

C

D

B, F - The Jahangiri Mahal is a solid four-sided and five-floored palace and is connected throughout by screened galleries. The rooms and their antechambers open onto an internal courtyard. Eight pavilions with towers on the fourth floor are topped by segmented domes crowned with the lotus and water vase. The last floor is made up of terraces and chattris.

C - The courtyard that Jahangir's Palace faces onto can be seen from the roof of the Raja Mahal. To the left, the wing of the Shish Mahal that used to be a guest-house and which is now a hotel can be seen. The dislocation of the apartments over several floors means that the separation of the male and female quarters is not so clear.

D - Although rather damaged, the royal palace contains lovely paintings on the ground floor. The pictures of animals are full of life, like the imaginary creature made up from a collage of real animals.

E - The "Ramayana," an epic poem based on the deeds of Rama, an avatar of Vishnu

and recognisable by his blue incarnation, was also a source of inspiration for the painters of the Raja Mahal.

G - The paintings on the walls of the ground floor of the Royal palace mainly illustrate Krishna, an important avatar (descent in another form) of the god Vishnu.

E

I

J - In the picture, the monkey god Hanuman can be seen beside Rama and his wife Sita.

K - Although the images are of sacred and mythical events, the settings, clothes, mounts, carriages and everything else give a clear idea of what life was like in this period.

The rather damaged Raja Mahal (royal palace) was also built by Madhukar. The ground floor rooms have marvellous, animated depictions mostly centered on the life of Krishna, another *avatar* of the god Vishnu.

His loves and his dances with the *gopis* (shepherdesses) celebrating the natural idyll in which the god lived make up the famous motif of the *rasalila*, the circular dance in which Krishna multiplies his image so that every girl can have him as a companion.

However, the masterpiece of Orchha is the Jahangiri Mahal built by Bir Singh Deo (1605-27) in honor

F

G

J

K

H

H - The gods are painted inside arched cornices; the edge of the doors shows false architectural motifs and a continuous frieze borders the painted ceiling.

I - The painting shows the elephant attacked by a crocodile and saved by Krishna descending from heaven.

of his friend and protector, the Mogul emperor, Jahangir. This five-floor, four-sided palace has a screened, overhanging gallery that runs around the outside of the third floor and connects the various rooms that open onto the inner courtyards.
The fourth floor has eight pavilions topped by towers that mark the directions of the compass and segmented domes capped by a lotus flower or water vase. The top floor is made up of terraces and *chattris* connected by narrow galleries made to look like crenellations around the building. Cornices, overhangs, corbels, parapets and door and window frames are finely carved into the ochre sandstone while floral and geometrical patterns and paintings of animals decorate the walls.

A - The heavily ornate temple is adorned with architectural details and both sacred and profane pictures. This picture shows the representation of cities and palaces in a mixture of perspectives – some frontal, some aerial.

B

C

D

B, H - Dedicated to Lakshmi, wife of Vishnu, the low, pentagonal Lakshminarayana temple built by Bir Singh Deo in 1618 is enclosed by a solid wall and topped by a shikhara in the center of the roof. Note that the design of the shikhara has now been transformed into a spire (H).

E

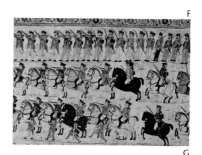

F

G

E, F - The arrival
of the Europeans,
in this case the British,
was also a source of
inspiration for artists
apparently impressed
by the fire-arms.

G - Vishnu rests on the
serpent Shesha watched
over by his wife Lakshmi.
The five-faced god
Brahma, creator of the
universe, sits on a lotus
flower which blooms
from Vishnu's navel.

I - The unarmed and
naked wrestlers grasp
each other in a furious
fight. Although the
characters are
mythical beings,
the scene is depicted
with great realism.

H

I

C, D - Hunting was
a favorite theme
of artists: here hunters
on fiery steeds follow
the animals.
Geometric or floral
bands separate the
narrative pictures.

Equally remarkable are the multi-
floor cenotaphs topped by pinnacled
shikharas along the banks of the river
Betwa where the royal family was
cremated, and the temple dedicated to
Lakshmi, bride of Vishnu, hidden behind
a large enclosure wall. This was built by
Bir Singh Deo in 1618 and is
embellished by pictures with holy and
profane themes which offer an
interesting overview of life during that
period.

A

B

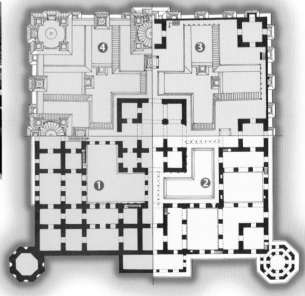

A - Raja Bir Singh Deo built Govinda Mahal at Datia, about 25 miles from Orchha. The palace distributed around the sides of the courtyard combines with the centralized structure of the fort.

The Govind palace at Datia, about 25 miles from Orchha, is also attributed to *raja* Bir Singh Deo. It combines the architectural model with rooms around the sides of the courtyards with the centralized structure of a fort where the ceremonial rooms are grouped together. The important parts of the building were on the upper floors while downstairs was for the service rooms and the *serdab* (the summer quarters) below ground.

Datia palace stands around a central courtyard in which a four-floor square block rises. This housed the royal apartments and the *darbar* (the room where the king held court). The block is crowned by a domed pavilion flanked by *chattris* and connected to the four wings of the palace by small bridges decorated by colonnades. Eight smaller pavilions stand at the corners and in the center of the third floor, like in the Jahangiri Mahal at Orchha.

This ingenious geometric arrangement gives glimpses of the interiors of room after room through open spaces and screened passageways, terraces and *chattri*, where a hidden recess, a stairway embedded in a wall or an unexpected interior courtyard evokes the romantic splendors and adventurous intrigues of the royal courts that have made India famous.

C

E - The central section, or prasada, *contains the representation rooms and is connected to the four wings of the palace by small bridges with elegant colonnades.*

D

B - Datia palace is arranged around the central courtyard in the middle of which stands a four-story block. This is topped by a domed pavilion flanked by chattris. *The most important rooms were on the higher floors. The lower floors contained the service rooms while the underground floors formed the serdab, the section for the summer months.*

C, D - The painted main gateway is a reproduction of a Moslem entrance framed by a pointed arch set in a rectangular cornice.

E

MAP OF GOVINDA MAHAL AT DATIA
THE PALACE IS BUILT ON A SYMMETRICAL PLAN: THE FIVE STORY CENTRAL BLOCK IS CONNECTED TO FOUR PAVILIONS VIA FOUR BRIDGES, EACH IN THE CENTER OF ONE OF THE FOUR SIDES.

A

B

C

A, H - The wall decoration of the Govinda Mahal includes painted mosaics and frescoed niches (H). In one of them we see the tree of life (A), the symbol that was important to both Hindu and Islamic worlds.

B - Parakeets chatter in the branches of a tree; these birds were popularly connected with Kama, the god of love. The colors of the birds are fixed by vegetable glue painted on a thick layer of plaster.

C - The elegant ampulla-shaped flower vase containing stylized and symmetrical flowers decorates the queen's apartments.

F

D

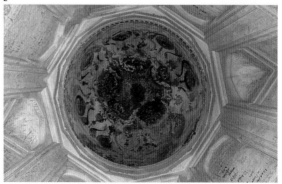

E

D - The strict geometrical composition offers attractive glimpses into other buildings and the courtyard as in the hypostyle bridges that lead to the prasada.

E - The apical pavilion in the Govinda Mahal is topped by a domed ceiling divided into sixteen differently shaped but symmetrical segments.

F - The raslila is one of the best known frescoes at Datia. The raslila is the round dance in which Krishna divides into many images so that every gopi (shepherdess) in love with him is able to have him as a companion.

G - Two elegant peacocks, solar birds that were dear to the lord Krishna, flank an enigmatic image in a floral festoon.

G

H

ORISSA, REALM OF THE GODS

UDAYAGIRI, THE CAVES OF THE ASCETICS

The ancient land of Orissa, formerly known as Kalinga, was characterized by a strong tribal presence. It was the conquest of Kalinga by Ashoka of the Mauryan dynasty that decided the emperor's conversion to Buddhism: evidence of this is given by the edict that

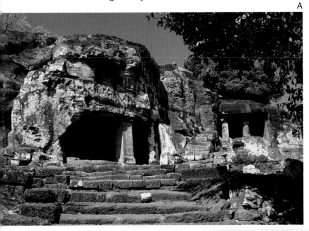

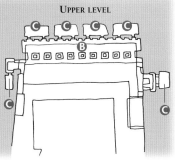

A - The hills at Udayagiri and Khandagiri contain many 1st-2nd century BC rock dwellings excavated by Jain monks under the patronage of Kharavela, king of Kalinga, ancient Orissa.

B - The cells were surrounded by columns and architraves topped by

lunettes with mythical scenes. The cells are connected by friezes containing court and hunting scenes and popular tales.

C - The picture shows a detail from a frieze in Cell No. 1 in Ranigumpha (the Queen's Cave). A hero saves, then marries, the princess who had climbed a tree to hide from her enemies.

MAP OF RANIGUMPHA AT UDAYAGIRI

THE CELLS ARRANGED ON TWO LEVELS (C) FACE ONTO A WIDE COURTYARD (A). VERANDAHS (B) ARE INCLUDED IN THE WINGS ON BOTH FLOORS.

Ashoka himself had carved on a rock in the shape of an elephant at Dhaul, near Bhubaneswar. Today, Orissa is home to some of the most outstanding examples of *nagara* architecture.

Boasting a history rich in changing fortunes, this state has a number of architectural wonders linked to different expressions of Indian spirituality: the rock settlements of Udayagiri and Khandagiri were the dwellings of Jain monks, the monasteries on Ratnagiri hill were a cultured and refined Buddhist center, at Bhubaneswar the majority of temples were dedicated to Shiva while at Puri it is Jagannath, a manifestation of Vishnu, who dominates.

The Chedi dynasty reigned in the Bhubaneswar area between 180-100 BC. The inscription in the "Hathigumpha" (the cave of the elephant) details the life and devotion to Jainism of their most famous king, Kharavela. It was Kharavela and his pious wife who decorated the

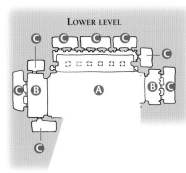

UPPER LEVEL

LOWER LEVEL

caves of Udayagiri and Khandagiri. The cells are ringed with columns and architraves topped by lunettes showing mythical landscapes and are connected by elaborate friezes showing busy scenes from court life, hunting expeditions and popular stories. The cells face onto colonnaded verandahs or directly onto courtyards like, for example, the ground floor of the complex at Ranigumpha (the cave of the queen). Ranigumpha and Ganeshagumpha (the cave of

Ganesh, the god with the head of an elephant) are the two largest and most important caves on the site; Ganeshagumpha is decorated with a lovely frieze and has carvings of two round elephants standing outside. The best conserved cave in Khandagiri hill is Ananta where the cells are protected by armed *dvarapala* (the guardians of the doors) and open onto a verandah overlooking a wide courtyard.

BHUBANESWAR, CITY OF THE THOUSAND TEMPLES

D, G - The Vaital Deul temple is famous for its depictions of heavenly nymphs in the niches of the paga, *the vertical sections that protrude from the* shikhara.

E - Detail of the torana, *the triumphal arch of Mukteswar temple at Bhubaneswar built from 950-75. A small head is included in the* kudu *(horse-shoe shaped niche).*

After the glorious reign of Kharavela, Orissa seems to have entered a period of decadence from which it emerged in the 7th century with the Shailodbhava dynasty. This was followed by the Bhaumakara dynasty and then by the Somavamshis in the 9th century. With the Eastern Gangas in power since the 11th century, Bhubaneswar became an important religious center filled with many temples in the *nagara* style.

The profusion of buildings - at one time there were 7000 grouped around the *Bindusagar*, the sacred pool, but today there are only a few hundred - and the long period of time over which they were built (from the 7th-13th centuries) is a perfect opportunity to study the development of *nagara* architecture. Its beginnings in the 5th century are demonstrated by temples like that dedicated to Shiva at Bhumara and another dedicated to Parvati at Nachna Kuthara in Madhya Pradesh. Their inner sanctums are based on a square ground plan, have flat roofs and ambulatories and

are each preceded by a porch with decorations on all walls. However, the first attempt at the construction of a *shikhara* was seen in the Vishnu temple built during the same period by the Dashavatura at Deogarh in the district of Jhansi, Uttar Pradesh. The temple has three false doorways decorated by panels and a real entrance surrounded by a frame. This was the architectural feature that triumphed at Bhubaneswar. The detailed treatises on local architecture name the various parts of the temple, the *deul*, which is generally split in two sections:

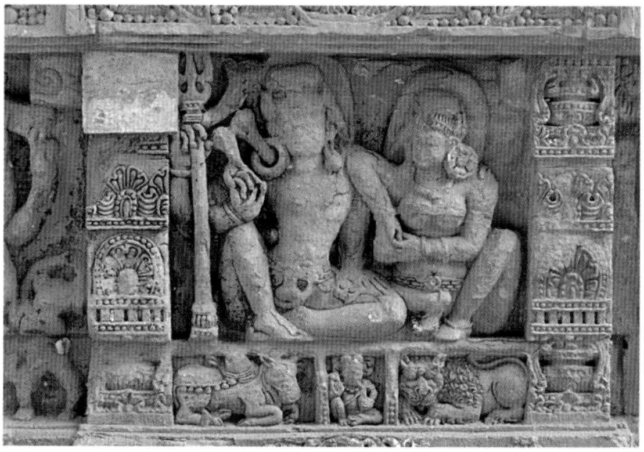

F - A panel on Parashurameswar temple showing Shiva with his bride Parvati. The vahanas *(mounts of the gods), a bull and a lion, are shown below in small boxes.*

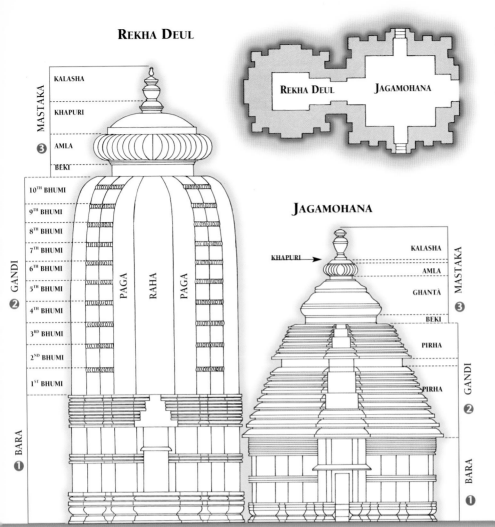

REKHA DEUL

MASTAKA
- KALASHA
- KHAPURI
- **3** AMLA
- BEKI

GANDI
- 10TH BHUMI
- 9TH BHUMI
- 8TH BHUMI
- 7TH BHUMI
- 6TH BHUMI
- 5TH BHUMI
- 4TH BHUMI
- 3RD BHUMI
- 2ND BHUMI
- 1ST BHUMI

PAGA RAHA PAGA

2 GANDI

1 BARA

PLANS OF THE DEUL AT ORISSA TEMPLE

REKHA DEUL   JAGAMOHANA

THE *DEUL* IS SPLIT INTO TWO SECTIONS: THE REKHA DEUL (INNER SANCTUM) AND THE *JAGAMOHANA* (PAVILION OF THE FAITHFUL)

THE *REKHA DEUL*:
1 *BARA*, WALLS
2 *GANDI*, COVERING INCLUDING THE *SHIKHARA*, OR MULTI-STORY *REKHA*, AND *BHUMI* (GROUND FLOOR OF THE *REKHA DEUL*)
3 *MASTAKA*, APEX SPLIT INTO THE *BEKI* (COLLAR); *AMLA* OR *AMALAKA* (GROOVED CUSHION) AND *KHAPURI* (SPHERICAL COVER) THAT SUPPORTS THE *KALASHA* (WATER VASE).

THE *JAGAMOHANA*:
1 *BARA*, WALLS
2 COVERING, ONE OR TWO SERIES OF *PIRHA* (PYRAMIDAL SHEETS OVER THE *JAGAMOHANA*)
3 *MASTAKA* (APEX) SPLIT INTO THE *BEKI* (COLLAR), *GHANTA* (BELL), *AMLA* OR *AMALAKA* (GROOVED CUSHION) AND *KHAPURI* (SPHERICAL COVER) THAT SUPPORTS THE *KALASHA* (WATER VASE).

HORIZONTAL SECTION OF THE *REKHA DEUL*:
PAGA (PROTRUDING SECTIONS) *RAHA* (CENTRAL *PAGA*), VERY LARGE AND OFTEN DECORATED WITH MONUMENTAL NICHES

JAGAMOHANA

KHAPURI →

MASTAKA
- KALASHA
- AMLA
- GHANTA
- **3** BEKI

GANDI
- PIRHA
- PIRHA
- **2**

BARA
- **1**

A

between the *garbhamuda* and the *jagamohana*. The *deul* and the *jagamohana*, which generally were built on a platform, were divided in three horizontal sections:
◆ the *bara*, the walls
◆ the *gandi*, the covering, which in the *deul* is composed of a multi-floor *shikhara* or *rekha*, the *bhumi*, and in the *jagamohana* by one or two series of *pirhas*, the sheets used for the creating the pyramid shape. To carry the weight of the *rekha*, the tower is set on a series of storys containing empty spaces with flat roofs called *ratnamudas*.
◆ the *mastaka*, the upper section divided into the *beki*, the neck of the column; the *amla* or *amalaka*, the segmented cushion-like element; and the *khapuri*, the spherical vault supporting the *kalasha*, the water vase. A further bell-shaped element, the *ghanta*, is set on the *jagamohana* in the *mastaka* between the *beki* and the *amla*.

◆ the *garbhamuda*, the inner sanctum covered by a spiral *shikhara* called a *rekha* for which *rekha deul* or *bara deul* (large temple) are the terms used to refer to the sanctuary and its covering;
◆ the *mandapa* or the *jagamohana*, *mukhashala*, *bhadra deul* or *pirha deul* in reference to the sloping covering made from horizontal sheets or *pirha*. Sometimes a connecting hall, the *antarala*, was built

Although the inner sanctum is always square, as is frequently the *jagomohana* too, the exterior of the temple is broken up by several projecting sections *pagas* or *rahas*. These create constructions with three, five, seven or more protrusions around the walls of the *shikhara*. Of these, the central *paga* often attains notable dimensions and may be decorated with niches accommodating statues.

A strong contrast exists between the profuse decorations of the exterior and the absolutely plain interior in a symbolic representation of the route to be taken by the initiate who must detach himself from exterior forms to be able to search inside his heart for divine truth.

Two further areas are added to the *garbhamuda* and *jagamohana* in the most important temples: these are the *natamandir* (dancing hall) and the *bhogamandapa* (room of offerings).

A - The temples of Bhubaneswar, here is the temple of Siddeswar, are for the most part built of sandstone without the use of cement.

C, D - The emphasis on the horizontal of the compact shikhara (background) in

B   Parashurameswar temple is compensated by the four pagas which each run up one wall. In foreground (D) is the rectangular jagomohana with double flat roofs at the rear.

B, E - The interiors of temples at Orissa are generally bare (E) in contrast with the profusion of external decoration (B). The god only becomes manifest in a heart that is free from passions.

C   F, G - The fretted windows at Parashurameswar depict dancers and musicians and are one of the site's most

lovely features. There is never much light in Hindu temples as the interior is supposed to evoke the idea of a cave, a womb or a heart.

G

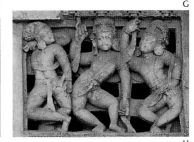

H

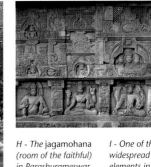

H - The jagamohana (room of the faithful) in Parashurameswar temple has abundant decoration arranged according to precise regulations so that it fits in with the architectural elements.

I - One of the most widespread decorative elements in Orissa temples is the miniature sanctuary adorned with kudus and statues as shown on the wall of Parashurameswar temple.

D

E

F

I

The temples of Bhubaneswar are for the most part built of sandstone without the use of cement, with plinths and enclosure walls made from laterite clay. They were constructed over three periods: the early period, 7th-10th centuries, of which important examples are Parashurameswar and Vaital Deul temples; the middle period, 10th-12th centuries, of which Mukteswar, Bhrameswar, Lingaraja and the Jagannatha temple at Puri are

archetypes; and the late period, 12th-13th centuries, of which Rajarani and Ananta Vasudeva are the principal monuments.

The 7th century Parashurameswar is one of the oldest temples of all. It is rather small and stands directly on the ground with no platform. The rectangular jagomohana covered by a double flat roof is an addition at the rear. The fretted windows depicting dancers and musicians are magnificent.

A

B - The khakhara *temple of Siddheswar at Bhubaneswar represents the mature architectural phase at Orissa.*

C - *This is a reproduction of a miniature temple at Vaital Deul. Shiva is inserted in the medallion of the spire topped by the* kirtimukha, *the monstrous face of the devourer of time.*

D - *The ancient image of riders grouped on gryphons at Vaital Deul is expanded with the addition of a third gryphon, attendants and cascades of pearls.*

Vaital Deul, dating from the 8th-9th centuries, is a lovely example of *khakhara deul*, i.e. a temple covered by a rectangular cupola similar to half a watermelon from which it takes its name *khakhara*. The harmoniously proportioned structure is preceded by a *jagamohana* covered by a two-story flat roof with *shikhara*-type sanctuaries on each of the four corners. Of the many architectural features, the lovely *chaitya* windows accommodate statues. Inside there is an image of Chamunda, one of Shiva's wife's most terrifying forms, accompanied by a procession of Tantric deities. The nearby Shishireswar temple, also decorated with elegant sculptures, is attributed to the same period.

B

C

A - *The 8th-9th century Vaital Deul temple is a typical example of a* khakhara deul *(temple covered with an oblong cupola).*

D

E - *Vaital Deul: Mahishasuramardini (She that kills the demon-buffalo) is a common representation of the Great Goddess in her warlike guise of the Keeper of Order.*

E

F

F - *Lions and elephants often represent reigning dynasties. The relative positions can indicate dominance over one another. This is Vaital Deul.*

The jewel in Orissa's architectural crown is Mukteswar, dating from 950-975 and standing on a low platform, a typical example of a *pancharatha* (a temple with five projections). Its *jagomohana* is based on the classic style of terraced covering; it is illuminated by windows with diamond-shaped fretwork and

G

has unusual internal decoration. The most characteristic element of this temple is the *torana* detached from the main building; the *torana* is presented as an arch built with horizontally- as opposed to radially-set stones, and decorated with reclining figures on two lovely floral capitals. A pool for ablutions stands nearby, particularly frequented by women afflicted by sterility.

Not far away and probably from the same period, Gauri temple, despite being a particular type of *khakhara deul*, is very similar to Mukteswar for its wonderful decorations.

J

H

K

I

G - Mukteswar temple is a typical example of a pancharatha *(a temple with five protrusions)*, with a well-proportioned shikhara *and a* jagomohana *topped by the traditional terraced covering.*

H - Mukteswar temple is considered the architectural gem at Orissa. It stands on a low platform next to a pool with waters that are supposed to cure sterility.

I - A special element of Mukteswar is the detached torana. It was designed as an arch but created by setting the stones horizontally rather than radially.

J - The 10th century temple of Gauri is another example of khakhara deul. It is dedicated to one aspect of Shiva's consort and is splendidly decorated.

K - The temples at Bhubaneswar are mostly built from dry sandstone with laterite plinths and enclosure walls. They were probably painted after being plastered with lime.

L - This detail of Gauri temple shows a heavenly nymph that peeps out from a half-closed door. The kalasha *(water vase)* that symbolizes the fertile womb of life is shown in the foreground.

L

C

A - Brahmeswar temple was built in the 11th century between two enclosure walls on a plinth with a panchayatana ground plan – a central temple with four smaller ones at the corners – with a square pool.

B - Decoration on the shikhara at Orissa is almost exclusively geometric except for the sardula and vyala, various types of gryphons, as can be seen in this detail of Brahmeswar temple.

A

B

C - Rajarani temple was built during the first half of the 12th century and is one of Bhubaneswar's masterpieces. At one time, 7000 temples stood around the sacred pool of Bindusagar.

D - Lingaraja temple was built from 1000-1040. It is forbidden to westerners but can be admired from a raised platform. Besides the rekha deul and jagomohana, it has a natamandir (dance hall) and bhogamandapa (hall of offerings).

D

Bhrameswar temple was built in the 11th century between two enclosing walls on a platform using the panchayatana layout - a central temple with four minor temples at the corners - and is reflected in a square pool. It is mainly decorated with mithunas (pairs of lovers) and kanyas (divine girls) but also has a rare form of internal embellishment: the jagomohana has a lotus flower ceiling with nagas at the corners and processional friezes around the top of the walls.

Fruit of the experience of centuries, Lingaraja temple is ascribed to the period between 1000-1040. It represents the quintessence of Orissa's nagara style. Forbidden to westerners, it can nevertheless be admired from a raised platform at the corner of the wall that encloses it.

A natamandir and bhogamandapa have been added to the garbhamuda and

jagamohana at a later date. The 146 foot high *shikhara* boasts 10 floors and its verticality is emphasized by the unbroken *anghashikhara* that overlay the projecting bands. The area between the *beki* and the *amla* is mediated by gryphons at the corners and four armed figures on the *raha*. The pyramidal roof in the *jagamohana* is split in two parts, increasing the monumentality of the whole. One of the many annexes surrounding the Lingaraja is the temple of Parvati from two centuries earlier; it has the same four-part structure and refined decoration of its larger neighbor.

The temple of Jagannatha in Puri is a center of devotion and forbidden to westerners. It was built in 1118 on the same basis as Lingaraja despite being much larger

sovereign of wealth, on seven jars of jewels to the north; and Ishana, a form of Shiva, with an emaciated figure to the north-east.

The *deul*, ornate with *nayikas* (female figures in seductive poses), contrasts with the very plain *jagamohana*. Only the entrance is embellished, with effigies of the nine planets in the architrave and flanked by two columns entwined with *naginis* (deities partly in the form of snakes).

With a ground plan similar to Lingaraja, Ananta Vasudeva is the only temple at Bhubaneswar dedicated to Vishnu. It was built in 1278 by the princess Chandradevi.

Many other temples are evidence of the past splendor of Bhubaneswar, revealing exceptional beauty in the details of their architecture, statues and decorations with beauty used as a vehicle for spirituality.

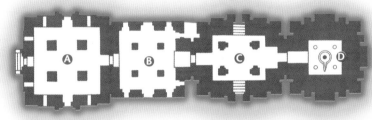

MAP OF LINGARAJA
TEMPLE
A *NATAMANDIR* OR THE
  DANCE HALL
B *BHOGAMANDAPA* OR
  PAVILION OF OFFERINGS
C *JAGAMOHANA* OR ROOM
  OF THE FAITHFUL
D *GARBHAMUDA* OR INNER
  SANCTUM

E - In one of the niches in Rajarani temple, Shiva is dancing the tandava, *the frenetic dance of cosmic dissolution. His mount, Nandi the bull, is at his feet.*

F - The statues on elaborate pedestals are separated from each other by moldings with a strong horizontal emphasis that balance the vertical thrust of the building.

G - Vishnu rests on the many-headed serpent Shesha-Ananta watched over by his wife Lakshmi. The god of the origin of the universe, Brahma, is shown on a lotus.

and incorporating about forty buildings. It was probably built over an ancient place of worship and linked to the tribal society that characterizes Orissa's culture. Restored several times, the temple houses three effigies of Jagannatha, the form Vishnu appears in as the Lord of the World, with his sister Subhadra and brother Balabhadra, a sort of totem with large round eyes.

The Rajarani, from the early 12th century, is famous for the beauty of its statues and differs from the other *deuls* in its unusual *shikhara*, similar to that of Khajuraho in that it has *angashikhara* added to the main body of the tower but here they do not overlap as in other temples and are emphasized as distinct parts lending volume and a soft fullness to the structure. The images of the *dikpalas* (protectors of space) on the corners jutting out from the walls of the inner sanctum are remarkable: we see Indra, king of the gods, on an elephant to the east; Agni, lord of fire, on a ram to the south-east; Yama, judge of the dead, with a buffalo to the south; Nirrti, goddess of death, holding a head over a headless body to the south-west; Varuna, god of the ocean, on the *makara* to the west; Vayu, deity of the wind, with a banner to the north-west; Kubera,

KONARAK, SURYA'S CARRIAGE

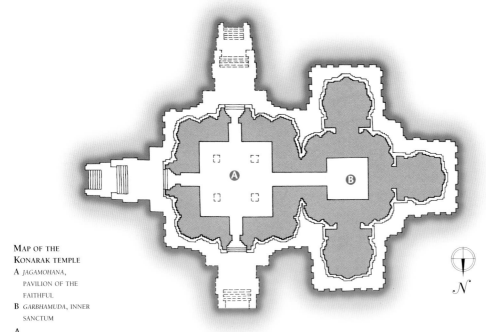

MAP OF THE
KONARAK TEMPLE
A *JAGAMOHANA*,
   PAVILION OF THE
   FAITHFUL
B *GARBHAMUDA*, INNER
   SANCTUM

A

B

C

"Let us meditate on this excellent light of the divine sun; may he enlighten our mind." This is one of the Hindu world's most holy prayers known as *gayatri* in reference to the poetic structure based on 24 syllables, and *savitri* as it was dedicated to Savitar, another name for Surya, the sun god. The temple of Konarak, 37 miles from Bhubaneswar, is a celebration of this prayer and the power of Surya built around 1250 by Narasimha I of the Ganga dynasty.

The district of Konarka, named after a particular position (*kona*) of the sun, for which *Arka* is another name, is linked to the myth that tells of the cure from leprosy of Shamba, son of Krishna, thanks to the help of Surya. The devastation of the temple during the 16th century by the Moslems is cited in many texts, including Islamic sources. Deserted as a place of worship after its profanation, Konarak was sacked by locals for construction materials and by neighboring rulers for statues and ornaments. The raja of Kurda excelled all others in this destructive diversion until the British stepped in to prohibit further removal. The Royal Navy supported this step as the temple served

A - The temple of Konarak is a colossal celebration of the power of Surya, god of the sun, built by Narasimha I around 1250. The jagamohana, pavilion where the faithful gather to contemplate the deity in the inner sanctum, still has its pirhas (horizontal covering sheets) although the shikhara of the garbhamuda has collapsed.

D

E

B - The temple entrance is framed by the pilasters of the natamandirs *sculpted with figures of musicians and* devadasi *(handmaidens of the god) also called* maharis *(experts in the sacred dance, the orissi).*

C - In front of the temple stands the natamandir *(dance pavilion).*

D, F - Next to the natamandir, *an elephant (symbol of the preceding dynasty) is crushed by a rampant lion (emblem of the Ganga rulers).*

E - Many other buildings surround the temple; the ruins of some can be seen near the natamandir. The latter construction was fundamental to the temple for the role played by dance in religious rituals.

F

as a landmark and was known to western sailors and travellers as the "Black Pagoda."

When Fergusson visited Konarak in 1837, part of the *shikhara* over the inner sanctum was still intact but a decade later a tropical storm brought it down. Clearance of the site from the jungle began in 1882 and some of the sculptures were taken to the Calcutta museum in 1894. Excavations were begun under the aegis of the Archaeological Department of Bengal in 1901 and despite the dangers associated with the invasion of sand and unstable stonework, the consolidation work was finished in 1910. Chemical treatment removed the sea-salt, mould

and fungus while the trees planted between the site and the sea limited the damage done by sea wind and sand. As soon as India declared independence, it set up a committee to continue the restoration work which is still in progress.

The temple of Surya is enclosed within a huge wall with entrances on three sides. It was conceived as the carriage of the sun pulled by seven horses: three on the north side and four on the south (two are still in place) and supported by twenty-four wheels almost 10 feet tall along the plinth. For some the wheels are symbols of the 12 months of the year by day and by night, for others they are the

24 hours of the day.

The large room for worshippers, the *jagomohana*, is today filled and sealed to prevent its collapse. It is crowned by a pyramidal structure and terraces and the even larger *deul*, the god's cell now without its *shikhara*. On the three free sides at the base of the *deul* stand additional sanctuaries with external stairways that lead to niches holding statues of Surya.

The temple is preceded by a splendid pillared pavilion on a high plinth. The pavilion, once covered by a pyramidal structure, has a panelled ceiling and is richly decorated.

The detailed representations of the dancers - *devadasis* (handmaidens of the god) or *mahari* in Orissa - have allowed the steps of the local classical dance, the Orissi, which were being lost by the beginning of this century to be saved. The pavilion, therefore, seems to have been a *natamandir* (dancing hall). As a basic ritual in the ceremonial of the temple, dance captures in movement the religious inspiration that statuary and architecture express statically, and while dance converts space into time, the other two transform time into space.

Other buildings complete the complex at Konarak. To the south stands the *bhogamandapa* with the remains of the kitchens, two tanks and a well; to the south-west of the main

C

A

D

C - The wheels are the symbol of the twelve months of the year by day and by night; alternatively, they represent the twenty-four hours in a day. Their eight main and eight

intermediate spokes act as a sundial. The wheels are beautifully carved and engraved throughout, including motifs on the hubs which are often erotic.

A - The Temple of Surya was designed to represent the carriage of the sun pulled by seven horses, two of which are still in place, on twenty-four wheels nearly 10 feet high set along the plinth.

B, H - The "colossal" statuary groups at Konarak were once positioned in front of the three flights of steps to the plinth of the temple: two nearly full-size elephants to the north and two war-horses with attendant and defeated warrior to the south.

The statues of the two rampant lions on kneeling elephants that are crushing a demon used to be situated to the east but now are next to the *natamandir*.

D - The exquisite quality of the work at Konarak temple can be seen in the details as shown in this lovely decoration of elephants in various and lively poses at the base of the wheels.

E - Three niches containing statues of Surya on the external sides at the base of the inner sanctum can be reached by stairways. The picture shows one of the god's attendants and a devotee.

F, G - The three enormous statues of Surya himself show the god at different moments of his journey across the sky. Whether mounted or in his seven-horse carriage, the Sun always looks regal and is characterized by a lotus flower, symbol of his rays, and by other trappings used in the Persian world from which the solar image comes.

B

temple there is a second, maybe older, temple later dedicated to Mayadevi, a wife of Surya; while fairly close by stands a small sanctuary dedicated to Vishnu.

The huge statuary groups of great power and plasticity are the last of the significant finds on the site. At one time they stood in front of three flights of steps around the plinth: on the eastern side are two lions climbing on crouching elephants as they crush a demon, to the north, are two almost life-size elephants while to the south, stand two war-horses with an attendant and a dejected warrior.

At Surya, sculpture and decoration play a fundamental role without, however, spoiling the well-proportioned architectural structure that balances the horizontal and vertical forces through the use of moldings, friezes, pillars and miniature pavilions. Statues of deities, princes, court dignitaries identified by their inscriptions, ascetics, *alashakanyas* (reclining girls), *nagas*, *naginis* and *mithunas* alternate with trains of elephants, military parades, hunting scenes and caravans. There are also portrayals of scenes in heaven and of everyday life intertwined with tangles of flowers and ordered geometric patterns. Every single inch of the walls is sculpted, from the plinth supported by trains of elephants to the very top where a segmented *amla* sits. The wheels are a masterpiece of carving and act as a sundial with their 8 main and 8 intermediary spokes.

Built on sandy soil paying scarce attention to the foundations, the temple was constructed using laterite slabs for

G

E

H

F

the plinths and blocks of kondalite - a type of gneiss - for the temples themselves. The stone blocks were brought from a great distance, possibly via a canal which has since dried up and grown over. They were then laid precisely without the aid of mortar and plastered with lime and sand. The sculptures were added at a later date and were sometimes made with the use of green chlorite. The most successful examples of sculpture are the cornice of the main gateway divided into seven elegant borders, the three statues of Surya in different poses over 10 feet tall in the external niches of the inner sanctum, and the base of the idol inside the sanctum.

The construction of the *shikhara* brought the height of the temple to

D

A

B

C

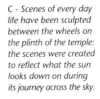

E

A - The jagomohana *entrance is towered over by an architrave with 7 cornices decorated with images of dancers. The emphasis on the horizontal is tempered by the 6 sanctuaries place on top of one another and covered.*

B - In an evocation of fertility, a girl leans against a fruit-laden tree, probably a banana tree. Festoons and floral decorations fill the surface, highlighting the horror of emptiness in Indian art.

C - Scenes of every day life have been sculpted between the wheels on the plinth of the temple: the scenes were created to reflect what the sun looks down on during its journey across the sky.

D - The uprights of the jagomohana *entrance are divided into seven bands each supported by a mythical figure beneath a canopy of leaves. This detail shows a demon to the left and a naga (part serpent god) to the right.*

E - This photo shows a rampant lion on an elephant. The group is found in a narrow niche bordered by floral decorations.

over 195 feet. Wrought iron girders were used to create a support frame for the *shikhara* but it was unable to prevent its collapse.

Despite being despoiled, Surya Deul continues to be a magical place and its portrayals, many of which are erotic, extol life and the living power of the sun. And if the ruler and the high priest had sexual relations with the *maharis* to invigorate and foster the fertility of the land and the population, thereby ensuring the perpetuation of life (*samsara*, which, like a wheel, turns incessantly), the ascetics saw in the sun the power of enlightenment which would liberate them forever from the cycle of rebirth.

LATINA

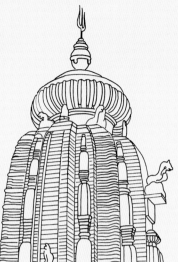

THE DRAWINGS SHOW THREE FUNDAMENTAL TYPES OF *SHIKHSRA*. *THE LATINA*, ON A SQUARE BASE, WITH *ANGASHIKHARA* OF EQUAL SIZES INCORPORATED IN THE SPIRAL CONSTRUCTION THAT CREATE ASCENDING BORDERS MARKING THE CORNERS.

THE SEKHARI, WITH *ANGASHIKHARAS* OF DIFFERENT SIZES THAT "INFLATE" THE *SHIKHARA* AND ROUND OFF THE ANGULARITY OF THE CORNERS.

THE BHUMIJA, BASED ON A CIRCULAR OR STAR-SHAPED DESIGN WITH PARALLEL ROWS OF STACKED MINIATURE *SHIKHARAS* SEPARATED BY VERTICAL BANDS TO GIVE THEM EMPHASIS.

SEKHARI

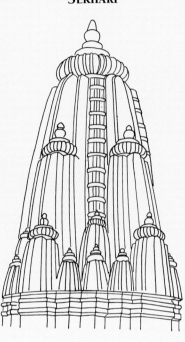

BHUMIJA

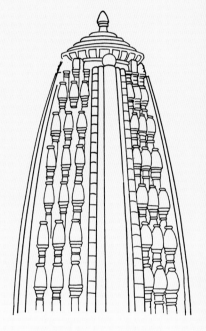

F

VARIOUS TYPES OF SHIKHARA

The *shikhara* underwent notable transformation over the centuries and from region to region.

Three main types can be identified:
◆ the *latina*, a term derived from *lata* (a climbing plant), has a square ground plan where small *amalakas* or *amlas* divide the tower into storys but without interrupting the upthrust of the parabolic curve. *Urushringas* or *angashikharas* (miniature *shikharas*) are incorporated in the spiral construction and create ascending borders in the intricate structure which mark the corners. One of the best examples of a *latina shikhara* is at Lingaraja at Bhubaneswar.

◆ the *sekhari*: groups a number of *angashikharas* of different sizes around the tower which accentuate the rotundity of the *shikhara* and smooth the angularity of the corners. Examples of this type are Kandaryamahadeva at Khajuraho and Rajarani at Bhubaneswar.
◆ the *bhumija* (daughter from the earth): has a circular or star-shaped ground plan with *shikharas* or other reproductions of miniature sanctuaries placed on top of one another in parallel rows interrupted by vertical bands. The most important example of this style is the Udayeswar temple at Udaipur in Madhya Pradesh.

F - The Mukteswar, with the latina *type of* shikhara, *is embellished with elegant statues and refined decoration.*

GUJARAT, CHISELLED MASTERPIECES

MODHERA, THE ABODE OF THE SUN

The importance of Gujarat as a site of ancient settlements is confirmed by the archaeological site of Lothal, a city of the Indus valley civilization inhabited in the 3rd and 2nd millennia BC. The city was divided into two parts, the acropolis constituted the upper section while the residents inhabited the lower. The street pattern and urban structure are evidence of an ordered and affluent society. Lothal was once a flourishing sea-port but today it lies 10 miles from the coast due to geo-

A

B

C

A - The temple of Modhera dedicated to the sun god is one of Gujarat's architectural masterpieces. It was built in 1026 by Bhima I of the Solanka dynasty and is famous for its splendid Ramakunda pool.

B - Vishnu is shown reclining on the serpent Shesha Ananta in one of the small temples of Revakunda. The chakra (a spoked circular weapon that characterizes the god) can be seen in the foreground.

GROUND PLAN
OF MODHERA
A RAMAKUNDA POOL
B MAIN ENTRANCE,
   STAIRWAY AND
   PILLARS
C *SABHA MANDAPA*, THE
   ASSEMBLY PAVILION
D PORCH
E *GUDHA MANDAPA*, THE
   COVERED PAVILION
F *GARBHA-GRIHA*,
   THE INNER SANCTUM
G AMBULATORY

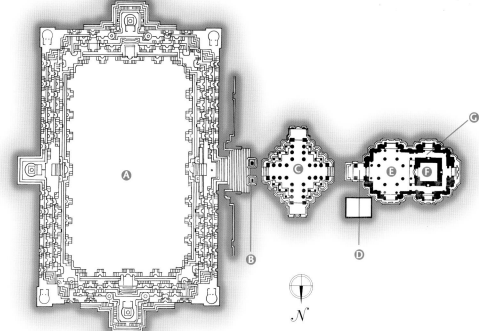

C - *The picture shows a holy kiosk on the steps of the pool: a goddess can be glimpsed between the sculpted decorations chiselled by the local master craftsmen.*

morphological changes. It has a huge, brick dockyard measuring 690 by 114 feet with a warehouse 136 by 130 feet and many other buildings designed to support a busy trading port.

Splendid temples in the *nagara* style were built over the centuries in various areas thanks to the munificence of local dynasties. For example, eight temples were built at Roda in the 10th century where each inner sanctum had a porch and was topped by a *shikhara* in which the simplicity of the structure was enriched by beautiful ornamentation. Equally noteworthy was the temple of Harischandrani Chori at Samalaji built a century later; this temple stands on a platform and includes an *ardhamandapa*, a *mandapa*, an *antarala* and a *garbha-griha* crowned by a slender *shikhara* and rounded off by gracious *angashikharas*. The marvellous decorations still *in situ* and the many lovely sculptures displayed in the museum in Baroda testify to the sophistication of local artists.

One of the masterpieces of Gujurati architecture is the temple of Modhera, dedicated to the sun god, Surya, the "Resplendent," one of the most ancient deities in the Hindu pantheon. Surya is the dispenser of life and death, the center of the universe and a symbol of knowledge; he derives his iconography from the Indo-European mythical repertory and it is not surprising to see

him on a carriage pulled by seven horses in both the Indian and Greco-Roman pantheons.

Many magnificent temples have been consecrated to Surya in India: Martand in Kashmir, Osia in Rajasthan, Modhera in Gujarat and Konarak in Orissa are the most famous.

Dedicated to Surya-Martanda, an esoteric form of the god, the now ruined temple of Martand at Anantnag is the

oldest and most impressive sun temple. Built by the Kashmiri king, Lalitaditya, in the 8th century, it has a rectangular courtyard with three-lobed arcades and chapels onto which the grey, stone temple opens. Probably covered by a pyramidal structure, its large statues and decorations show the Greco-Roman influence exerted by the nearby Indo-Greek kingdoms of Bactria and Gandhara.

D - *The lovely geometric pattern of the steps of the Ramakunda is embellished with kiosks for the deities along the sides and by miniature shikhara at the corners. At the equinoxes, the rising sun skims the surface of the*

D

water and its rays progressively rise up the steps until the statue of the god Surya is illuminated in the temple.

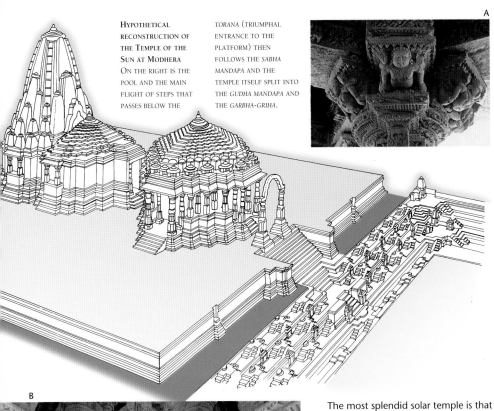

HYPOTHETICAL
RECONSTRUCTION OF
THE TEMPLE OF THE
SUN AT MODHERA
ON THE RIGHT IS THE
POOL AND THE MAIN
FLIGHT OF STEPS THAT
PASSES BELOW THE

TORANA (TRIUMPHAL
ENTRANCE TO THE
PLATFORM) THEN
FOLLOWS THE SABHA
MANDAPA AND THE
TEMPLE ITSELF SPLIT INTO
THE GUDHA MANDAPA AND
THE GARBHA-GRIHA.

A

A - The columns inside the temple are formed by drums sculpted with streams of dancers and celestial nymphs.

B, C - Inside the temple, the cross of the columns supports a ceiling in which the octagonal arrangement of the beams supports the dome.

D

B

C

The most splendid solar temple is that of Modhera, easily reached from Ahmadabad even though it stands in an isolated spot of great beauty. It was built at the behest of Bhima I of the Solanki dynasty in 1026. Two separate structures stand on a high plinth, the *subha mandapa*, an open hypostyle "pavilion of the assembly" in the shape of a cross, and the sanctuary itself split into the *gudha mandapa*, or "covered" pavilion preceded by a porch, and the *garbha-griha* (inner sanctum) surrounded by an ambulatory. The *subha mandapa* is covered by a pyramidal roof and the *garbha-griha* by a *shikhara*. The external walls are decorated with images of Surya on his seven-horse carriage, deities, heavenly nymphs, animals, mythical figures and exquisitely carved symbolic objects. There are numerous pairs of lovers who are always associated with the worship of the sun and fertility.

The *subha mandapa* was perhaps used for dancing; it is open on all four sides with stairways that lead to entrance arches. The pillars inside stand in the shape of a cross and support a central domed ceiling. The pillars are composed of several column-drums sculpted with groups of dancers and heavenly nymphs in a profusion of jewel-like decoration.

D - The Modhera temple stands on a high plinth and comprises two structures: the assembly pavilion and the inner sanctum. The sabha mandapa (assembly pavilion) is an open structure possibly used for dancing with four flights of steps that lead to four three-lobed entrance arches.

E

F

E - One of the typical
features of Gujarati
architecture is the
festooned torana,
the gateway formed
by a three-lobed arch
below the architrave,
that looks like a
garland.

G

F - Eight columns
stand in a circle inside
the gudha mandapa
to support the domed
ceiling. In the niches,
heavenly nymphs hold
up the column drums
that merge into the
ceiling beams with
anthropomorphic
capitals.

G - The external walls
of the temple of
Modhera are
decorated with gods,
heavenly nymphs,
mythical figures and
animals. This picture
shows Parvati, wife of
Shiva and, like her
husband, a trident
bearer.

The most spectacular construction
though is the Ramakunda, the splendid
rectangular pool facing the temple which
has geometrically patterned stairways with
small kiosks for the god along the sides and
miniature *shikharas* at the corners. When
the sun rises at the equinoxes, it skims the
surface of the water and its rays rise
progressively up the stairways until they
pass under the *torana*, the triumphal
entrance to the *subha mandapa*. The light
then penetrates the colonnaded rooms,
reaches the inner sanctum and illuminates
the statue of Surya. The radiant splendor of
the sun transforms the pool and the temple
into a site worthy of the sun god.

H

I

H - The ground plan
of the gudha
mandapa and the
garbha-griha is
described as
pancharatha (with
five projecting parts).
The shikhara over the
inner sanctum no
longer exists.

I - The sanctuary
is divided into the
gudha mandapa
(covered pavilion),
porch and garbha-
griha (inner
sanctum with
ambulatory).

THE SACRED MOUNTAINS OF THE JAINS

Gujarat state has more Jains than any other. Jains are the followers of the religion instituted by Mahariva in the 6th century BC. One of Gujarat's most ancient settlements is located on Mount Girnar where Jainist caves and temples stand on the 3,630 foot high summit. Once the visitor has passed the rock where Ashoka had 14 edicts engraved, the climb continues up a paved path. The site also contains Hindu temples but not inside the Deva Kota, the gate in the enclosing wall that protects the 16 Jain temples. The most important of the Jain buildings is the Temple of Nemintah which

A

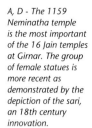

B

A, D - The 1159 Neminatha temple is the most important of the 16 Jain temples at Girnar. The group of female statues is more recent as demonstrated by the depiction of the sari, an 18th century innovation.

B - The most famous Jain holy site is Palitana on the hill of Satrunjaya. There are more than 800 temples and 7000 images which originally date from the 9th and 10th centuries but which were rebuilt after the Moslems destroyed them from the 16th century on.

C - One of Gujarat's oldest Jain communities is located on Mount Girnar with caves and temples where the followers of Jina (the Victor) lived. Jina was an advocate of an ascetic existence.

C

D

contains the black stone image encrusted with gems of the 22nd *Tirthankara*, an honorary title given to Jain prophets. The temple was built in 1159 within an enclosure onto which 70 cells face; it has two hypostyle *mandapas* with domed ceilings, and a *garbha-griha* surrounded by the *pradakshinapatha* with beautiful pillars made from white marble.

The Temple of Tejahpala and Vastupala, two pious ministers during the Solanki dynasty that built the temple in 1230, is composed of a large *mandapa* onto which three cells open: the eastern cell is dedicated to Mallinatha, the 19th *Tirthankaras*; the southern cell to the holy Jain mountain, Parasnatha, that rises in Bihar and

depicted on the circular plinth, while the northern cell is dedicated to the mythical Mount Meru on a square plinth. Outside the enclosing walls and almost at the top of the mountain stands the Temple of Amba Devi, dedicated to the maternal and female aspect of the god borrowed from the Hindu world.

However the most famous holy city in the Jain world is Palitana, a symbol of ascesis and a destination for pilgrims. Palitana includes over 800 temples and 7000 images on the sacred hill of Satrunjaya. The temples are spread over two hilltops inside eleven *tuks* (solid defensive walls). The constructions were for the most part built during the 9th-10th centuries,

then destroyed by the Moslems and rebuilt from the 15th century on. Surprisingly, within the perimeter walls is the tomb of a Moslem holy man who, it is said, protected the site. The Angar Pit is still a place of devotion and the many miniature cots illustrate the fame of the man as a bestower of children.

The typical structure of temples at Palitana includes an enclosing wall in which the chapels of the *Tirthankaras* are built, an elegantly paved courtyard and the central temple on a plinth. The typical temple will have an *ardhamandapa* with festooned arches, highly decorated hypostyle *mandapa* with a magnificent ceilings and a *garbha-griha* topped with a *shikhara* and *angashikhara*.

E - The temples are spread over the two hilltops of Satrunjaya inside a series of eleven massive defensive walls built with towers and crenellations.

F - A typical temple in Palitana stands within an enclosing wall in which Tirthankara chapels stand. A hypostyle ardhamandapa and mandapa, and a garbha-griha, are built on top of a plinth, on the right of the photograph, a typical Jain architectural feature is the temple built on two or more floors with a chaturmukha sanctum (open on four sides) so that the image of the four-faced Tirthankara can look out.

G, H - Decorations at Palitana cover the entire Hindu repertory, from the typical Indian motif of the elephant to that of the dvarapala (guardian of the door) that protects the entrance to the temple. Although Jains do not believe in a supreme God, they are not opposed to the main themes of the Hindu religion.

A

B

A - Adinatha temple is a chaturmukha *type with an inner sanctum housing a statue of the 1st Tirthankara, Adinatha. The statue's four faces look out protectively towards all regions of the universe.*

B - The temple of Adinatha, built on two floors in 1618, is crowned by a shikhara *flanked by angashikharas, repeatedminiature shikharas.*

C - The deities that crowd the temple walls are not the final point in the devotee's search for spirituality but help him to proceed on that path as they are endowed with superior awareness.

C

D

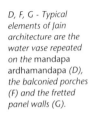

D, F, G - Typical elements of Jain architecture are the water vase repeated on the mandapa ardhamandapa (D), the balconied porches (F) and the fretted panel walls (G).

E - The Tirthankara chapels protected by dvarapalas open onto graceful colonnades that run along the perimeter walls of the temples.

H - The figures of the four Tirthankaras arranged in a cross around a pillar topped by a canopy symbolize the universal diffusion of the Jain doctrine from the eternal center of the truth.

F

E

G

H

The Moslem influence is present in the false domes which sometimes crown the *mandapa* or the corners of the perimeter wall. Another typical feature of Palitana which is rare elsewhere in India is the two or more story temple with a *chaturmukha* cell (open on four sides because it contains a four-faced image of the *Tirthankara*) preceded by four *mandapa* with a porch each.

The Chaumukh temple of Adinatha, built in 1618 on two floors with a cell open on four sides facing the four cardinal points, is based on this plan. The cell is connected to the *mandapa* on the eastern side and holds a statue of the 1st *Tirthankara*, Adinatha, whose four faces turned

A

B

C

D

E

F

towards all regions of the universe have a defensive function.

The principal temple on the site is that of Adishvara. It is made from *arasa* (the local marble), located on the holiest spot in Palitana and is also dedicated to the first *Tirthankara*. It was originally built in 960 but rebuilt in 1530 after being destroyed by the Moslems.

The two story temple is enclosed

C - First built in 960, Adishvara temple was rebuilt after the Moslem destruction in 1530. It stands inside a wall encircled by chapels and has a courtyard paved with colored marble.

D - This relief shows the dhoti, a piece of cloth wrapped around the waist and held in place by a heavy girdle; it is the traditional clothing of men and women.

F - Adishvara is the main temple on the site. It is made from arasa, the reddish local marble, and stands on the holiest site in Palitana. It is dedicated to the first Tirthankara.

G - The sculptures and decorations of Adishvara temple are some of the most beautiful in Palitana. The temple walls are divided by different moldings and alternate processions of statues, cordons and geometric friezes.

A - Along with the traditional shikhara the false dome is also used at Palitana, principally as a covering for the mandapa or placed at the corners of the enclosure wall as a consequence of Moslem influence.

B, E - The two floors of the temple dedicated to the first Tirthankara are topped by a very slender shikhara tempered by numerous angashikharas. The hypostyle mandapa and other sections of the temple are crowned with pyramidal structures and domes.

by a wall containing chapels; the verticality of its slender *shikhara* is tempered by *angashikharas*. The hypostyle *mandapa* is ornamented with delicately carved statues and beautiful ceiling decorations.

Small details in the many other sanctuaries make up for their recent construction, for example, intricate marquetry on window screens or *mandapa* walls, floor mosaics, the corbels on the columns, entrance archways, floral decorations and statues reveal the genius and faith of the local artists. The white marble statues of the *Tirthankara* are especially lovely, their wide open eyes are made from glass paste with silver pupils to give the prophets the crystal transparency of the enlightened.

H - These scenes refer to the vast world of Hindu mythology: apart from the prod and water container, Shiva holds the vajra, a double scepter with three points.

I - The groups of statues on the projecting parts are set in cornices that reproduce temples in miniature. The picture shows the elephant god, Ganesh, the remover of obstacles.

I

J

G

H

J - Shiva Nataraja (Lord of the Dance) is one of the more dynamic figures in Hindu iconography. It is through dance that the god dissolves the world at the end of each cosmic cycle.

JAINISM, THE WAY OF THE ASCETICS

A - The Jain
community is
divided into two
congregations:
the shvetambara
(clothes of white)
and the digambara
(clothes of heaven),
i.e. without clothes.
The statues in Temple
No. 13 at Deogarh
are inspired by the
digambara.

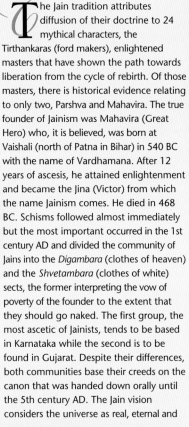

A

C

B, C - For the Jainists,
the Tirthankaras are
not gods but
enlightened spirits
whose example can
help humans to free
their souls from the
influence of matter in
order to liberate
themselves from the
cycle of reincarnations.
The 24 Tirthankaras
can only be
distinguished by the
symbols accompanying
them. Seen here is
Parshva (B), identified
by a cobra crown, in
the temple of
Parshvanatha at
Khajuraho.

The Jain tradition attributes diffusion of their doctrine to 24 mythical characters, the Tirthankaras (ford makers), enlightened masters that have shown the path towards liberation from the cycle of rebirth. Of those masters, there is historical evidence relating to only two, Parshva and Mahavira. The true founder of Jainism was Mahavira (Great Hero) who, it is believed, was born at Vaishali (north of Patna in Bihar) in 540 BC with the name of Vardhamana. After 12 years of ascesis, he attained enlightenment and became the Jina (Victor) from which the name Jainism comes. He died in 468 BC. Schisms followed almost immediately but the most important occurred in the 1st century AD and divided the community of Jains into the *Digambara* (clothes of heaven) and the *Shvetambara* (clothes of white) sects, the former interpreting the vow of poverty of the founder to the extent that they should go naked. The first group, the most ascetic of Jainists, tends to be based in Karnataka while the second is to be found in Gujarat. Despite their differences, both communities base their creeds on the canon that was handed down orally until the 5th century AD. The Jain vision considers the universe as real, eternal and increate (that it has always existed and was not created). Jainists analyze the components and phenomena of the universe in a series of classifications of which the most important are: the soul, inanimate matter, the influence of the *karma* on the soul, the servitude which ensues from that, the halt of karmic effects, elimination of karmic matter accumulated in the soul, and liberation. Matter that has form is increate and indestructible and its smallest components only differ at the level of the molecule. Time, space and the principles of motion and stasis permit the development of the universe which passes through six stages of evolution as it proceeds from perfection to degeneration and vice versa. Although all things are eternal and immutable according to the Jain philosophy, their fundamental qualities can be altered and are submitted to the process of production, transformation and destruction. The world is therefore unity and diversity, universal and particular, permanent and changeable and because of this continual evolution, the only knowledge possible is relative knowledge. This is the innovative Jain doctrine based on "points of view" or the pluralism of the forms of being. Depending on the position from which it is considered, a manifestation may assume any of seven different aspects and it is the "could be" that becomes the foundation of this doctrine of relativity of understanding. Absolutism of any kind is therefore erroneous and only by considering reality from all points of view can true understanding be arrived at. This is the aim of the *jiva* (souls) which are infinite in

B

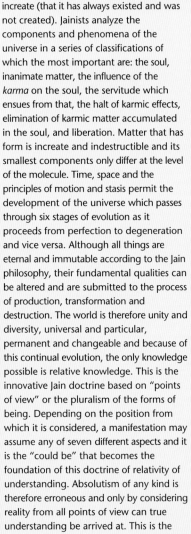

D - The eyes of the
white marble statues
of the Tirthankaras
are made from glass
paste corneas and
silver pupils to give
the prophets the
transparency of the
enlightened.

number, eternal, immaterial and extensible. They contract and expand like light in order to inhabit bodies of different sizes and they can assume divine, human, infernal, animal or subhuman form depending on the merits. Consequent upon a process of attraction the *jivas* exert on matter, the two elements come into contact and the soul, solicited by the passions, remains ensnared in the world conditioning the mental, corporal and verbal behavior of its vehicle and accumulating *karman*. This creates the influx of karmic matter on the soul and the ensuing servitude. Depending on the entity of the influx exerted by the *karman*, the *jiva* may be reduced to an inferior condition, that of the subhuman or the ignorant; or to an

the soul rises towards the top of the universe, the empyrean, where all freed souls exist in a condition of fulfilment. At the opposite end of the cosmos, minuscule vegetal essences, the *nigoda*, wait to begin their journey of evolution.

This framework excludes the presence of a Divinity given that the universe is eternal and increate, the law of *karma* explaining the mechanism by which the universe operates. The *siddhas* (perfect liberated souls) are themselves a sort of infinite multiplication of the Divine. Within the Jain world, the Tirthankaras are the ideal models for the more illuminated devotees as well as being the object of ritual veneration. Images of the

considered an aid to those that are still involved in the human world, they are only forms of superior existence and must be reincarnated as men if they wish to attain final liberation.

The most important symbols in Jainism are the *svastika* (the four arms symbolising the four levels of rebirth - divine, human, feral and infernal), the three points refering to the triple jewel, and the half-moon that is the symbol of liberation.

The Jain moral path is rigorous and requires profound commitment for the monks and nuns who take the vows of non-violence, adherence to the truth, abstention from theft, chastity and the absence of worldly desires. In addition, they are

D

intermediate condition, that of men who observe the doctrine and who are on the path to enlightenment; or to the superior condition, the sublime state of those who have freed themselves from material matters. To prevent new *karma* from extinguishing the existing *karma*, it is necessary to cultivate correct understanding, correct faith and correct conduct - the three "jewels" of Jainism. When liberation has been achieved,

Tirthankaras are seated in the *shvetambara* places of worship and standing in those of the *digambara*; they are each associated with an animal or prophetic symbol and with a *yaksha* or *yakshini*, guardian spirits of the trees. The Jain world also includes female and male deities which have been borrowed from the Brahman context as a concession to the devotional demands of the masses. Although the gods are

bound by rules governing the minutiae of everyday life such as the obligation for the most orthodox to wear a mask so as not to swallow insects inadvertently, and the requirement to sweep the ground in front of them as they walk so as not to stand on living creatures. There are very close relations with the rich and cultured lay community which has actively supported the monastic congregations for centuries.

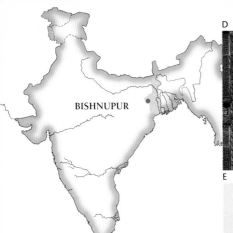

BISHNUPUR

A - At Bishnupur, the city dedicated to Bishnu (the god Vishnu), there stands a complex of terracotta temples of which Madan Mohan is the most important.

B -The 1694 temple is based on a square ground plan and topped by a single spire. In front there is a verandah with three rows of finely worked arches.

THE TERRACOTTA TEMPLES OF BENGAL

A

B

C

G

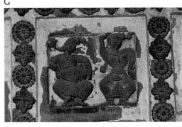

Although Bengal falls within the area influenced by *nagara* architecture, as shown by the temple site at Barakar 140 miles from Calcutta where the *shikharas* are similar in design to those of Bhubaneswar, the local artists developed a particular style of their own over the centuries. This is best demonstrated in the incredible complex of temples in the *pur* (city) of Bishnupur dedicated to Bishnu, or Vishnu, situated about 112 miles from Calcutta. Off the beaten track in rural countryside of great beauty, Bishnupur is the site of the ruins of a palace and holy buildings constructed by the local Malla dynasty during their period of splendor from 1622 to 1758.

The brick and clay temples standing on laterite plinths are more recent imitations of the ancient structures made of less durable materials. They faithfully reproduce the wood, bamboo and straw houses of Bengal with a particular fondness for their curved lines. The sanctuaries are square or rectangular, crowned by distinctly convex roofs with one or more pinnacle towers on top. They also have verandahs generally composed of three arches on pillars either set on the facade of the temple or around all four sides.

Madan Gopal, for example, built in 1665 in laterite, has five towers that make it resemble the Orthodox churches of Macedonia while Madan Mohan, from 1694, has a square ground plan, a verandah and a single pinnacle. One of the most spectacular constructions is Shyam Ray built in 1643 with five pinnacles; it has splendid wall decorations made from terracotta tiles that take on different shades of warm colors at various hours of the day. Jor Bangla (Twin Hut), built in 1655, is based on a typical *do-chala* (twin structure) layout with two connected sections within a rectangular building. Its tower stands in the valley between the

C - The Shyam Ray of 1643 is one of the most spectacular examples of a regional style of architecture that remained uninfluenced by the classical sites: four corner spires are added to the central dome.

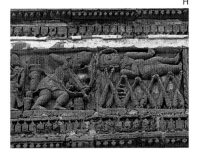

F - The images depicted at Madan Mohan are simple and fresh: there are friezes with alternating rows of animals, warriors and hunters. The hamsas (geese-swans) that symbolize the soul are a favorite image.

D - As Bishnupur is a site dedicated to Vishnu, decorative themes connected with the mythical cycle of Krishna are common: the picture shows the Raslila, the dance of the gopis (shepherdesses in love) around the god.

E - The Jor Bangla (Twin Hut) has a do-chala (twin structure) ground plan with two zones connected within a rectangular building. Above there is a small tower in the valley between the two roofs.

roofs of the twin sections.

The same design is found at Bansberia, about 30 miles from Calcutta, where the temple of Ananta Vasudeva is square with a verandah on all four sides and a central pinnacle while the temple of Hanseswari is built to the *naravatna* (nine jewels) design in reference to its nine towers.

The decoration centers for the most part on the mythical episodes relating to Vishnu and his principal incarnation as Krishna - shown in the *raslila* (Krishna's dance with the shepherd girls which symbolizes souls yearning for the god) - and on life at the time the temple was built: it includes scenes of royal processions, hunting expeditions and the affairs of daily life, all produced in profuse detail and with a pleasing freshness.

G - Dance is prayer in movement, sculpture is prayer petrified: dancer and musician images are recurrent in Hindu decoration. This is the Jor Bangla temple.

H - This scene is probably taken from an episode in the "Mahabharata," the Indian epic poem; Bhisma, the great ancestor of Bharata, lies on a bed of arrows before dying.

I - This boat may be transporting soldiers: apart from its mythical meaning, the scene is a glimpse of life in the 17th century.

J - The whole surface of the Rasmancha temple is covered by splendid wall decorations made from terracotta tiles that take on warm colors depending on the time of the day.

K - The 16th century Rasmancha temple has an unusual structure: it is raised on a plinth, surrounded by a continuous verandah on three sides and has a pyramidal form.

L - The arches of the verandah of the Rasmancha temple rest on thickset pillars of shaped bricks and the unlined walls reveal the careful arrangement of lime bricks.

83

LADAKH, THE LAND OF THE DIAMOND SCEPTER

A COMPLEX ICONOGRAPHIC WORLD

B - A small chorten (a Ladakhi stupa) stands among mani walls (made with stones engraved with mantras) near Tangse. The rock on the right has a stylized Wheel of Life.

C - Monks play a fundamental role at Ladakh; as the major landowners, they also guide the people socially and politically.

D - A group of young monks in the monastery school of Phiyang is intent on learning the sacred characters of Tibetan writing. Culture has always been an important part of life in monasteries.

E - The mandala is a symbolic pattern that reflects the ordering of the psyche and cosmos and plays an important role in local tradition. Its design is a ritual operation as shown in the monastery at Tikse.

LADAKH

A - A lama meditates at the monastery of Phuktal. The lama ("venerable master") is synonymous with the Sanskrit word guru; he is the highest exponent of Tibetan and Ladakhi Buddhist thought.

Buddhism has left few traces of its passing in India. Although its founder was Indian, historical and cultural events have led to its almost complete disappearance from its land of origin. Ladakh, however, continues to be a stronghold of Vajrayana Buddhism, the form that evolved around the 5th-6th century AD as a result of the influence of Tantrism. Tantrism is a complex Hindu ritual movement aimed at restoring primordial Unity by recomposing the polarities of existence - essentially male and female - using sexual and extreme initiatory practices.

Although it has elements in common with Hindu Tantrism, Vajrayana Buddhism differs fundamentally because the *prajna* - intuitive wisdom or perfect awareness realized during enlightenment when one becomes intuitively conscious of the *shunyata* (emptiness), the only true essence of all phenomena and absolute Reality that incorporates and transcends opposites - is static and passive and is identified with *nirvana* (extinction of the cycle of existence). In comparison, the Hindu *shakti* (divine female energy) is active. Both concepts are deified and assume female characteristics in a more or less evident evocation of the Great Goddess who has always been present in the sphere of spiritualism as she is the origin and the end of every cosmic process.

The female gods such as Tara and *Prajna*, or Prajnaparamita, assume great importance in this way. The union of *Prajna* and the Buddha Vajrasattva, who together symbolize the manifest and immanifest worlds, generates the reawakening of supreme consciousness and the total sum of bliss.

If the *prajna* is passive, the Vajrayana devotee becomes active (unlike his Hindu counterpart who is passive) and, in accordance with this dynamism, is able to personify the concept of *upaya* (means) because compassion and love towards all beings become the instruments of salvation and transformation of the *samsara* (place of birth and death). Only compassionate wisdom, the synthesis of head and heart, brings enlightenment. The indestructible and immutable knowledge of the truth, luminous and pure as a diamond scepter, the *vajra*, springs from the union of *prajna* and *upaya*, often represented by the embrace of deities of the opposite sex. It is from this current of Buddhist thought that the term Vajrayana is taken.

In order to best exercise one's *karuna* (compassion) and attain intuition of

C

always represented with their hands held in particular positions, and secondly on *mani* walls where *mantras* are engraved in long strips of stone. The most famous *mantra* is "Om Mani Padme Hum" (The Jewel in the Lotus) in which the two terms can be interpreted in different and symbolic ways, for example, Buddha and the world, male and female, compassion and knowledge, truth and the heart and so on. *Mantras* can be found around the Ladakhi countryside, in wall paintings and in *tankas*, where the *mandala* have a pre-eminent place.

Tankas are painted on different types of material - cotton, silk or linen - and are widespread in Ladakh. The traditional technique of making them is still used in certain monasteries although modern processes have been introduced which have meant a loss of quality and have encouraged a collector's market which has nothing to do with their holy aspect.

After spreading the cloth with a mixture of chalk and glue, then rubbing and polishing it with a shell or smooth stone, the design of the *mandala* is traced out. Another piece of cloth on which the design is mapped out by small holes is placed over the first. Coal dust is sprinkled so that it will pass through to the prepared cloth below to leave the pattern marked out which is then completed with black or red ink. The more extensively used technique is printing in which the design is engraved onto a metal or wooden matrix and then reproduced on the cloth.

At this point, the cloth is laid out on a frame and painted using water colors mixed with vegetable glue. The completed *tanka* is not the work of one person but of a team in which members specialise in one field.

The iconography of Vajrayana Buddhism is based on the theory of the three bodies of the Buddha according to which the Enlightened One manifested himself on earth in the fictitious personage of Siddhartha Gautama, the Buddha that could be perceived by man. He also appears in divine forms in the heavens for the benefit of the *bodhisattvas* (enlightened ones that help humans free themselves from *samsara*) while as the Absolute, he manifests himself in the body of the *Dharma* (Doctrine) which can only be known by

the other Buddhas. No longer, therefore, one Buddha, but innumerable and assisted by innumerable *bodhisattvas* in an iconographic expansion influenced by the surrounding Hindu religious environment.

This leads to a complex unravelling of divine forms that emanate and return to the Adhibuddha, the ineffable symbol of universality, and which is symbolized by the five cosmic Buddhas emanating from the body of the *Dharma* - Vairochana, Akshobhya, Ratnasambhava, Amitabha and Amoghasiddhi - from which are derived the five *bodhisattvas* produced from the body of bliss, reflections and active principles of the previous Buddhas - Samantabhadra, Vajrapani, Ratnapani, Avalokiteswar and Vishvapani - which in their turn are manifested on earth in the five human Buddhas - Krakucchanda, Kanakamuni, Kashyapa, Shakyamuni and the Buddha of the future Maitreya - produced from the body of transformation.

The theme of the five *Dhyanibuddhas*, or Buddhas of

D

E

meditation, is very frequent in Ladakhi representations.

Vairochana (He that shines) is a depiction of the Emptiness that contains and transcends all. He is shown in white with the eight-spoked wheel of the Buddhist path in one hand, sitting on a throne of lions, embraced by the "Divine Mother of Infinite Space" and linked with the first of the building elements of the universe: space/ether. The gesture

shunyata, full control of the "three doors" of knowledge, the body, the word and the mind, is needed. This control is practised by means of different techniques including *yoga*, with its psycho-physical exercises, and a series of supporting instruments which aim to encourage discipline and purification. Exercise of the *mudra* (hand gestures representing the main aspects of the spiritual path), the constant repetition of *mantras* (syllables and holy verses) aimed at purifying and concentrating the mind, and the tracing of the *mandala* (a circular symbolic design crowded with gods and symbols) used to plumb the depths and control and activate latent potential.

The *mudra*, *mantra* and *mandala* are the three elements that are depicted firstly, in the statues of Buddha and others in the Buddhist pantheon who are

A

B

A - Among the characters in the pantheon of Vajrayana Buddhism, the lokapala (guardians of the world) are royal figures protecting the regions of the universe. Their symbolic design, borrowed from Tibet, shows Chinese influence.

B - Besides showing signs of spiritual supremacy (the bulge between his eyebrows and the protuberance of the skull), the Buddha at the monastery at Shey also has three folds on his neck, a symbol of supreme beauty.

C - Images evoke the initiate's spiritual descent into the depths of the psyche in order to achieve enlightenment.

that is associated with him is the *dharmachakramudra* (the putting into practice of the doctrinal wheel) or the teaching that leads to supreme wisdom and enlightenment, of which Vairochana is a symbol.

Akshobhya, protector of the east, is as blue as the sky and radiates from his heart the pure white light of wisdom that is as limpid as a mirror in which all things are reflected without any alteration of its surface. This is the reason he is called Akshobhya (Immutable, Imperturbable). He is connected with water and seated on a throne held up by elephants. In his left hand he holds the five pointed *vajra* while the right hand is turned away with his fingers touching the ground in a gesture of firmness. He embraces Locana (Divine Mother, Eye of the Buddha).

Resplendent in the color of the sun, Ratnasambhava, protector of the south, has his hand loose towards the ground but shows his palm in the gesture of

offering the three jewels of Buddhism: the *Buddha*, the Doctrine and the community of monks. This is the origin of his name which means "Origin of the jewels." The color yellow refers to the earth of which Ratnasambhava is protector together with his female counterpart, Mamaki, whom he embraces on a throne supported by horses, solar animals associated with the star at the zenith.

Amitabha (Infinite splendor) is the Lord of the west, as red as the sun at sunset and associated with fire. His hands are laid palms up in his lap in the gesture of meditation while holding a lotus, symbol of the intuitive vision that springs from purification of perception. Seated on a throne of peacocks, he embraces Pandaravasini (She that is dressed in white). The contrast of the red and white symbolize the blaze of discriminating vision and the luminosity of pure perception.

Amoghasiddhi, guardian of the north, is the incarnation of the mystery

of the "Sun at Midnight" or the presence of the invisible light that guides enlightenment. The yellow of the sun and the night blue are mixed to create green, the color of active wisdom, which this fifth Buddha radiates from his heart. Enlightened doctrine leads to activity aimed at liberating all living things. The double *vajra* that Amoghasiddhi holds in his hand symbolizes benevolence and compassion, the two cardinal virtues of Tantric Buddhism that Amoghasiddhi (Infallible perfection) realizes in full. The raised hand showing the palm, in the gesture *abhayamudra* common to so many cultures, invites us not to be afraid. Seated on a mythical creature part bird and part man, he flutters in the air with which he is associated. He is united with Tara (Star), compassionate Lady of supreme salvation.

The primary function of the *Dhyanibuddha* is to stir vibrations, encourage mental associations and open to new experiences by means of the widest possible range of symbols and archetypes. The use of colors has clear psychological intent and is one of the most controversial and varied applications in the Buddhist sphere as they are used in different ways in different contexts. With regards to mind control, colors are associated with the five main alterations that afflict the psyche: white with ignorance, blue with hate, yellow with pride, red with lust and green with envy. By concentrating on the color, one is able to stimulate the related mental state and therefore become aware of it and pacify it. Pacification is achieved by referring to the Buddha of the same color who, with his serene and luminous image, shows how it is possible to transform negative psychic states into positive ones.

Portrayal of gods is used as a support to the processes of voicing and dissolving passions through cultivation of the "five judgements" and therefore choice of the sacred image to meditate on cannot be casual. Having made his choice, the practising devotee comes to share the qualities of the deity to the point of identifying himself with the god in a transmutation of his human personality into the divine personality.

C

D

D - Protection of the dharma (doctrine of Buddha) is entrusted to the dharmapala (custodians of the dharma). This photo shows the monastery at Hemis.

E - Dhritarashtra, the lokapala of the east, is here shown in the monastery at Spituk. He is the lord of the gandharva (celestial musicians) in India's oldest tradition.

Consequently, there are innumerable portrayals of the divine figures. There are angry and frightening divinities as guardians of doors, proud ones that govern regions of space, the four main ones, four intermediate ones, the many bodhisattvas that make up the cohort around the central image, the celestial Buddhas that preside over the five great families of deities and which encourage a precise form of meditation, and there are their companions, the dakinis, who are expert yoga ascetics and endowed with great powers.

Two of the most striking elements in the iconography of Vajrayana Buddhism are the terrifying behavior of the gods and the erotic entwining of the male and female figures.

In the first case, the frightening aspect of a god is not to be understood as demonic but is supposed to suggest the power and appalling struggle conducted to overcome fear, anguish and mental alienation. The Herukas are such an example: these are angry, aggressive figures that personify the masculine qualities of the Buddha and the dynamic and combative aspect of enlightenment. They have three eyes that refer to the many symbolic triads: past, present and future; the world of the coarse, the ethereal and that without form; attachment, aversion and ignorance, and other examples still.

The retinue of dakinis that accompanies the Herukas arouses the forces able to overcome the narrow and conventional human personality by cutting its karmic links and projecting into another dimension. In this way, panic becomes an indispensable condition for approaching realization. Terrifying in their nudity, which refers to the need to confront truth without mystification, the dakinis personify the most explosive and powerful forces of nature, dangerous for a normal man but capable of ensuring salvation to an initiate able to control them through awareness and knowledge and able to use them as instruments for breaking down barriers.

The blood-filled cup that these figures often hold symbolizes the red solar element that is the emblem of awareness and which here has a double meaning: it can be an intoxicating poison if exclusively the product of

intellectual processes and self affirmation, yet it becomes the elixir of salvation when it is combined with the virtues of compassion and love. These aspects are fully represented by the union of the male and female deities.

The terrible attitude of the Herukas and Dakinsi lasts only as long as the struggle or until integration is achieved. At that point, the angry gods show their true, benevolent, selves. It is no longer the dark impulses that control and condition the mind but the mind that has dominated and destroyed the impulses. It does this by emptying them

E

of their contents and moving in the direction of shining purity that is the prelude to achievement of shunyata (emptiness).

The embracing gods refer to the overcoming of polarities represented by male and female, Yab-Yum (father and mother) or the god and his companion. Their union emphasizes the reintegration of the Unity and therefore the attainment of enlightenment. The erotic ecstasy suggests the ineffable moment of bliss and fulfilment that accompanies achievement of supreme consciousness.

A

B, C - A monk (B) from the Gelug-pa congregation, the "Yellow Caps," uncovers a fresco in the monastery of Lingshed. The "Yellow Cap" monks are the most austere and closest in their interpretation of the original message of Buddha. They were founded by the Tibetan monk Tsongkha-pa, shown in the tanka in Likir monastery (C), to fight back against the relaxation of customs of the first monks, the "Red Caps," who tended towards tantric and magical practices.

D - This row of chortens is to be found at the monastery of Phuktal in Zanskar, one of the three districts of Ladakh. The chorten (receptacle of offerings) is the symbol of the dharma and is made up of geometric sections which refer to cosmic elements.

E - Leh, dating from the 14th century, is dominated by the fort and royal palace built between the 16th - 17th centuries. The nine floor palace has today been abandoned.
D

GÖNPAS, SOLITARY PLACES

Ladakh is a barren land situated between 9,750 and 19,500 feet above sea-level, suspended from the sky by rugged, majestic mountains with an air of crystalline clarity. Throughout the country, a chain of *gönpas* (monasteries) is responsible for guarding the Vajrayana version of the message of Siddhartha Gautama, the historical Buddha.

The originally Mongol population has embraced Buddhism since the first centuries of the Christian era and was therefore influenced by the Lamaist Buddhism that spread through Tibet following the preaching of the 8th century Indian monk Padmasambhava, the *guru* Rimpoche. He founded the congregation of the Red Caps, monks who wore a red head-covering and followed Tantric doctrine

B

C

A - Maitreya, the Buddha *of the future that according to Tibetan tradition will appear in the West,* is a much-loved figure *in Ladakh. This statue is in the monastery of Sani, the oldest in Zanskar.*

and practices combined with certain elements of the older Tibetan religion, Bon-po shamanism.

A particular form of Buddhism was therefore created which came to be called Lamaism, from the term *lama* (venerable master), which is synonymous with the term *guru* and given to the most advanced exponents of Buddhist thought. The Red Caps were the first to spread through Ladakh when the country was divided into several centers of power. During the 11th century, king Utpala unified the kingdoms of Spiti, Zanskhar and Ladakh as far as the Mustang. Following relaxation of the customs of the Red Caps, king

Trakbumde (1410-1440) embraced the reforms that Tsongkha-pa had carried out in Tibet creating the congregation of Gelug-pas (Yellow Caps) which adhered to a more austere interpretation of the original message of the Buddha with less emphasis on Tantric and magical practices. The message of the Yellow Caps that spread into Ladakh with the founding of the *gönpa* of Spituk and Tikse. At the end of the 15th century, the Moslems reached western Ladakh and, after a short-lived period of glory under king Senge Namgyal (1570-1642), the kingdom was forced to accept the protection of the Moguls to prevent a Mongol-Tibetan invasion. In

F, G - The cham, *ritual Vajrayana Buddhism dances influenced by the ancient Tibetan religion, Bon-po, is the central event at monastery festivals. They are danced by monks to the sound of various instruments, including large cymbals.*

built from brick, stone and wood; they have wall paintings but the many restorations that have been carried out over the centuries make dating difficult.

Gönpas often include one or more *chortens* (receptacles for offerings and symbols of the *Dharma*). This is a Tibetan development of the *stupa* that incorporates various geometrical shapes representing cosmic elements. The cubic base refers to the earth, the drum to water, the construction above to fire, the umbrella-shaped part to air and the pinnacle in the form of a vase - the mythical container of *amrita*, the nectar of immortality or supreme consciousness - to ether/space. Another reading sees the lower part symbolising earth, the upper part sky and the middle part man who is placed

F

G

1834, *raja* Jammu annexed the country and the British intervened to establish a border with Tibet.

As land-owners and centers of organisation and power, the *gönpas* always remained the cornerstones of the country. Built between the 10th-17th centuries on caravan routes that connected to the Silk Road, the monasteries are often actually forts protected by their position on rocky outcrops: they are built in several storys, plastered white in the color of purity and meditation and often have their window frames and doors painted in the lucky color of light blue. Dark red stripes are also

sometimes painted below the guttering to ward off evil influences. The monasteries are divided into a courtyard with porticoes, a meeting hall (the oldest and most important section), the Buddhist temple, the monks' cells, the library and a print room; sometimes there is also a royal apartment. Many monasteries have a temple for the *Gonkhangs* (guardian spirits) which is prohibited to women; this is an interesting and contradictory element as women in Ladakh enjoy the same consideration as men and yet, the custom of polyandry whereby brothers may marry the same woman still exists. The monasteries are

between the two on a path of ascesis.

The benefit of the building is received by walking around it clockwise. Niches containing holy images or other aids to meditation are placed in the walls and there are long lines of prayer or "*Dharma*" wheels which are spun by the faithful with a twofold objective: to celebrate and perpetuate the "putting in practice of the wheel of the Doctrine" by Buddha centuries before when he disclosed the path to liberation, and spreading of the positive vibrations contained in the holy *mantra* engraved on the wheel or painted on rice paper.

A

A, E, F - At the monastery of Kharsha, many frescoes decorate the Lhabrang or residence of the senior lama. The recurrent themes are the various Buddhas, most importantly Shakyamuni with his bowl (E); the bodhisattvas, the enlightened ones who help other humans to free themselves from the cycle of rebirths; and important members of the faith, like Tsongkha-pa shown in the yellow cap (F).

D

B - Monastery interiors, like this one at Leh, are generally dark and the rooms receive their light from the entrance. Doorways are often flanked by images of the dharmapala whose aggressive attitudes emphasize their function as protectors against negative influences.

E

G

F

B

C

Leh, the capital of Ladakh, can be reached from Srinagar by following the ancient caravan route that joined Kashmir, Ladakh and Tibet.

There are several centers of interest along this road. At Baltal, is the path leading to the cave of Amanarth, a famous pilgrimage destination for followers of Shiva who worship a *linga* made from ice there.

At Dras, Buddhist reliefs including those of Avalokiteswar and Maitreya can be found on the rocks. At Kargil, still a Moslem town, the path leaves for Zanskar, a semi-desert region ringed by marvellous mountain scenery; it is an ideal place for trekking.

The roads are lined with small villages

C - The repetition of the Buddha in the motif of the "Thousand Buddhas" in the monastery at Leh suggests the unique relationship each person has with the Enlightened One.

D - Karsha is home to the most important monastic city of Yellow Caps in Zanskar.

H

I

G - Note the severe style of the tapered buildings in this view of the citadel at Leh. The pinnacle of a chorten can be seen in the foreground: the pinnacle is associated with fire (the base with earth and the bell-tower with water) while the half-moon symbolizes air and the apex ether or space.

H - Scattered along the caravan routes, monasteries were often built on rocky outcrops like Bardhan in Zanskar and frequently acted as forts.

I - Houses of lay people were grouped around the monastery as in this photograph of Phuktal. Built between the 10th - 17th centuries, monasteries comprise a meeting hall, a temple, the monks' rooms, a library, a print room and sometimes a royal apartment.

J - The 7th century AD relief of Maitreya on the rock at Mulbek announces that the Moslems had arrived at the border of the Buddhist countries.

J

where the women still wear attractive local costumes and head-scarves studded with turquoise stones, and by numerous monasteries, many of which can only be reached via a gruelling trek up a mountainside.

On the road from Kargil to Padam, capital of Zanskar, two monasteries can be seen: Pititing, from which there is a marvellous view, and Sami, which it is thought was founded by Padmasambhava in the 8th century. From Padam, one can reach Zangla passing by the monastical city of Karsha where the most important congregation of Yellow Caps in Zanskar is situated. At Zangla itself, the ruins of the palace of the king of Zanskar and an

unassailable fortress can be seen. Returning to Padam, the ancient capital Thonde can be visited where a monastery is set in a marvellous natural location, then the monastery of Bardhan, the village of Reru and the monastery of Mane before reaching Phuktal Gönpa in a setting of wild and incomparable beauty.

Following the caravan route further towards Leh, the visitor reaches Mulbek at an altitude of 10,400 feet. Here the figure of Maitreya, 23 feet high and sculpted out of the rock, guards the entrance to the Buddhist villages.

A

B

The next stop is the Lamayuru Gönpa at 11,193 feet, founded by the Red Caps in the 11th century. Now partially ruined, it still has a beautiful statue of Buddha Vairochana, many wall paintings and an impressive meeting hall. The statues of Naropa, one of the founders of Vajrayana Buddhism, of Marpa, the monk that introduced it to Tibet, and of his disciple Misla Raspa, known as Milarepa, are kept in a small cave.

Near Nurla, the remains of the 11th century citadel of Temisgang dominate the caravan route with the temples of Maitreya, Avalokiteswar and Padmasambhava spangled with images and paintings from the Tantric Buddhist pantheon. At Yuletokpo it is possible to deviate to the monasteries of Ridzong and Mangyur, and then continue to Alchi.

Founded in the 11th century by Rinchen-bzang-po, a cultured monk who translated many Buddhist texts from Sanskrit into Tibetan, Alchi monastery contains splendid murals showing court scenes and *mandalas*

crowded with deities in its meeting hall with the beautiful, multi-colored wooden door. There are also statues including those of the five *Dhyanibuddha* - Vairochana with four heads in the center, Akshobhya and Ratnasambhava, Amoghasiddhi and Amithaba on either side - and the goddess Tara and Maitreya. The wood lined temple of Sumstek is much more interesting; it has a *chorten* and enormous, multi-colored statues of *bodhisattvas* which can only be seen entirely from the frescoed top floor. To the right of Sumstek stands Lhakhang Soma (New Temple) covered with paintings and boasting several *chortens*.

C

D

E

A - The 19th century Ridzong monastery can be reached from Yuletokpo. It houses a collection of tanka (sacred paintings on cloth) and some outstanding statues.

B -These chortens are at Ridzong: a second interpretation of their component parts views the base, bell-tower and pinnacle as representing the earth, man and heaven, i.e. the path from the profane to the sacred.

C - Founded in the 11th century, the walls of the monastic complex at Alci enclose five temples, chortens and monks' houses.

D - The wooden buildings at Alci are of great beauty, particularly the porches of the Dukhang (assembly hall) with its splendid entrance portals.

E - Another dharmapala, this time in the monastery of Lamayuru at the entrance of the Gonkhang, the temple of the guardian deities, where the influence of the Bon-po religion is evident.

F - Lamayuru Gönpa was built in brick by the Red Caps in the 11th century. At one time it was one of the biggest cultural centers in Ladakh and had more than 400 monks. Today there are only about 40.

G

H - Sacred images can be seen in the main Lamayuru of Lhakang (house of the Divine) which also acts as a temple. The place in the foreground is where the orchestra sits during ceremonies.

I - Lamaist Buddhism believes that some lama reincarnate themselves voluntarily to continue preaching the doctrine. Their statues stand in line in front of the library shelves of the Lamayuru where the texts of the "Kangjur" (the precepts of the Buddhist faith) are kept. They hold white shoes, traditionally offered by the faithful.

H

I

A - The remains of
the 15th century fort
of Basgo include the
Temple of Maitreya,
decorated with
splendid pictures.

B - The monastery
at Phiyang is worth
visiting for its
collection of 14th
century bronze
statues.

C - This symbol of the
Buddhist doctrine can
be seen at Sankar
monastery: it shows
two gazelles on either
side of a wheel set in
a rest and
commemorates the

first sermon that the
Buddha gave in the
Wood of Gazelles at
Benares. The sermon
is called "The Setting
in Motion of the
Dharma Wheel."

D

A

B

C

Past Saspol, further down the road to Leh, there is a deviation for the Yellow Cap monastery of Likir, probably dating from the 15th century. Then comes Basgo where the 15th century fort was besieged in vain by the Tibetans and helped by a Mogul army. The 15th century Chamba Lhakhang (Temple of Maitreya) inside is decorated with splendid pictures and is the see of the seven Brug-pas, an emanation of the Red Caps, which are widespread and dominant in Bhutan. The temple of Serzang ("of gold and of copper") stands amidst the ruins of the royal apartments. It gets its name from the hundreds of manuscripts of the "Kangjur," canonical Buddhist texts, and the "Tangjur," their commentaries, printed with gold, silver and copper letters. All around are *chorten* and *mani* walls. Beyond Nyemo, the large monastery of Phiyang contains a collection of 14th century bronze statues and an attractive Gonkhang.

Six miles past the monastery of Spituk, famous for its holy dances, the visitor arrives at Leh at an altitude of 11,446 feet. The city was mentioned for the first time in the 14th century when the king of the nearby kingdom Shey carried out some building there. Once the Ladakhi kingdoms were united, a fort was built at Leh by King Tashi Namgyal (1500-32) on Victory Peak which overlooks the city. A century later, Senge Namgyal (1570-1642) built a palace there that still stands and Leh became one of the most important trading centers between China, Tibet and India. Its fortunes continued during the 19th century when the *raja* of Jammu conquered the country. Its trading importance ended when China annexed Tibet.

The nine floor palace, now abandoned, stands in the old city dotted with *chortens*. In front of the palace stand the temples of Maitreya and Avalokiteswar with interesting statues and pictures. Climbing up to the ruins of the fort, there is another temple dedicated to Maitreya and a disquieting Gonkhang with the guardian deities at their most terrifying.

Various important buildings surround Leh: the monasteries of Sankar, Matro and Stakna; the 19th century palace of Stok; Shey with the ruins of what used to be a royal residence until the 15th century, standing among many *chortens* and *manis*; in the deserted 18th century royal palace at Shey there is still a frescoed temple and another with a colossal statue of Shakyamuni; at the foot of the palatine hill there is a rock sculpted with the *Dhyanibuddha* and, further on, another temple with the frescoes of the main figures in Buddhism and a second colossal statue of Shakyamuni.

D - A view of Stakna monastery and its village.

E - The monastery of Spituk at Leh, one of the oldest in Ladakh, is famous for its cham. The monastery is built around a courtyard, the fulcrum of the congregation's life, with wooden loggias. The traditional terraced roof supports a bell-tower which symbolizes femininity, intuition and transcendent wisdom.

F

E

G

H

F - The first capital of Ladakh, Shey, is located near Leh on a holy lake. There are ruins of a royal palace, a pair of remarkable temples and many chortens and manis.

G - Offerings of clothes and precious materials to decorate statues, like this one at Shey, is part of the Ladakhi ritual that honors images in a sort of regal ceremony.

H - Stok was the seat of the royal family from 1834 when the raja of Jammu conquered the country. The palace and the monastery show the taste for compact buildings of several storys with wooden balconies.

A

B

C

A - The library at Tikse holds manuscripts of Buddhist precepts and their commentaries.

B - The monastery at Tikse is famous for its January celebrations. The drums are used to keep the rhythm of the cham.

C - The buildings within monasteries are arranged in a physical hierarchy with the main temples in the highest section of the citadel as a manifestation of Ladakhi theocracy.

D - The procession of lama with their traditional white shoes opens the display at Tikse.

D

E - Access to the temple is generally gained via steps and a porch. These architectural features symbolize the passage from the sacred area to the profane. The picture shows the stairway of the Lakhang at Tikse.

F - Trumpets are the other main instrument in the cham orchestra. Also included are different types of drums, short trumpets, oboes, cymbals, bugles and bells.

G, H - Many individuals figure in the cham: some are fixed and appear in every display while others vary from monastery to monastery. Classical Indian and Tibetan shamanic dances have given rise to an interesting iconographic fusion. Preparation of the masks takes a long time as the details are strictly laid down by tradition.

F

G

H

Especially noteworthy are the monasteries of Tikse and Hemis, 15 and 34 miles respectively from Leh.

Tikse was built as a fortress in the 15th century but its murals were painted 400 years later. In one of the two meeting halls there is a library; a small temple with splendid *tanka* can be visited in the apartments of the monastery's superior.

I - The face of Maitreya, the last of the five historical Buddhas who yet has to appear in person, smiles enigmatically in the monastery of Tikse. The five Dhyanibuddha (the Buddhas of meditation) are represented by the five sections of the crown.

J - Fearsome deities, like the mysterious Herukas wrapped in flames, are not demonic forces but represent the terrible struggle to overcome mental anguish. They also incarnate the male virtues of the Buddha and the dynamic and combative aspects of enlightenment.

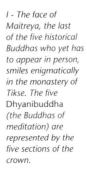

A - *Hemis monastery is characterized by long rows of carved and painted wooden loggias that show the influence of Kashmir.*

B - *The small houses built on the ridge belong to farmers that work on the monastery estate. The relationship between the monastery and the farmers is still feudal in nature.*

C - *Hemis is famous for the* cham *held in mid-June.*

A

B

C

D

Passing by other fortified monasteries, we come to Hemis, founded in the 17th century by Tagtshang Raspa of the Brug-pas congregation. Famous for its festival held in its large courtyard at the end of June, the monastery has two meeting halls with sculpted wooden verandahs, one containing the silver *chorten*, the other the throne of the *lama* who directs the *gönpa* and who it is believed is the reincarnation of Tagtshang Raspa. The Old Temple with 200 year old pictures, the main meeting hall or Lhakhang, other small temples, the *lama*'s apartments and an ancient royal residence are all installed on the upper floors.

G

E

F

D - The long rows of prayer wheels are spun to symbolize the "setting in motion of the Wheel of the Doctrine" and to spread the positive vibrations of the holy mantras engraved on the cylinders or painted on rice paper.

F - The sacred images at Hemis are displayed in line under the porch.

E - The door has a unique architectural symbolism: it is the threshold between two spiritual levels, exterior worldliness and interior spirituality.

In the foreground, the Buddha touches the ground to call it to witness his victory over the demon Mara and his resulting enlightenment.

G - The mandala is prepared by letting mineral powders pour

from a metal cone. It requires great precision and patience.

H - Animal masks at Hemis are indicative of the shamanic roots of Bon-po in the tradition of Red Cap Buddhism.

H

BUDDHISM AND ITS DEVELOPMENT

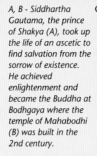

A, B - Siddhartha Gautama, the prince of Shakya (A), took up the life of an ascetic to find salvation from the sorrow of existence. He achieved enlightenment and became the Buddha at Bodhgaya where the temple of Mahabodhi (B) was built in the 2nd century.

Siddhartha Gautama was born in Lumbini wood near Kapilavastu in present-day Nepal towards the middle of the 6th century BC. He was the son of Mayadevi and Shuddhodana, head of the Shakya clan. Siddhartha was married at the age of 16 and became a father. He soon felt the futility of the life of luxury he had been brought up in and, following symbolic meetings with an old man, a sick man, a dead man and a wandering ascetic, he decided to abandon his life as a prince. He became Shakyamuni (ascetic of the Shakya) and dedicated his life to the search for truth. Having failed to find answers in either the philosophical speculations of the age or from the ascetic beggars, he gave himself to meditation which "awakened" him to the truth and therefore "Enlightened" him; this is the origin of the name given to him, Buddha,

A

B

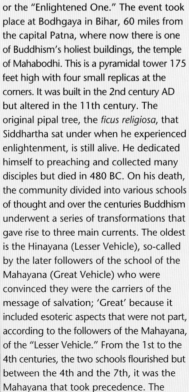

C

or the "Enlightened One." The event took place at Bodhgaya in Bihar, 60 miles from the capital Patna, where now there is one of Buddhism's holiest buildings, the temple of Mahabodhi. This is a pyramidal tower 175 feet high with four small replicas at the corners. It was built in the 2nd century AD but altered in the 11th century. The original pipal tree, the *ficus religiosa*, that Siddhartha sat under when he experienced enlightenment, is still alive. He dedicated himself to preaching and collected many disciples but died in 480 BC. On his death, the community divided into various schools of thought and over the centuries Buddhism underwent a series of transformations that gave rise to three main currents. The oldest is the Hinayana (Lesser Vehicle), so-called by the later followers of the school of the Mahayana (Great Vehicle) who were convinced they were the carriers of the message of salvation; 'Great' because it included esoteric aspects that were not part, according to the followers of the Mahayana, of the "Lesser Vehicle." From the 1st to the 4th centuries, the two schools flourished but between the 4th and the 7th, it was the Mahayana that took precedence. The

Vajrayana (Diamond Vehicle) emerged in the 5th-6th centuries and reached its peak in the 9th but declined in India at the end of the 14th century when its adepts were absorbed into Hinduism. It has remained strong, however, in Tibet and in neighboring regions.

All three schools refer to the "Four Noble Truths" enunciated by the Buddha. They are: that sorrow is the universal experience of mankind in a world in which everything is impermanent, painful and without sense; that the cause of sorrow is desire; that the removal of sorrow can only come from the removal of desire; that desire can be abandoned by following the Noble Eightfold Path - right views, right resolve, right speech, right behavior, right occupation, right effort, right mindedness and right meditation as a program leading to salvation.

Hinayana Buddhism, or Theravada (Doctrine of the Elders), is considered the depositary of the teachings of the Buddha and focuses on moral training and the monastic rule. The Theravadin (followers of Theravada) consider the universe overwhelmed by a perennial becoming and, to break out of this changing circle of phenomena and sorrow free from all spirituality, they cultivate detachment from life to follow a Middle Way which condemns materialism and spiritualism but which considers ascesis and metaphysics as useless. The individual does not exist as a

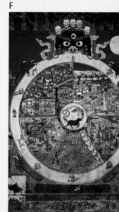

E - The positions of the hands, mudra, refer to a particular spiritual dimension and a moment in the life of the Buddha: the victory over Mara and the Buddha's consequent enlightenment are celebrated here at Bodhgaya.

C - The Buddha was not depicted in person until the 2nd century. One of the symbols to indicate his presence were footprints, as in the temple of Mahabodhi. These are the object of great veneration.

D - The development of Buddhism brought with it new conceptions into the doctrine: the bodhisattva (guides towards liberation) appeared with the Mahayana, the "Great Vehicle." The 16th century painting in the monastery at Karsha shows Padmapani, the "Lord of the Lotus."

substantial entity and psycho-physical unit; what is defined as a man is a phenomenal personality in a continuous becoming. At death, a new series of compounds follows, conditioned by the effects of the karma accumulated in the previous aggregates which acts as a catalyzing and determining element. The concepts of a permanent soul subject to reincarnation or of the Absolute have no place in this context. The opponent of the sorrowful phenomenalism of the material world is nirvana, total extinction of empirical existence and of its fictitious consciousness. Nirvana is also indefinable as it is beyond the limited comprehension of man. Only the monk who has become an arhat (a venerable saint) with an austere and detached life is able to achieve it.

The Mahayana starts from the same point as the Hinayana with the doctrine of the early Christian era. They are less intransigent in their interpretation of rules, averse to the ideal of the arhat and convinced that the possibility of salvation is not a prerogative of the arhat alone - from which the term "Great Vehicle" is derived as all beings are included in the embrace of salvation. The followers of Mahayana look for answers to two irrepressible needs: one speculative and the other mystical. They consider the ego to be illusory; it is a negative concept fed by the "three poisons" -

attachment, aversion and ignorance - and the momentariness of each phenomenon free of any spiritual basis is empty. The concepts of shunya (empty) and shunyata (emptiness) end up referring to the only true essence of all phenomena, to the absolute Reality that incorporates and transcends all opposites, that is beyond all definition and which can be experienced only with a process of enlightened intuition. Within this context, the samsara (conditioned existence) and nirvana (its extinction) no longer oppose one another in an irreducible antagonism but become the two interdependent aspects of the same internal reality, consciousness, now a raging sea under the impulse of desire, now a serene mirror that reflects its emptiness. In a strong reassessment of laymen, the Mahayana proclaims the right of every being to be capable of attaining enlightenment with the help of the bodhisattva, literally "He whose essence is enlightenment." Although enlightened and ready to achieve nirvana, the bodhisattva prefers to postpone his immediate liberation in order to indicate the path of salvation to others in the fulfilment of compassion and benevolence, the cardinal virtues of Mahayana Buddhism. The figure of the bodhisattva plays a full part in the religious context of the "doctrine of the three bodies:" the human body of the historical Buddha that could be perceived by mankind, the glorious and divine body that is enjoyed by the bodhisattva, and the body of the Dharma (Doctrine) that can only be known by Buddhas.

The addition of female deities marks the advent of Vajrayana which extends the concept of shunyata and suggests complex ritual passages to attain it. The various goddesses symbolize prajna (perfect intuitive wisdom), followed by upaya, the right "means" which is constituted by compassion and love for all beings. The union of prajna and upaya brings enlightenment or the pure and unchanging knowledge of the truth.

F - The Wheel of Life is one of the most characteristic elements of Ladakhi iconography. It symbolizes the different levels of awareness in existence and sets them in the various kingdoms, from the infernal to the divine, under the control of time, the fearsome three-eyed Mahakala.

G - Gilding and inlaying of semi-precious stones are an essential part of the creation of a statue as earthly treasures are especially befitting of the sacred.

A

HARYANA: IN THE HEART OF ISLAMIC INDIA

The mosque, the tomb and the fort

The huge differences between the Hindu and Moslem worlds can be seen when comparing the structure of a temple to that of a mosque. Strictly monotheist, the Islamic religion excludes any anthropomorphic representation so that decoration is

B

C

exclusively based on geometrical or floral patterns and calligraphy. The Hindu temple, however, is filled with the figures of gods, humans, demons and animals that almost obliterate the lines of the construction. The significances of its strongly centralized design are often difficult to understand at first glance and the path that leads to the meeting with the Divine in the dark inner sanctum is almost maze-like.

However, while the symbolism of Hindu architecture is only understood in its entirety by initiates, Islamic symbolism is much more explicit: the mosque is a linear and luminous building always aligned with Mecca (which in India is to the west) and has particular emphasis on the facade so that it can be easily understood by all.

From a technical point of view, the Hindu architect prefers the use of flat roofs and a false vault as a covering while

the Moslem uses the arch and creates a true vaulted roof. The former also builds without the use of binding materials, the second uses lime.

Islamic architecture is for the most part expressed in three basic constructions: the *masjid* (mosque), the *maqbarah* (mausoleum), and the *qila* (fort). The oldest mosques are built with a courtyard with a central tank for ritual ablutions and with a prayer hall opposite the entrance. The direction of Mecca, the *qibla*, is shown by the *mihrab*, a sometimes ornate niche built in the western wall before which the faithful prostrate themselves. The *minbar* is generally placed next to the *mihrab* and is a form of pulpit from which readings of the Koran are made and prayers led.

The perimeter wall is embellished with porticoes and cells for pilgrims while the prayer hall is covered by one or more cupolas and enriched by the

iwan, a facade of Persian derivation which frames the entrance in a pointed arch. A *madrasa* - originally the house of the Koranic master that has evolved into a residential college with courtyard and hypostyle buildings - and the cemetery in which the tombs of the men and women are separated are often annexed to the mosque.

Minarets, towers from which the *muezzin* calls the faithful to prayer, may be built separate from the rest of the mosque, at the four corners of the perimeter wall, in the two frontal sections only or possibly included as part of the prayer hall at the corners of the facade or as towers flanking the *iwan*.

Also of great holiness are the tombs of the *sufi*. *Sufi* are islamic ascetics that devoted themselves to mystical practices either in monastic communities or as individual wandering beggars. They belong to a religious movement that appeared in the 8th century in the Bassara (Iraq) region of Arabia and particularly throughout Persia. Their tombs are often a place of pilgrimage and many rulers and their courtesans had themselves buried in the same area so as to benefit from the holy influence of the place.

Although Islam requires simple burial

HARYANA

B - The tomb of Humayum in Delhi foreshadowed the classical design of the mausoleum. It stands on a high plinth in the center of the garden; its burial chamber has a double dome and annexes for relatives.

C - The fort evolved from a gloomy, solid defensive citadel into a palace split into hypostyle pavilions in the style of a marble encampment. The Red Fort in Delhi is a blend of the two models.

D - The minaret is one of the basic elements of the mosque. It was in origin a separate structure but ended up being incorporated into the main building and used to mark the corners and the facade. Here is the Qutb Minar from the Quwwat-ul-Islam Mosque at Delhi.

A - Islamic architecture is expressed in three main constructions: the masjid *(mosque),* maqbara *(mausoleum) and* qila *(fort). This photo shows the mosque of Aurang Zeb at Lucknow, Uttar Pradesh. The mosque in its simplest form is composed of a courtyard with a central tank for washing, and a domed prayer hall with a monumental facade and minarets.*

in the ground facing Mecca, the mausoleum soon became an object of great architectural interest. It is generally situated in the center of the *char bagh* (the park divided into "four gardens") at the crossing of four raised avenues which have waterways coursing along them. This layout evokes the Pairi Daeza (the walled place) - from which the Greek term "Paradeisos" comes - or the Persian Paradise. The fountain of life plays in the center of the park from which the four holy rivers gush. If a tomb is placed in this position, the deceased would be placed in the lap of eternity. The conception of the Pairi Daeza explains the fundamental importance underlying gardens and the play of water in Indo-Islamic architecture.

The central room of the *qubba* (mausoleum) is generally cubic and covered by a domed ceiling. The passage from a square to a circle occurs by means of an octagonal drum in which an arch or a semi-dome at the corners of the *qubba* transforms the square into an octagon.

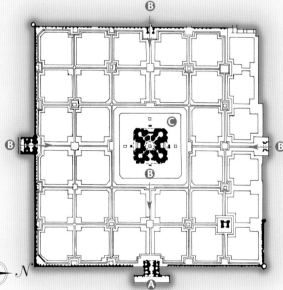

D

PLAN OF THE TOMB OF HUMAYUM
THE GEOMETRIC STRUCTURE OF THE GARDEN IS DIVIDED INTO SYMMETRICAL SECTIONS WITH FOUR MAIN AVENUES
A ENTRANCE GATEWAY
B FOUR AVENUES
C PLATFORM WITH MAUSOLEUM AND AROUND THE GARDEN WITH CHESSBOARD LAYOUT

This may, if necessary, be further divided into a figure with sixteen sides to as to create an adequate base for the ring of the dome. The repetition of miniature splays in a sort of honeycomb is a classical ornamental motif referred to as *muqarnas*.

The fort was derived from the evolution of a massive defensive citadel into a palace split into hypostyle pavilions similar to marble

encampments, attesting to the psychological transformation the Moslems underwent in India. The first sultans and provincial governors were hated conquerors who felt isolated in the great Hindu sea around them and it is hardly surprising they defended themselves with thick walls, blind windows, arches and low, threatening domes. The Mogul emperors on the other hand considered themselves rightful lords of a land that belonged to them and the open pavilions and increasingly slender cupolas reflected their feelings of security and familiarity with India. In the nearly two centuries of their reign, though their peak lasted less than one, they developed the unique and fabulous Mogul style of art.

In general, there were three sections to the courts in the style of the "Thousand and one Arabian Nights," each of which had its own mosque: the courtyard of the public audiences with the *diwan-i-am* (ceremonial hall); the buildings and gardens of the *daulat khana* (house of the master) where the ruler lived around the *diwan-i-khas* (hall for private receptions); and the *haram saray* or *zanana*, the quarter reserved for the women with splendid gardens, pools and fountains. The contrast between the solid walls made from red sandstone and the graceful, white marble pavilions is one of the most indicative aspects of Mogul architecture.

The development of Moslem architecture in India is documented by the remains of the sultanate of Delhi, provincial buildings and Mogul masterpieces. The Seljuk influence is evident in the oldest Moslem buildings, while the influences of Tamerlane and the Safavid dynasty underlay Mogul art with the exception of the constructions built by Akbar which were inspired by a fertile union with Indian art. Mogul architecture became more showy than substantial under Aurangzeb and its Baroque and rococo flourishes signalled its end.

The use of the arch, the vault and the dome were the most important innovations of the Moslems. The materials they used were sandstone (the best coming from Sikri) and black marble from Surat and white marble from Makrana in the state of Jodhpur in what is today Rajasthan.

DELHI

THE EIGHT CITIES OF DELHI

One of the most important places for the study of the development of Indo-Islamic architecture is Delhi. Of the eight cities that traditionally constitute Delhi, leaving out of consideration the first two (the mythical Indraprastha celebrated in the epic poem "Mahabharata" and the older Lal Kota or Qil Rai Pithora of the Hindu dynasties) and the last (the Delhi of British India), the other five were built by Moslem rulers.

Having installed himself in the citadel of Lal Kota, Qutb-ud-Din began building the oldest mosque in India, Quwwat-ul-Islam (Power of Islam) and Qutb Minar, its splendid minaret in 1193. He used columns

C

C - The remains of the "Power of Islam" facade with five ogival arches extend to the foot of the Qutb Minar. Originally designed with three floors, it was completed with another two in marble. With groups of columns and tapered edges, the minaret dominates the site of Quwwat-ul-Islam. The mosque was later enlarged by Iltutmish who added a courtyard.

D - Ghiyas-ud-Din Tughlaq built his tomb in the center of a pool at the citadel of Tughlaqabad (1321-1325). The tomb was enclosed by turreted walls and made from red sandstone with a marble, bulb-shaped dome.

E - Iltutmish built his own mausoleum in the site of the "Power of Islam" mosque in 1235. This was a grey stone building with no dome, composed of eight ogival arches decorated with geometric patterns derived from Hindu designs.

D

A - Settled in Delhi, the sultan Qutb-ud-din started construction of Quwwat-ul-Islam (the Power of Islam) and its minaret, the Qutb Minar, in 1193. This is the oldest mosque in India.

B - The first Moslem constructions in India made wide use of materials taken from destroyed Hindu temples. An example is the porches in the courtyard of Quwwat-ul-Islam.

recovered from destroyed Hindu temples for the walls and placed small cupolas where the walls met. The prayer hall was given a facade with five pointed arches and decorated with bands of Koranic script. The minaret originally had three floors made from sandstone of different colors with balconies supporting groups of stalactites; later, two more floors made from marble with reddish sandstone inserts were added.

In 1235, Iltutmish increased the size of the mosque with the addition of another courtyard and the mausoleum. The latter was made from grey stone, had no cupola but eight pointed arches and was decorated with geometrical patterns showing Hindu influences. The mosque of Sultan Ghari in the district of Mehroli was another mausoleum in grand style: it had a hypostyle enclosure with a tower at each corner and a simple yet austere prayer hall in front of which an octagonal plinth was built. Below the plinth was the burial chamber of the son of Iltutmish.

Ala-ud-Din moved his capital from Lal Kota to Siri though almost nothing remains of it now. The name of the sultan is linked to the building works undertaken in the area of Quwwat-ul-Islam of which only the first

floor of an unfinished minaret and the "Ala-ud-Din gate" to the splendid Ala-i-Darvaza mosque of 1311 remain. A *qubba* (a cubic room topped by a cupola) was made from sandstone with marble highlights and split into two tiers, one with arches framing *jali* (fretted marble screens), the other with blind windows. Four large arches with double archivolts frame the entrances.

Tughlaqabad is an impressive citadel built by Ghiyas-ud-Din in 1321-1325. It contains the tomb of its founder enclosed by turretted walls in the center of a now dry pool. This slightly tapering and sober building is made of sandstone with marble inserts and is crowned by a bulb-like marble cupola in the Tartar style.

The oldest section of the marble burial chamber of *sufi* Nizam-ud-Din Auliya,

F

H - The Khirki Masjid (Mosque of the Windows) is an austere structure built in the shape of a cross on an arched plinth.

G

F - Ala-ud-Din planned a mosque to stand beside Quwwat-ul-Islam. Only the entrance was completed, the Ala-i-Darvaza, made from sandstone with marble inserts in 1311.

G - The complex of Nizam-ud-Din stands in the center of the one of Delhi's oldest quarters. It comprises a mosque, a mausoleum and the tombs of other notables.

H

MAP OF DELHI
A LAL KOTA
B SIRI
C JAHANPANAH
D KOTLA FIRUZ SAHA
E DINPANAH
G SHAHJAHANABAD

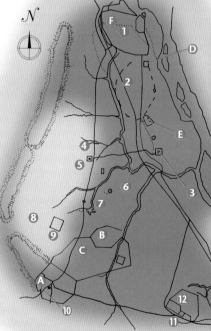

connected to the red sandstone mosque, was erected in 1325. Over the centuries many people have been buried there including Jahanara Begum, the daughter of Shah Jahan.

Muhammad Tughlaq built a new capital at Jahanpanah, an unknown site somewhere between Lal Kota and Siri, but then decided to transfer the population 745 miles to Daulatabad near Aurangabad in the state of Maharashtra in a terrible march lasting 40 days. Dalautabad was once known as Devagiri when it was the citadel of a Hindu Yadawa dynasty destroyed by Ala-ud-Din in 1296. The new sultan, Muhammad, transferred all the citizens of Delhi there in 1327 but then moved them all back again in 1330 causing unspeakable suffering. In 1345, Dalautabad fell into the hands of a Turkish governor, Zafar Khan, who founded the Bahmani dynasty destined to last a little over a century. Five defensive bastions make the fort unassailable. To reach the top of the fortification, it is necessary to climb a spiral stairway cut out of the rock.

The fifth city of Delhi was built under Firuz Shah in 1354. The city was called Firuzabad or Kotla Firuz Shah. It was built from poor materials and in a very plain style in which flat-roofed pavilions replaced

vaulted ceilings and *apadanas* (square, hypostyle Persian rooms with porticoes). The *talar* (a building with columns with a wall at one end where the throne stands) was the fore-runner of the *diwan-i-am*. Firuz Shah also founded the *madrasa* at Hauz-i-Khas, a Koranic college with a mosque and octagonal tomb.

Construction of Khirki Masjid, the "Mosque of the Windows," is attributed to one of Firuz' dignitaries. The mosque owes its name to the number of screened openings in the walls of the austere building raised on an arched plinth. The ground plan of the mosque is in the shape of a cross with four courtyards lined with three rows of columns and cupolas at each junction. Three of the four entrances to the mosque project from the main body of the building and are flanked by minarets, the fourth, blind, entrance is the location of the *mihrab*. This design did not bring enough attention to the *qibla* and was never repeated.

Tughlaq's buildings were menacing and heavily anchored to the ground as though defensive in nature.

1 RED FORT	7 MOTI MASJID
2 CITY OF SHER SHAH	8 HAUZ-I-KHAS
3 TOMB OF HUMAYUM	9 TOMB OF FIRUZ SHAH
4 TOMBS OF LODI	10 QUBT MINAR
5 TOMB OF SADFAR JANG'S	11 TOMB OF GHYAS UD-DIN
6 TOMB OF NIZAM-UD-DIN	12 TUGHLAQABAD

A - Built in red sandstone with marble inserts and with a prayer hall with lobed arches, the Jami Masjid is the religious center of Shajahanabad, the seventh of the eight cities of Delhi.

B - Closed off by an enclosure wall and further bounded by a low wall, the tomb of Isa Khan uses eight chattri to allow the square shape of the mausoleum room to merge into the circular dome.

C - The cenotaphs of Isa and his closest relatives are dimly lit by fretted windows inside. In keeping with Islamic tradition, the bodies are simply buried in the ground.

The development of the design of the mausoleum took place under Sikander of the Lodi dynasty who moved his capital to Agra. The best examples are the tombs of the Sayyid and Lodi families in the Lodi Garden in Delhi. There were two main types: the first had an octagonal plinth and a single story with a verandah, this was probably meant to be used for rulers. The second had a square plinth and two or more storys but no verandah which was perhaps meant for nobles. Both had a cupola although these sometimes seemed a little flattened. This disadvantage was overcome by raising the drum the cupola rested upon and then surrounding the cupola itself with eight small cupolas on *chattris* (kiosks with small columns).

A classic example of the octagonal design is the Sikhander tomb of 1517 which stands in Lodi Garden. It is surrounded by a triple-arched verandah which lightens the mass and is screened by a wide continuous overhang. The cupola is the first example to have an internal ceiling over the burial chamber and a separate external cupola of the size required by the architecture of the new style. Sikhander was also responsible for the Bara Gumbad Masjid built in 1494. It had a guest-house attached, was decorated with beautiful arabesques and joined on a high plinth to the large, square, two-story Bara Gumbad ("Tomb with a Large Cupola.")

D - The tombs of the Sayyid and Lodi dynasties in the garden of the same name in Delhi is indicative of the evolution of the mausoleum. The 1494 Bara Gumbad built by Sikander is an example of a tomb with a "large dome" on two floors.

E - The verandah that runs all around the tomb has the double function of creating large areas of shade and of using its arches to lighten a rather heavy building.

F - Between the 13th and 16th centuries there were two types of sultanate mausoleum: one with a square plan, many floors and no balconies; the other was octagonal, one floor high and with a verandah. The tomb of Isa Khan is one of the second type of design.

G - Humayum founded Dinpanah, the sixth city of Delhi. His mausoleum became the model for those to follow. The octagonal tomb with marble dome stands in the center of the garden on a high, arched plinth.

G

preferred in Delhi during this period as shown by the 1547 tomb of Isa Khan, a dignitary of Sher Shah, built in an octagonal enclosure containing a mosque decorated with enamelled tiles.

Humayum returned to his throne in 1555 but was only able to enjoy his power for a year. On his death, his wife, Hamida Banu Begum, had a mausoleum built for him which became a model for those to follow. A perimeter wall with four large entrances bounded a garden divided into four sections by avenues which led to the tomb from the gates. The tomb itself was made from red sandstone and white marble in the center of the garden on a high plinth decorated with arches. The octagonal burial chamber with four monumental *iwan* was crowned by a Persian-style cupola made from white marble and flanked by four, terraced, two-story corner structures with additional *iwans* and *chattris* for the remains of other members of the royal family.

Construction of the Jami Masjid, the largest mosque in all India, was also the work of Shah Jahan between 1650-56. It stands on a high plinth with flights of steps that are home to shops and services. The enclosure wall had by this time developed into an open colonnade and the prayer room in red sandstone and marble inlays was dominated by an imposing *iwan* flanked by two wings of five arches each and topped by three enormous marble cupolas.

The era of the Lodi dynasty ended with the Moth-ki Masjid, a well-proportioned building in red sandstone and grey stone, with five arches, each with a triple archivolt and separated by vertical bands of decorative niches.

In the 16th century, Babur, descendant of Genghis Khan and Tamerlane, established the dynasty of the Moguls and his son, Humayum, founded Dinpanah, the sixth city of Delhi. Dinpanah was centered on Purana Qila (Old Fort) whose construction was finished by Sher Khan of the Suri dynasty after dethroning Humayum in 1540. The most interesting buildings in the fort are the Qila-i-Kuhna from 1541, built in grey and red sandstone with white and black inserts, which has a beautiful facade with five arches of different sizes and octagonal turrets at the rear corners, and

H

the Sher Mandal, a two-story, octagonal building with arches and *chattris*, which was used by Humayum as a library.

Sher Shah's tomb stands in Sasaram, Bihar, on a high plinth in the center of an artificial, square pool. The enormous monument has an octagonal lower story and hexagonal upper story with *chattris* between. The huge cupola stands 146 feet high and is nearly 72 feet wide. The octagonal ground plan was also

I

H - The Jami Masjid, completed in 1656, is the largest mosque in India. It is dominated by the massive iwan flanked by two arched wings and overlooked by three enormous domes.

I - The completion of Purana Qila was the work of the usurper Sher Shah. The massive fort was begun by Humayum on what was once possibly the site of Indraprastha.

The seventh city of Delhi, Shajahanabad, was created by Shah Jahan. It is centered on the Red Fort and the Jami Masjid. The fort is protected by more than a mile of walls and by the course of the river Yamuna. It has two beautiful entrances, the Lahore Gate and the Delhi Gate. Once past the area where the palace bazaar used to be held, a square courtyard leads to the *naubat khana* (place of the drum).

This is a two-story building where the musicians who announced the movements of the emperor lived. Further on, a wide courtyard opens onto the *diwan-i-am* (public audience hall) built in sandstone plastered with powdered marble. It has lobed arches and a back wall inlaid with semi-precious stone against which the

D

A

B

C

marble canopy for the throne rests on a high platform.

Private apartments line the river bank behind the *diwan-i-am* connected by the Nahar-i-Behisht (Channel of Paradise) which carried water to the various parts of the fort: the Rang Mahal with the wonderful fountain in the shape of a lotus flower made from marble and precious stones; the Khas Mahal, three marble pavilions built between 1639-49 as a private residence for the emperor with the Muthamman Burj, the octagonal tower from which the ruler appeared to his courtesans each day; the *diwan-i-khas* which contained the famous peacock throne stolen in the sacking of Delhi in 1739 by the Afghan adventurer Nadir Shah; the *hammam* (baths) with mosaic floors permanently covered by a film of water and walls reflecting glass tiles; the Hayat Baksh Bagh, the Mongol garden with geometrically shaped flower beds filled with colorful flowers and small marble pavilions; and the Shah Burj, the octagonal tower that carried water to the palace along an acqueduct stretching 50 miles.

The Moti Masjid (Pearl Mosque) which stands in front of the *hammam* is a jewel of milky marble enclosed by red sandstone walls.

It was built on the wishes of Aurangzeb in 1662 with three pear-shaped cupolas and slender minarets. Unfortunately, the *haram saray* has been almost totally destroyed.

A - The Red Fort in Delhi was the product of the aesthetic genius of Shah Jahan. It is protected by over a mile of crenellated walls and by the river Yamuna.

B - The diwan-i-am (public audience room), built from sandstone and plastered with powdered marble, has wide overhangs to which large awnings were hung to increase the area of shade.

C - The marble canopy of the throne stands on another platform against a wall inlaid with semi-precious stones at the end of the lobed arches. The seat of the Grand Vizir, the emperor's first dignitary, is placed in front.

E

D - Inside the fort, the naubat khana (Place of the Drum) stands at the far end of a square courtyard. This two story building was for the musicians who announced the movements of the Emperor.

E - Elegant marble panels decorate the walls of the Red Fort. A favorite theme was symmetrically arranged flowers in slender archways.

F - Access to the fort is via two monumental gates (the Lahore Gate and the Delhi Gate) with an iwan entrance. This photograph shows the Delhi Gate.

F

G - The marble diwan-i-khas (private audience pavilion) was where the precious peacock throne was kept before it was stolen by the king of Persia, Nadir Shah in the sacking of Delhi in 1739.

H - The Khas Mahal was the emperor's private residence. It consists of three marble pavilions built between 1639-1649 inlaid with semi-precious stones and lined with precious metals.

G

H

K - The private apartments are found behind the diwan-i-am; the apartments were connected by the Nahar-i-Behisht (Channel of Paradise) that carried water as far as the lotus-shaped fountain made from marble and precious stones in the Rang Mahal.

I

PLAN OF THE
RED FORT
A LAHORE GATE
B NAUBAT KHANA
C *DIWAN-I-AM*
D RANG MAHAL
E KHAS MAHAL
F *DIWAN-I-KHAS*
G HAMMAM
H HAYAT BAKSH
I SHAH BURY
J PAVILIONS
K HARAM SARAY
L DELHI GATE

J

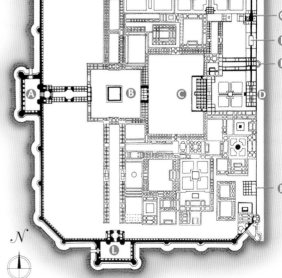

I - The Red Fort needed great quantities of water every day. To ensure enough was supplied, the Shah Burj was built, the octagonal tower that carried the water into the palace from an aqueduct 50 miles long.

J - The Moti Masjid (Pearl Mosque) was built in the Red Fort by Aurangzeb in 1662. It is a jewel of milky white marble and encircled by red sandstone walls with three pear-shaped cupolas and slender minarets. The floor in the prayer hall resembles prayer rugs.

K

N

FATEHPUR SIKRI, THE IDEAL COURT

FATEHPUR SIKRI

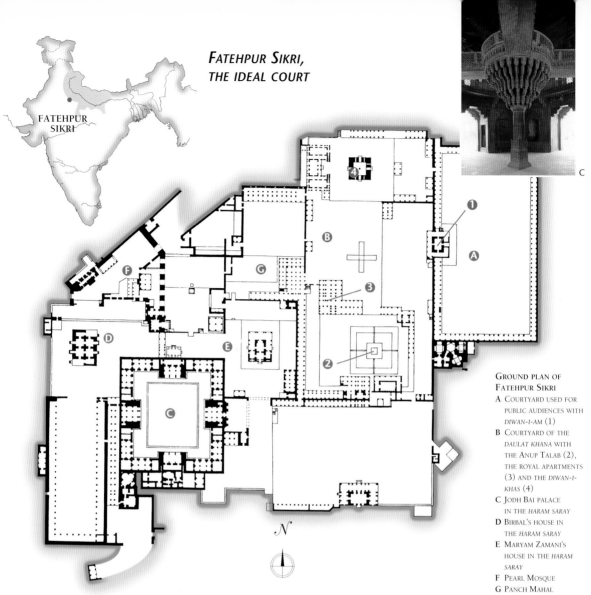

C

GROUND PLAN OF FATEHPUR SIKRI

A COURTYARD USED FOR PUBLIC AUDIENCES WITH *DIWAN-I-AM* (1)
B COURTYARD OF THE *DAULAT KHANA* WITH THE ANUP TALAB (2), THE ROYAL APARTMENTS (3) AND THE *DIWAN-I-KHAS* (4)
C JODH BAI PALACE IN THE *HARAM SARAY*
D BIRBAL'S HOUSE IN THE *HARAM SARAY*
E MARYAM ZAMANI'S HOUSE IN THE *HARAM SARAY*
F PEARL MOSQUE
G PANCH MAHAL

A

B

The town of Fatehpur Sikri was founded by Akbar who wished to build it near the village of Sikri where a Moslem ascetic named Sheikh Salim Chisti (1480-1572) had predicted the birth of the heir. Thus in 1568 a fledgling court was erected beside a small lake and, on his return from a victorious military campaign in 1573, the emperor officially named the site Fatehpur (City of Victory). Akbar had to leave the site however in 1585 to move his capital to Lahore to contain the danger from Afghanistan. The perfect city, at least on paper, did not therefore have a long life but what remains of the place, comprehensively pillaged by locals for building materials, is a testament to a happy period of Indo-

Moslem union. The fusion between redundant Hindu figurative decoration and the Moslem geometrical patterns expresses the tolerance and syncretism in art that characterized the enlightened reign of Akbar.

Designed especially to be a ceremonial capital, Fatehpur Sikri was the manifestation of the emperor's architectural ideal and in that guise resembles certain European Renaissance cities: the links between the various sectors overlooking gardens and wide, courtyards were paved not only at road level but also on passageways between terraces and roofs.

The town spread over a rectangle measuring 2.2 miles by 0.9 miles and was in part protected by a wall 4 miles long. It had 9 gateways, the best preserved of which is Agra Gate. Passing the *caravanserai* and the *naubat khan*, the visitor reaches the royal stables and workshops, including the mint. The palace proper begins with the *diwan-i-am*, a sober building with five arches, beyond which the *daulat khana* extends.

The *daulat khana* stands in two blocks around a courtyard divided into two parts: one with a cross-shaped platform for the game of *pachisi*, the other containing the Anup Talab pool with an exquisite pavilion of the same name with decorated overhangs. The northern block of the *daulat khan* contains the Pavilion of Jewels and the Ankh Michauli, the place of the "closed eyes." The first is a two-story building with balcony supported by elaborate projections and four *chattris*; it was probably the *diwan-i-khas* and has an interesting internal structure: in the center a pillar with capital formed by groups of corbels holds up the platform of the throne. The platform is connected to the four corners of the building by four suspended arms. The second block is popularly believed to have been used

D

E

F

for the game "hide and seek" though perhaps it contained the royal treasure in its three underground sections. The "astrologer's kiosk" next door is decorated with festoons supported by *makara*, the mythic aquatic Hindu monsters.

On the south side, enclosed by porticoes, were Akbar's apartments which included the *hammam*, a couple of rooms with a use that has not yet been identified, and a *baradari*, a two-story pavilion with "twelve columns" and some frescoes. On the balcony of the upper floor, which included the canopy of the throne, the emperor used to look over the Daftar Khan (Courtyard of the Offices) to show himself to his courtesans.

The Panch Mahal stood between the two blocks of buildings. The Panch Mahal had five storys of loggias, the last of which was made up of *chattris*; this typically Hindu structure was probably completed with sliding walls, curtains or screens. The miniature paintings of the era often showed the use of large curtains - hung from stone rings still to be seen above the sloping roofs. Light wooden walls and fabric screens were also used. Carpets, drapes and awnings in rich materials furnished the rooms in which bays in the walls acted as wardrobes and cupboards.

A closed passage led from the *daulat khana* to the court of the *haram saray* where Akbar slept. This was a wide four-sided space where various pavilions, apartments, bathrooms and service rooms stood. The most famous sections of the *haram saray* are the house of Maryam Zamani, known as the Golden Pavilion for its frescoes enhanced with gold-leaf, and the nearby palace of Jodh Bai. Preceded by a large doorway and built around an internal courtyard, the palace is composed of four wings. The closed rooms on the ground floor are accessible from covered verandahs and were probably used during the winter months. The cooler, arched rooms on the upper floor faced onto terraces built with *chattris* and were reserved for the hotter months. Like all the other buildings, the palace is built in sandstone with blue enamelled tile details; the decorations were probably by Hindu masters from Gujarat.

From the Jodh Bai palace, it is

G

H

A - The courtyard of the daulat khana at Fatehpur Sikri with the Anup Talab pool and the main buildings arranged around its sides: on the left are the royal apartments with the Panch Mahal behind, at the far end the diwan-i-khas, and on the right the Anup Talab pavilion.

B - This detached building in the northern section of the Anup Talab courtyard was probably the diwan-i-khas. Note the balcony supported by elaborate projections and the four chattris.

C - The interior of the diwan-i-khas was very unusual: in the center a pillar with a capital formed by groups of corbels supported the dais of the throne. The dais is connected to the four corners of the building by four suspended arms.

D - A detail of the Panch Mahal, a five-story palace with loggias, the last of which was built of chattri. This typically Hindu structure was probably completed by movable screens, curtains and awnings.

E - Various pavilions and palaces stood in the courtyard of the haram saray. The palace of Jodh Bai is the most remarkable; it was preceded by a portal with jharoka (bay window balconies) and chattris.

F - Jodh Bai palace is arranged around an internal courtyard: wide overhangs protect the ground floor rooms from the sun; the arched rooms on the upper floor open onto terraces with chattris.

G - This interior is one of four wings of the sandstone Jodh Bai palace; rugs, drapes and awnings made from rich materials furnished the rooms. The niches in the walls were used as wardrobes and shelves.

H - The interior of the palace was decorated with balconies supported by ornate projections, niches with pediments decorated with geometric and floral patterns, pilasters and beams with hanging capitals.

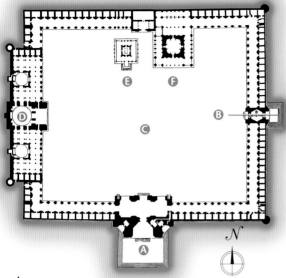

PLAN OF JAMI MASJID
A BULAND DARVAZA (GATE OF MAGNIFICENCE)
B BADSHAHI DARVAZA (EMPEROR'S GATE)
C COURTYARD
D PRAYER HALL
E MAUSOLEUM OF SALIM CHISHTI
F MAUSOLEUM OF ISLAM KHAN

A - The lovely mausoleum of Salim Chishti stands in the courtyard of the Jami Masjid. This is a pavilion made from white Makrana marble with wide overhangs and serpentine projections screened by elegant jalis.

B - The jalis (fretted ornamentation in wood and stone) are an ancient Indian tradition which the Moguls brought to perfection. The grilles that screen the mausoleum are a lacework of marble.

C - The cenotaph of the holy man is a canopy made of ebony encrusted with mother of pearl. It is a pilgrimage destination for both Moslems and Hindus, particularly childless women.

D, E - The decoration emphasizes the niche in the mihrab that shows the qibla (direction of Mecca) that the faithful face when they pray. Next to the mihrab stands the minbar, a form of pulpit that prayers are conducted from.

F - The ban on representing the human figure encouraged Moslem artists to develop floral decoration and calligraphy. Written in different styles, calligraphy became an ornamental element as seen in the marble inserts of the Chishti mausoleum.

G, I - The Jami Masjid has two entrances in the crenellated walls: the Buland Darvaza (Gate of Magnificence) and the Badshahi Darvaza (Emperor's Gate) in the picture G. This is the inside of the Buland Darvaza, a testimony of the power of the Moguls. It faces onto the courtyard of the mosque and is lined with cells for students and pilgrims.

possible to pass to the Hava Mahal (Pavilion of the Winds). This is a *jali* construction designed to permit good air circulation. Not far away, the Nagina Masjid was available for the women of the *haram saray* to use for private prayer.

One of the most ornate palaces was the so-called House of Birbal, a Hindu *raja* favored by Akbar, who could hardly live in the women's quarters. Akbar perhaps had it built for his daughter but more probably this was where one or more of his wives lived. There were four rooms and two entrances on the ground floor and two rooms with cupolas and bay windows on the upper floor. Additional features were overhangs and projections and the whole house was profusely decorated with Hindu motifs. Questions regarding the use made of the nearby Stable Court are still unanswered, given the "unseemly" proximity to the women's apartments.

A screened cloister that passed by the Pigeon-loft and *caravanserai* led to the lake shore at Hiran Minar (Deer Tower), built over the remains of Akbar's favorite elephant and decorated

H - The prayer hall is entered via a large iwan with marble inserts that nearly hide the three cupolas decorated with arabesques. The purpose of the chattri-style pediments is to temper the discrepancy between the facade and the wings.

G

J

with tusks built into the walls. Close by are the polo field and the Hathi Pol (Elephant Gate), the emperor's private entrance.

The grandeur of Fatehpur Sikri is completed by the Jami Masjid of 1572, entered from the Badshahi Darvaza (Emperor's Gate) and the Buland Darvaza (Gate of Magnificence). At over 170 feet high, it is dazzling testimony to Mogul power emphasized by the grand entrance stairway and imposing *iwan*.

The square courtyard is bordered with a line of porticoes with *chattri*-

style pediments offering accommodation cells to pilgrims and students. A single *iwan* in front of the sumptuous prayer hall almost hides the three cupolas decorated with painted arabesques.

Two other buildings enrich the mosque: the lovely mausoleum of Salim Chisti, a white marble pavilion with cupola, ample overhangs and serpentine projections all screened by elegant *jali*, and the red sandstone mausoleum of Islam Khan, Salim Chisti's nephew and dignitary of Jahangir.

J - The fusion of the redundant figurative decoration of Hindu art and the calibrated geometric patterns of the Moslems is an expression of the tolerance and syncretism that characterized the enlightened reign of Akbar. The columns made from differently sized geometrical sections inside the mosque were inspired by the traditional architecture of Hindu temples.

AGRA, AESTHETIC PERFECTION

PLAN OF THE TOMB OF ITIMAD-UD-DAULA THE TOMB IS SYMMETRICAL THROUGHOUT. THE CENOTAPHS LIE IN THE CORNER ROOMS AND THE CENTRAL CHAMBER ON THE FIRST FLOOR.

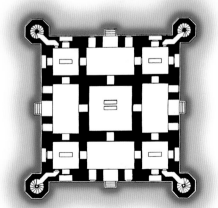

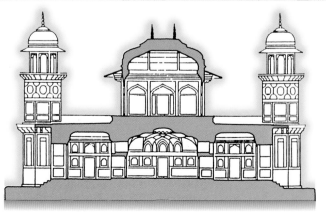

A, C - Jahangir's favorite wife, Nur Jahan, had this tomb built in 1626 in Agra for her father, Itimad-ud-Daulah. The mausoleum of the "Pillar of the State," as he was called, was the first to be built completely in white Makrana marble.

B - The design of the "Pillar of the State" is simple with elegant octagonal minarets at the corners topped by chattris and a small pavilion with lowered dome and wide overhangs on the first floor terrace.

D - The cenotaph of Itmad ud Daula is held up to the open sky on the upper terrace paved with two-colored mosaic tiles and surrounded by an ambulatory. It is probable that the original project included a cupola which was never built.

E - Akbar built his own mausoleum at Sikandra which was completed by his son, Jahangir, in 1613. It stands in a garden entered through an attractive gateway made from red sandstone and framed by four white marble minarets.

The monuments of Agra testify to the perfection achieved by Mogul art in the 17th century. The city's ancient Hindu past, including all traces of its brief period of glory as the capital of the sultanate at the time of Sikander Lodi (1488-1516), has been eradicated. It was with the great Mogul emperor Akbar that Agra began to acquire its glorious place in the history of Indo-Islamic architecture, and its splendor increased still further under his successors Jahangir and Shah Jahan. Despite being linked almost exclusively with the ineffable Taj Mahal, the fame of Agra is strengthened by other splendid buildings.

The first to be built was the colossal mausoleum of emperor Akbar, finished by his son in 1613, at Sikandra, 6 miles from Agra. The mausoleum has a perimeter wall with four entrances; the most splendid built from red sandstone, flanked by white marble minarets and decorated with geometrical patterns in marble and colored stone. The mausoleum stands 71 feet tall in the center of the char bagh and is divided into 3 parts: the plinth with arches and a huge iwan with slender minarets, three storys built in red sandstone with

comparison, appears small and frail, suggests that the original design was to have been topped by a large cupola. The impression given by the mausoleum is of a contrast in personalities - sober and powerful in the construction of the plinth, designed by Akbar himself, while the alterations made by Jahangir to his father's design are refined and introverted.

F

G

Another splendid jewel is the mausoleum of Itimad-ud-Daula (Pillar of the State) whose actual name was Mirza Ghiyas Beg, father of Jahangir's favorite, powerful and refined wife, Nur Jahan, who had him build the tomb in 1626. One of the four sandstone gateways in the enclosure wall is a guest-house with bathrooms, fountains and waterfalls which confirms that Moslem burial sites not only had no macabre connotation but were actually chosen and enjoyed as peaceful residences.

The mausoleum in the center of the char bagh was for the first time built entirely from white marble from Makrana. It has extremely simple lines with elegant octagonal minarets topped by chattris standing at its corners. The superb inlaid and multi-colored decoration and semi-precious stones such as cornelian, jasper and topaz reproduce the motif of a flask of wine and vase of flowers beloved of Jahangir. The burial chamber with alabaster cenotaphs stands on a first floor terrace in a small pavilion with lowered cupola, long overhang and windows screened by elegant jali. Mirza Ghiyas Beg and his wife are laid out on a colored and inlaid marble floor that imitates a floral rug.

E

F - The mausoleum of Sikandra stands in the center of a char bagh (four part garden). It consists of an arched base with a colossal iwan, three floors decorated with arches and chattris, and a pavilion on the top.

G - In Akbar's monument the arched ambulatory around the cenotaph is screened by square marble jalis which give the appearance of a cloister.

arches, chattris and small cupolas in white marble, and a final story built exclusively in white marble.

Narrow stairs lead to the upper floors and to the highest terrace, paved with two color mosaic tiles and surrounded by an ambulatory screened by marble jali, where the cenotaph is raised towards the open sky. The form of the monument may have been inspired by the ancient Persian ziggurat (stepped pyramid). The evident lack of harmony between the massive, solid first story and the middle section with terraces and chattris which, in

A - The Taj Mahal is the peak of Islamic burial architecture. It is dedicated to Mumtaz Mahal, the "Noble One of the Palace," beloved wife of Shah Jahan, who died in childbirth.

B - The mausoleum was moved back from the center of the char bagh to the end to take advantage of the perspective. The Taj has two wings made from red sandstone.

Superior in every respect, the Taj Mahal represents the apex of Islamic burial architecture and the unrepeatable fulfilment of the very highest artistic vision of the Mogul era. It is dedicated to Arjumand Banu, niece of Nur Jahan and wife of Shah Jahan, and known as Mumtaz Mahal (Chosen One of the Palace). She died in childbirth while following her husband on a military campaign in southern India. The nearly forty-year-old emperor was prostrate with grief and had the Taj Mahal erected in her honor.

The name of the architect who finished it in 1648 is unknown although several have been put forward: two brothers, Ustad Ahmad and Ustad Hamid, probably Persian to judge by the honorary title *ustad* (master); a Turkish disciple of the great Sinan; the Venetian, Geronimo Veroneo, remembered by the Spanish Augustinian father, Sebastiano Manrique; and a certain Augustin de Bordeaux. It is probable that each of them had a certain task to complete as part of the whole and that many others were also used to oversee the various sectors of the project which employed, it is said, 20,000 men.

The *caravanserai* adjoining the mausoleum is entered through the Taj Ganj gate which leads to the large garden gateway with octagonal towers and eleven *chattri* made from red sandstone decorated with arabesques and inscriptions from the Koran in white marble. Skillfully set at the back of the *char bagh* for reasons of perspective, the Taj Mahal itself can be glimpsed at the end of the gardens through the archway of the *iwan*.

The four exceptionally wide avenues cut by canals meet in the center of the

A

B

C

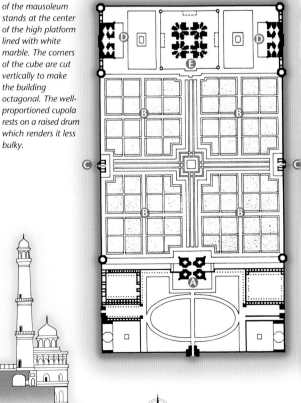

PLAN AND ELEVATION OF THE TAJ MAHAL
THE ELEVATION SHOWS THE DOUBLE SKIN OF THE COVERING WITH THE BIG GAP BETWEEN THE CEILING OF THE MORTUARY CHAMBER AND THE CUPOLA. THE PLAN SHOWS THE PERFECTION OF THE *CHAR BAGH* AND THE CHANGE IN POSITION OF THE MONUMENT TO THE END OF THE GARDEN.

A ENTRANCE
B *CHAR BAGH*
C WATER PAVILIONS
D MOSQUE AND GUEST-HOUSE
E MAUSOLEUM

C - The cubic structure of the mausoleum stands at the center of the high platform lined with white marble. The corners of the cube are cut vertically to make the building octagonal. The well-proportioned cupola rests on a raised drum which renders it less bulky.

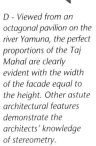

D - Viewed from an octagonal pavilion on the river Yamuna, the perfect proportions of the Taj Mahal are clearly evident with the width of the facade equal to the height. Other astute architectural features demonstrate the architects' knowledge of stereometry.

E - Access to the Taj is through an impressive red sandstone entrance decorated with arabesques and Koranic inscriptions in white marble. It has octagonal towers and eleven chattris like pediments.

D

E

garden in a lotus pool: the two lateral canals are connected to other water pavilions in the enclosure walls while the two that run lengthwise are enlivened by a series of fountains and emphasize the approach to the main building with its reflection in the canals and central pool.

Two symmetrical buildings in red sandstone with white marble domes - a mosque and a guest-house - act as wings to the Taj Mahal and have behind them a terrace with a pavilion that overlooks the river Yamuna.

The Taj Mahal itself is a cubic structure 185 feet square with cut corners to give it the appearance of an octagon. It stands on a high white marble plinth 305 feet wide. The central building is crowned by a cupola 84 feet high and 58 feet wide which stands on a tall drum. The cupola is flanked by four *chattris* and is topped by an overturned flower that holds up a gilded, double vase pinnacle; this feature is repeated on the *chattris*. The minarets at the corners of the platform frame the magnificent mausoleum.

Huge entrances with bowl-shaped vaults decorated with *muqarnas* lead through each of the four main, 107 foot

tall facades. The refined ornamentation includes niches, stalactites, panels with shoots of flowers in relief, scriptures from the Koran in black marble, polychrome wave patterns, arabesques and floral braiding created using inlaid topaz, sapphire, cornelian, jasper, chrysolite and heliotrope stones.

Standing in the center of the octagonal funeral chamber, connected by radiating corridors to the four entrances and four corner chambers, are the cenotaphs of Mumtaz and Shah Jahan protected by fretted marble transennas, reproductions of those in gold which were melted down by Aurangzeb. It would appear that the bodies are not held in the crypt below where there are two more cenotaphs but

are hidden in the foundations composed of a succession of 17 sealed underground rooms.

Features like the width of the facade equal to the height of the construction, the drum that the cupola rests on being hidden by the parapet of the *iwan*, and the four *chattris* moved inwards demonstrate the architects' understanding of stereometry. The attention paid to the proportions and perspective, the use of Makrana marble that changes color with the light and the well-proportioned curve of the dome of the double-skinned cupola with its enormous internal space help to dematerialize the mass of the building giving the impression that the mausoleum emerges from the sky behind and almost floats on the green carpet of the garden

A

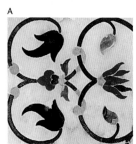

A, C, D - The ornamentation in the Taj Mahal is extremely elegant: the stalactites and panels featuring carved shoots of flowers (C) are all monochrome; the verses from the Koran are in black marble; the wave patterns, arabesques and floral designs are multi-colored with inlaid turquoise, malachite, lapis lazuli, carnelian, jasper, chrysolite and heliotropes.

B - Four huge entrances each give access to one of the mausoleum's four sides. Inside, a corridor leads from each entrance to the octagonal cenotaph room in the center from which four other corridors lead out radially to the rooms in the corners of the structure.

B

C

D

E

F

G

H

I

J

E - The white structures of the Taj Mahal are here seen from the Portico of North Gate.

F - The cenotaph of Mumtaz and Shah Jahan stands in the center of the octagonal room protected by fretted marble transennas which are reproductions of the original ones made from gold which Aurangzeb had melted down.

G - The bodies of the royal couple were buried in the foundations of the building somewhere in the seventeen underground rooms. These were bricked up to prevent intrusion.

H - Two symmetrical buildings – a mosque and guest-house - stand on either side of the Taj. They are made from red sandstone with white marble domes. In the distance, the octagonal towers of the enclosure wall can be seen.

I, J - The inside of the mosque is richly decorated, here one can see the marble mihrab. The floral decoration was especially dear to Shah Jahan who was an expert naturalist. This is a stylized reproduction of the tree of life. Note the strict symmetry of the parts.

A

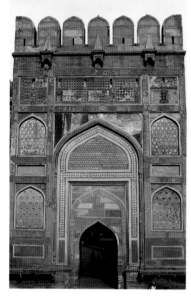

B

C

like a romantic vision.

While the evolution of the design of the mausoleum is amply documented at Agra, its Red Fort is the most interesting example of the evolution of civil architecture. Akbar commissioned it from Mohammed Qasim Khan between 1565-74 on the site of the fortifications of the Hindu Chauhan dynasty. A moat and double perimeter wall 1.5 miles long encircle it. Of the four original, 96-foot high entrances with external bastions, two are still useable: Delhi Gate and the Gate of Amar Singh. The latter was named after a heroic Hindu *raja* and is the present entrance; it stands between two towers and is followed by another gateway with a ramp for use by elephants.

D

E

A, C - Akbar built the Red Fort between 1565-74 on the fortifications raised by the Hindu Chauhan dynasty. Of the four original entrances, only the Delhi Gate, (A) and the Amar Singh Gate (C) survive.

B - The fort has a double enclosure wall with bastions and towers over a mile long and surrounded by a dyke. The entrances had a double defensive structure and a special ramp for the elephants.

D -The imperial apartments look towards the river; at one time, the Yamuna could be reached via a door used exclusively by the women of the haram saray.

F

G

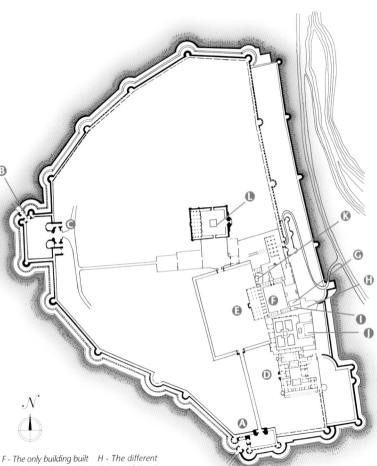

E - Jahangir's palace comprises two-story buildings along two courtyards. One of the courtyards faces the river and gives access to the serdab *and, below that, the* fansighar, *a maze of cells of unknown use.*

H

F - The only building built during Akbar's reign to remain in one piece is Jahangir's palace. The facade was designed in Hindu style, with blind arched verandahs and white marble decoration in the ochre-colored sandstone, but the ornamentation is Islamic.

G - The room of Jahangir's first wife, Jodh Bai, is the most beautiful: it is decorated with rajput style patterns and has a splendid domed ceiling.

H - The different designs of the dome, probably inspired by the tents of nomads on the steppes, characterize the various periods of Moslem architecture.

I - Three perfect bulb-shaped cupolas rise over the red walls that give the fort its name. The domes belong to the Moti Masjid (Pearl Mosque) which faces onto the Mina Bazar, the market courtyard.

I

A, B - Flat-topped
pavilions connected
by a screened gallery
stand on the terraced
roof of Jahangir's
palace. The fretted
parapets and the
projections that
support the top floor
are beautifully made.

B

C

C - The main building
material during this
period continued to
be sandstone with
tiles or marble inserts.
Decoration was
probably the work
of Hindu master
craftsmen from
Gujarat.

D - Monochrome
decoration is used on
projecting parts which
are for the most part
blind arches and
shallow niches. The
inner surface of the
architraves and corbels
are decorated with a
shallow floral pattern.

E - One of the most common images at the time of the building of the Red Fort, was the blind denticulated arch made from marble in a rectangular cornice with two rosettes at the top.

F - This is one of the open rooms in Jahangir's palace which was at one time closed with drapes.

D

G - Although the Moslems had introduced the use of the arch and the vaulted ceiling, Hindu builders working for the first Moguls still preferred to use the architrave and a false vault covering.

The other two gates have been walled up: one was the river gateway used by women, and the other the one used by the emperor to show himself to the crowds.

Within the Red Fort, one sees a huge tank in front of the Jahangir Palace, the only building from Akbar's era still intact. The Hindu-style facade has a verandah on blind arches and white marble highlights in the ochre sandstone while the ornamental motifs and geometric engravings are Islamic. One passes through an *iwan* to a hall, then a domed room and into a courtyard surrounded by two-story buildings. The room of Jodh Bai, Jahangir's first wife, is the most beautiful room in these buildings with ceilings and decor in the *rajput* style inspired by the courts of the Hindu *raja*. A second courtyard faces the river and allows access to the *serdab*, the cool rooms below ground, and to the *fansighar*, a maze of cells of uncertain use even further below ground.

The magnificent open marble pavilions in the gardens, light as silken curtains, were the work of Shah Jahan. The palace is based on the two traditional sections, the private and the public. The *diwan-i-am* is the linch-pin of the public part; it is built from red sandstone with white plasterwork, a portico with three rows of columns and lowered, festooned arches which stand on a wall with a three-light window. It was from the wall that the emperor would hold audience. Nearby, two rooms with screened windows

allowed the women to be present at the ceremonies without being visible. Despite living separately from the world of the men, the women took an active part in political life, for example, Nur Jahan effectively reigned in place of her husband Jahangir who was often lost to the pleasures of wine and opium.

E

F

G

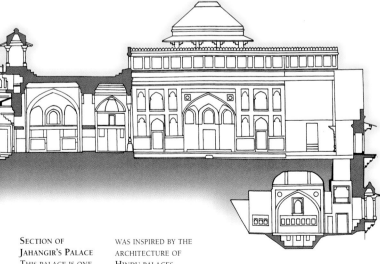

SECTION OF JAHANGIR'S PALACE THIS PALACE IS ONE OF THE OLDEST SECTIONS OF THE RED FORT AT AGRA, AND WAS INSPIRED BY THE ARCHITECTURE OF HINDU PALACES. THE RESIDENTIAL SECTION IS SPLIT OVER THREE FLOORS.

123

A - Shah Jahan had the existing large palaces knocked down and replaced with smaller marble pavilions. The diwan-i-am remains in red sandstone with white plasterwork.

B - The prayer hall with nave and two side aisles in the Moti Masjid (Pearl Mosque) faces onto a large marble courtyard enclosed by high red sandstone walls.

C - The private apartments were built around two gardens: the Machli Bhavan in the photograph with the diwan-i-khas in the background, and the Anguri Bagh (vineyard).

D - The Muthamman Burj is an octagonal tower facing onto the river Yamuna enclosed by a columned verandah area. Despite plundering, the beautiful patterns inlaid with semi-precious stones represent the apex of Mogul refinement.

E - Two floors of small rooms with verandahs run around three sides of the Anguri Bagh (vineyard) which the women of the harem used for their personal belongings.

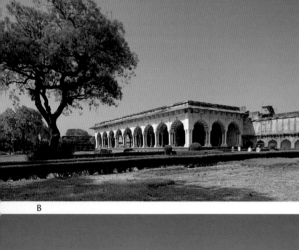

The Mina Bazar (court market) extends outside the *diwan-i-am* to the Moti Masjid (Pearl Mosque), a white marble dream enclosed behind sandstone walls and topped by three perfect bulb-shaped cupolas.

The section of private apartments stands around two gardens, the Machli Bavan (Fish Palace) and the Anguri Bagh (vineyard). The former is another sandstone building from which one passes, by means of the first floor, into a courtyard with a lovely milky-white marble mosque, the Nagina Masjid, built by Aurangzeb for his imprisoned father.

The *diwan-i-khas* faces onto the garden of the Machli Bhavan. It is an elegant building in white marble decorated with delicate floral braiding with hard stone inserts. Two thrones in black and white marble face each other on the terrace, the first was Jahangir's, the second Shah Jahan's.

Further on, the Muthamman Burj was an octagonal tower standing over a courtyard where Mumtaz Mahal lived, Shah Jahan's favorite wife, with Shah Jahan himself after being deposed by his son Aurangzeb. The splendid floral and geometric decorations inlaid with precious and semi-precious stones has suffered looting but still represents an admirable example of Mogul elegance.

The Anguri Bagh is set out in the traditional design of four raised avenues leading to a central fountain. It was made up of intersecting flowerbeds framed by brick edging and filled with flowers to

F - The area composed of three lines of columns with lowered and festooned arches is the diwan-i-am where the emperor held his public audiences.

G, H - The diwan-i-khas is an elegant building lined with white marble and decorated with a delicate intertwining flowers with inserts of semi-precious stones. The details of the pictures demonstrate the refined matching of the ivory-colored marble and the frame of the colored flowers.

I - The fourth side of the Anguri Bagh was closed by the three pavilions of the Khas Mahal placed on a high platform. The arched central pavilion has a flat covering and is made entirely of marble. It is covered by a terrace with wide overhangs while the two side pavilions have Bengali style roofs.

J - The two side pavilions of the Khas Mahal were perhaps used by Shah Jahan's daughters. They are built in the bangaldar style, topped by overhanging Bengali roofs made from copper and crowned by water vases.

terrace with wide overhangs and its splendid fretted marble windows overlook the Yamuna river.

The curves and sensuality of the festooned arches on slim groups of columns, the Persian bulb-shaped cupolas and the gentle Bengalese roofs express the refined personality of Shah Jahan.

Outside the fort, the Jama Masjid is also worth a visit. This mosque was built on the orders of Jahanara Begum, eldest daughter of Shah Jahan, in 1644. It is a sober design in red sandstone with bands of white marble, chattri pediments and three bulb-shaped cupolas topped by the classical design of the overturned flower and a water vase pinnacle.

create patterns of colors. Two floors of buildings line three sides of the Anguri Bagh alternating with verandahs that were used by the ladies of the harem to leave and reach their individual small rooms. At the bottom of the Anguri Bagh stands the Shish Mahal (Palace of Mirrors) which was in effect a hammam or Turkish bath: it had two sections, one hot and one cold, and was lined with glass mosaic tiles.

The fourth side of the garden was lined with the three elegant Khas Mahal pavilions built in 1636 on a high platform. The pavilions at either end were perhaps for the use of the daughters of the empress and are crowned by copper roofs in the Bengalese style with pinnacles in the shape of water vases. The central pavilion with arcades is covered by a

ISLAM IN INDIA

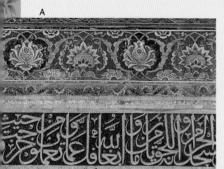

The year 1192 was a crucial date in Indian history. The men led by Muhammad - a Turkish commander descended from the Seljuk line who had conquered Ghazna and Lahore from his principality of Ghor, north of Kabul - routed the Hindu coalition led by Prithviraj III, the Chauhan king of Ajmer and Delhi, on the plain of Tarain north of Delhi.

The Moslems had been pressing at the gates of India for some time; their military expeditions had begun in the year 650 with the conquest of Kabul and surrounding territories, and then continued with the invasion of Sind in 712. In the meantime, the Turks had appeared in the limelight of history. They were of Europoid and Mongoloid extraction and had settled the Asiatic steppes. Converted to Islam in the 11th century, they became *ghazi* (Moslem soldiers) and were the true assault troops of the caliphs of Baghdad. Taking advantage of the weakness of the Persian empire, in 962 a Turkish general founded an independent principality in Ghazna (Afghanistan), from which his successors conducted a series of devastating raids on India. Ghazna was conquered by Muhammad of Ghor who then descended on India.

Having obliterated Delhi, Muhammad installed as governor his general Qutb-ud-Din Aibak (1202-1210) who became the sole ruler of Indian territories detached from the Turkish, central Asiatic kingdom on the death of his leader. His son, Iltutmish (1211-1236), was recognised as sultan by the caliph of Baghdad and so the first Moslem dynasty in India, the Mamelukes, was begun. Raziya (1236-1240), the daughter of Iltutmish and one of the few examples of a woman ruler, took over on the death of her father. She was followed by Mahmud (1246-1266) and Balban (1266-1287), the most outstanding of the sultans of Delhi, but after his death the dynasty petered out under Kaiqubad (1287-1290). Power passed into the hands of an Afghan general, Firuz (1290-1296) who instituted the Khalji dynasty with Ala-ud-Din (1296-1316), responsible for many of Delhi's Islamic monuments. Mubarak followed (1316-1320) but was assassinated by a converted Hindu. General Ghiyas-ud-Din (1320-1325) brought order back to the city and founded the Turkish-Indian Tughlaq dynasty which included his son Muhammad (1325-1351), Firuz Shah (1351-1388) on whose death riots broke out, and Mahmud (1394-1413). In 1398, Tamerlane sacked Delhi in one of Indian history's most tragic events, and after an era of civil unrest, the Sayyid dynasty took power (1414-1451) followed by the Lodi dynasty with the great sultan Sikander (1488-1517) who founded the new capital at Agra. The last Lodi ruler was Ibrahim (1517-1526), whose enemies solicited the help of Babur, lord of an Afghan principality, who invaded India in 1526 and founded the Mogul dynasty; the name is derived from its Mongol origin. On the death of the warlike Babur, the extent of the kingdom exceeded by far that of the old sultanate, and included

شبیه حضرت جهانگیر ا----ه که شبیه حضرت اکبر ا---ه رامی ببند

Afghanistan, the Punjab and the Ganges plain as far as the Bengal borders.

Babur's son, Humayum, reigned in Delhi from 1530-1540 but was dethroned by Sher Khan, an Afghan leader and governor of Bihar, who took the throne using the name of Sher Shah (1540-1545) leaving his son Islam Shah (1545-1554). In the meantime, Humayum had taken refuge in Persia and returned in 1555 to reclaim his throne with Persian help but died a year later. The crown passed to his son Akbar (1556-1605), the greatest of the Mogul emperors, an able commander and a patron and lover of the

C

arts. By marrying many Indian princesses, he consolidated links between the Moslem dynasty and the Hindu aristocracy and, as a result of his great religious tolerance, he even created a new religion, a sort of royal theosophy, that ended with his death. His son Jahangir (1605-1627) left government in the hands of his wife Nur Jahan, a Persian princess who ruled until the death of her husband and who had a profound influence on the artistic taste of the era. Jahangir's successor, Shah Jahan (1627-1658), the best known of the Mogul rulers, was a refined aesthete and invested in the construction of buildings, the most famous being the Taj Mahal. Shah Jahan's son, Aurangzeb (1658-1707) imprisoned his father and killed his brothers to take the crown. His bigoted policies led to the political and artistic decline of the realm. On his death, the empire crumbled and local factions reemerged.

D

A, E - Islam prohibits representation of the human figure which means artists have had to use geometric and floral designs and calligraphic representations praising God or of verses from the Koran for decoration.

B - The Mogul dynasty had Mongol origins. It began with Babur who invaded India in 1526. The most illustrious emperor was Akbar (1556-1605), seen here in a portrait held by his son Jahangir (1605-1627).

C - Islam underwent re-evaluation in India to such an extent that during the Mogul period, the human figure was represented. At least two artists would work on a miniature: one would paint the face, and the other the body. This is how the faces of the emperors have been handed down to us. Shah Jahan can be recognised in the miniature on his war-horse and wearing a plumed turban.

D - Shah Jahan (1627-1658), was a refined aesthete and a great builder who emptied the state coffers to finance his glorious marble edifices. The decadence of the Mogul empire began with his death. Shah Jahan can be recognised in the miniature on his war-horse and wearing a plumed turban.

E

127

RAJASTHAN, LAND OF THE RAJPUT

THE WARLORDS

A - The forts were the centers of power of the various Rajput clans. The solid defensive walls enclosed beautiful palaces which often had a plan of the building painted on the walls, like this example at Bundi.

B - The "Ramayana" is a famous chivalric poem of the exploits of Rama, an incarnation of the god Vishnu, and was an important source of inspiration for Rajput artists. This 18th century fresco in the palace at Bundi depicts the arrival of the gods for the wedding of Rama and Sita.

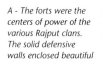

RAJASTHAN

B

ajasthan, the best known Indian state, became the center of a magnificent chivalrous civilization of *rajaputras* (princes). This people was of mixed origin, probably of tribes from the steppes of central Asia, who settled in the north-west of India around the Thar desert even though it is one of the hottest areas of India and receives so little rain that it is known as

A

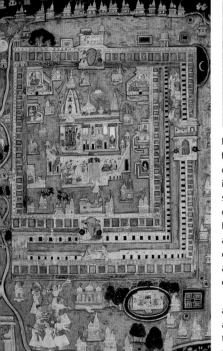

Marusthali (the Land of Death). It is in fact an arid steppe rather than a true desert and a single burst of monsoon rain is all that is required to transform the scorched earth into a carpet of grass dotted with *babul*, the acacia trees of Rajasthan. It is a land suitable for grazing and for farmers capable of collecting and carefully distributing the little water available; it is also a transit area for the caravans on their way to central Asia.

Around the year 1000, the *rajaputras* abandoned their semi-nomadic farming and grazing life to settle in the region that came to be called Rajaputana and which was later transformed into

Rajasthan. Divided into several clans, they created a series of feudal kingdoms: the king or *raja* assigned land to his relatives and the most loyal leaders in his clan in which the feudatory had absolute power. The only obligation of the feudatory was to pay a part of the forthcoming tributes and supply men and equipment in times of war.

Skilled horsemen, the Rajputs based their existence on a complicated chivalrous code in which battle represented the crux. The fame they earned for their many courageous actions was celebrated in the bardic poems that flourished in the Hindi

C infanticide, the use and abuse of opium, the eating of all types of meat except beef, the ancient tribal meeting of the war council, the rite of *jauhar* (voluntary immolation of women and children in the event of military defeat) while their men sought death on the battlefield.

The rite of *agnikula* (fire lineage) held on Mount Abu belonged to four powerful clans: the Pratihara from the south of Rajasthan; the Chalyuka or Solanki, lords of Gujarat who were defeated by the Moslem Ahmad Shah in 1411; the Paramara, rulers of Malva who were dethroned in 1401 by another Islamic warrior, Dilvar Khan Ghuri; and the Chahuan or Chahamana of western Rajasthan who were also present in Delhi, Ajmer, Bundi, Kotah and Sirohi.

Other important clans claimed they were descended from the sun through the sons of Rama, the incarnation of Vishnu, ideal prototype of a ruler and protagonist of the "Ramayana" epic: they were the Guhila or Guhilot, later called the Sisodia, who had been known

D - If heroism was the inspiration of the culture of Rajasthan, love was its worthy corollary. Krishna, another incarnation of the god Vishnu, was one of the preferred mythical subjects for amorous pictures. His erotic adventures with the gopis, the shepherdesses who were his companions in youth, were the subject of many pictures like these of the Bundi Palace.

D

C - The chivalric society of the Rajputs was dominated by the ideal of the warrior hero whose highest aspiration was to achieve glory in battle. The nobles and their rulers loved to be portrayed in warlike attitudes on their war-horses, as in this 18th century picture of a maharaja *in the palace in the city of Udaipur.*

language during the late Middle Ages.

It was, however, this very battle ethic that was responsible for a lack of development in their fighting techniques and tactics which, combined with the narrow allegiance of the clans, caused the defeat of the Rajputs at the hands of the Moslems.

Although the Rajput soon became perfect models of the second Indian caste, that of the warriors, and were celebrated in the Hindu world with a lavish ritual of fire on Mount Abu by the Brahmans, their Asian origins were evident in some of the customs that were foreign to Brahmanism such as female

since the 2nd century AD and were founders of the powerful state of Mewar which had Chittor and Udaipur as its capitals; the Kachhavaha of Amber and Jaipur; and the Rathor, lords of the state of Marwar which had Jodhpur as its capital and other centers of power such as Bikaner and Kishangarh. The Bhatti of Jaisal, on the other hand, claimed descendance from the moon through Krishna. The terms used to distinguish the various sovereigns were *raja* (king), *maharaja* (great king) and a range of synonyms such as *rana, maharana, raval* and *maharaval* depending on the dynasty in question.

E - Polychromy which was achieved via coloring or the inlaying of different materials was one of the decorative methods used in courts and the houses of nobles. This example is in the Chokhani Haveli of Mandava in Shekhavati.

E

As a result of this warrior culture, Rajasthan is sprinkled with interesting castles and forts while the cities are famous for their labyrinthine palaces which seem to have grown in size over the centuries without any particular ground plan in mind. The oldest buildings are the *garhs* (forts) enclosed by bastions, buttresses and solid walls with enormous *pols* (gates). The royal palace would be situated in the center of the defences on a fairly regular ground plan with *rajabhavana* buildings for the public life of the ruler facing onto an external courtyard while the complex of royal apartments, the *rajaniveshana*, was arranged around a number of internal courtyards.

Typical of Hindu palatine architecture was the *prasada* (multi-floored palace) with the *zanana* (women's quarters) at the top. It seems that no clear separation existed between the men's and women's quarters before the advent of Islam and it was only due to the influence of the Moslem rulers

A – One of the principal features of Rajput architecture was water, an essential element for the survival of the stronghold. Many capitals of the small kingdoms in Rajasthan were built next to lakes, like Udaipur that overlooks Lake Pichola.

B – Water is an attractive backdrop to the marble palaces that appear to float. This is the idea that inspired the Jai Mahal between Jaipur and Amber, an 18th century "pleasure-dome" for the maharaja.

C – The Rajputs created numerous artificial lakes to water their cities, leaving small islands to build small temples and pavilions on. A mile or so from Jaisalmer, the ladies of the court would amuse themselves with trips to a romantic construction built in Garhisar lake.

D – The countryside of Rajasthan is dominated by garh, forts, at the feet of which stand the living quarters of the people. An example is Meherangarh, the fort at Jodhpur, which dates from the 15th century.

D

A

B

C

that palaces began to be built with the *zanana* separate from the *mardana* (the men's quarters).

The *prasada* type of palace built on several floors was further enlarged with ideas taken and adapted from the Mogul courts. These new ideas featured open and often isolated pavilions of one or two floors at most, resembling tents, and were probably derived from the encampments of their past. The palace would therefore be made up of three blocks called *mahals* or *mandirs*, a service courtyard, surrounded by stalls, stores, kitchens, an armory and a temple close to the principal courtyard featuring the *darbar* (the public audience area which corresponded to the Islamic *diwan-i-am*), one or more courtyards lined by the ruler's apartments, a private reception area (the *diwan-i-khas*), the treasury and a small sanctuary and the *zanana* with terraces and gardens. The reduced size of

the rooms, particularly in the *zanana*, shows that life was led for the most part outside. The narrow and tortuous corridors linking the various parts of the palace were so-designed for defensive purposes because, inside the palace, the king risked assassination by his own relatives.

Although there was an Islamic influence in the forts and palaces of Rajasthan, their structure is also not untypical of Hindu design. The complicated and maze-like ground plan; the spread of the palace facilities over several floors; the profusion of protrusions and indents in the architecture of the palace's facade with bay windows, *jalis* (fretted screens), overhangs, *bangaldar* roofs and *chattris*; the darkness of the interior; the preference for curved lines as in the lobed arches; and the profusion of decoration that hid the architectural forms, particularly the use of glass and mirror tiles which made a *shish mahal* (palace of mirrors), a building to be

found in every palace. All are elements that contributed to create a sense of mysterious ambiguity.

If the huge funereal complexes erected where the Rajput rulers were cremated owed much to the Islamic influence, the *chattri* and *shikhara* style cenotaphs were very much a feature of the Hindu world; likewise the palaces and enclosures of the *mahasatis*, places of commemoration of the *satis*, the virtuous wives who followed their dead husbands onto his funeral pyre so that they would burn to death with him, and the *jauhar*, the ceremony that demonstrated the highest conception of honor, the fundamental virtue of the Rajputs and especially their women. Innumerable princesses and queens who preferred death than to fall into the hands of the enemy while their husbands fought to the bitter end on the battlefield.

One of the oldest forts seems to be that of Ajmer, built in the 7th century and linked to the fame of Prithviraj III, the ruler of Chahuan who attempted to stem the Moslem invasion but who lost his life

Ambika at Jagat, 35 miles from Udaipur, built in 960. This temple is built on a high plinth, with a porch, a hypostyle pavilion and an inner sanctum topped by a *shikhara*. The temple is decorated with strongly erotic groups of beautiful *surasundaris* and was constructed during the dynasty of the Gurjara Pratihara (740-1036). This dynasty was also responsible for the temples at Osia, 36 miles from Jodhpur. These temples are smaller and more linear: they have a high plinth, a porch and open hypostyle

H

H – The Rajputs were profoundly tied to Hindu tradition and built many temples. Those at Ranakpur are among the most beautiful, the most important of which was built in the 15th century.

I – Ranakpur temple is dedicated to Adinatha, the 1st of the 24 Tirthankara or prophets that preached an ascetic doctrine called Jainism. The doctrine was named after Mahavira, called the Jina (Victor). The photograph shows one of the Tirthankaras.

E, F – One of the most interesting elements of Rajasthan buildings is the jharokha, a bow window with small lace-like balconies and a bangaldar (Bengalese roof) with convex overhangs similar to a hut. Fine brackets decorated with banana leaf motifs supported the jharokha. The photo shows details of the Patva Haveli (E) and Moti Mahal Haveli (F) at Jaisalmer.

G – The sites where rulers were cremated were marked by buildings inspired by both temple and palace architecture. This is the enormous Jasvant Thara built at Jodhpur for the maharaja Jasvant Singh II in 1899.

at the battle of Tarain in 1192. The current building was constructed by Mogul emperor Akbar in 1572: the Museum of Rajputana is housed inside which is noted for its collection of statues, paintings, weapons and other various objects. Ajmer was and continues to be a pilgrimage destination because it accommodates the *dargah* (tomb) of Khaja-ud-Din-Chishti, the founder of a Sufi order. The massive silver cenotaph is located on an enormous site that includes two mosques from the 16th and 17th centuries.

The rulers of Rajasthan were profoundly religious and the enormous number of temples built by them and their ministers is evidence of their devotion. Jain temples are among the most splendid but there are also many Hindu examples, like the 11th century remains of the temples of Kiradu in the district of Barmer and of Abaneri in the district of Jaipur. There is also the temple dedicated to the goddess

mandapa. The inner sanctum is crowned with *shikharas* and small subsidiary sanctuaries featuring a wide range of architectural styles and fine decoration. The most impressive of these temples are those dedicated to Surya, Vishnu and Mahariva.

At Eklingji, 15 miles from Udaipur, the 10th century temple of Lakulisha, rebuilt in the 15th century, is a well-proportioned structure dedicated to Shiva with white marble *shikharas*. A black marble statue of Shiva with four faces is kept in the inner sanctum together with the *linga*. The more recent temple of Krishna in Nathadvara, 34 miles from Udaipur and a popular pilgrimage destination, contains a black marble statue of the shepherd god brought from Mathura by *raja* Singh I of Udaipur in 1669 to save it from the iconoclasm of the Mogul emperor Aurangzeb.

G

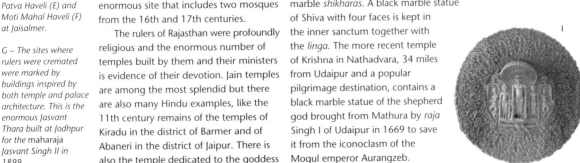

I

MOUNT ABU

B

C

D

by an entrance pavilion and elephant stalls, the white marble construction stands in a courtyard surrounded by a colonnade with 59 cells. The cross-shaped temple has an open, 48-column porch in front of a magnificently carved hypostyle *mandapa* adorned with statues. This *mandapa* is followed by another with a domed ceiling supported by 8 pillars and composed of eleven concentric rings. It is decorated with a frieze of marble dancers, musicians, knights, deities, birds and an open lotus flower supported by sixteen statues of the Vidyadevi, the goddesses of awareness. A few steps lead to a hall in front of the inner sanctum where the statue of Adinatha, the first *Tirthankara*, is kept.

The Luna Vasahi temple dedicated to Nemintah, 22nd *Tirthankara*, whose colossal black marble statue towers over the inner sanctum, was built two centuries later. It is also known as the Tehahpala after the minister to king Vivadhavala Solanki who with his brother built it in 1230. It stands in a colonnaded courtyard with 52 cells and is similar to Vimala Vasahi in layout. It has the same type of decoration and the composite

A – In a niche of the temple of Rishabdeo, the goddess Durga is shown as Mahishasuramardini, "He that kills the buffalo demon."

B – One of the main features of the marble temples of Dilvara is their domed ceilings.

C, D – The temple of Rishabdeo about 38 miles from Udaipur was inspired by the architecture of Jain temples in Gujarat. They are split into a hypostyle mandapa and inner sanctum with a shikhara covering.

E

T he most spectacular holy buildings in Rajasthan are Jain temples, the oldest and most celebrated site being Mount Abu. The 3,960 foot high mountain dominating the Aravalli highland has been a holy site from earliest Indian history. It is venerated by Jains, because Mahariva stayed there when he was 36, and by Hindus because it is the site of the *agnikula* from which the four main Rajput clans were born.

The group of Dilvara temples stands on Mount Abu within a high enclosure wall. The oldest of these temples is dedicated to Adinatha and is called Vimala Vasahi in honor of Vimala Shah, who built it, minister of king Bhimadeva I of the Solanki dynasty from 1032-45. Preceded

elements are each built to perfection.

The nearby temple of Bhima Shah is dedicated to Rishabadeva, another name for the first *Tirthankara*, whose statue is famous for being made of an alloy of five metals. The Chaumukha temple consecrated to the 23rd *Tirthankara*, Parshvanatha, is also remarkable with its splendid ceiling in filigree marble and the scenic view over the Divara site from its third floor.

Another prominent example of Jain architecture is the temple dedicated to Adinatha at Rishabdeo, 41 miles from Udaipur. It is built in Gujarati style with numerous hypostyle *mandapas* topped by *shikharas* and with statues of *Tirthankaras* inside including the black marble Adinatha known as Sri Kalaji (Black Lord).

F

E – The temple of Adinatha at Ranakpur is one of the masterpieces of Jain art. Its complex structure incorporates several floors and centers on the square sanctum that is open on all four sides.

F – The twenty-nine mandapas of the temple of Adinatha and its related porticoes have pillars sculpted with a profusion of statues and decorations. Their simple meaning often hides another, esoteric interpretation.

G – The western mandapa, the most important, has a beautiful domed ceiling supported by sixteen columns with sixteen female figures forming a halo.

H – Eighty-four chapels housing statues of Tirthankara were built into the perimeter walls of the temple of Adinatha. Of special note are the door frame and the step of the threshold.

G

H

Jain art peaked at Ranakpur, 56 miles from Udaipur. To reach the Jain temples one passes the 13th century Hindu temple dedicated to Surya, a fine example of the *nagara* style with an *ardhamandapa*, a *mandapa*, a *garbhagriha*, a *shikhara* and profuse decoration with solar motifs. There are three Jain temples: the first dedicated to the 22nd *Tirthankara*, Nemintah, from the 15th century but with a modern *mandapa*, the second, Suparshvanatha, the 7th *Tirthankara*, also from the 15th century but also with a recent *mandapa* and decorated with statues in erotic poses, and the third, the temple dedicated to Adinatha. This last was built from 1433-39 by the architect Dipaka for the rich merchant Dharana during the reign of Kumbhakarna. It is the first example of a *chaturmukha* temple in which four hypostyle rooms are placed in front of the *mukhamandapa* (the inner sanctum open to the four cardinal points) containing a *chaturmukha* (four faced) statue of Adinatha.

The structure of the temple is, however, much more complex: it is split over 36,000 square yards with 29 *mandapas* on different levels centered on the *mukhamandapa*. On each of the axes of the *mukhamandapa*, there is a *sabhamandapa* (an open hypostyle assembly room) and a *gudha mandapa* (a closed or "covered" hypostyle room on three floors) preceded by an open and a closed porch. Other buildings radiate between the axes alternating between dome and *shikhara* coverings with the highest *shikhara* on the central chapel. 84 small chapels stand along the perimeter walls, each topped with a *shikhara*. The main *sabhamandapa*, the western one, is the largest and has a magnificent ceiling with a pyramidal covering resting on 16 columns.

The temple's 420 pillars transform it into a kind of marble forest in which every surface is decorated with filigree motifs that resemble engravings in ivory. Every ceiling is different and the domes embellished with statues are true works of sculpture. Crowds of figures and symbols make up a host of holy images that can be seen from every angle, a sight that has few equals in all India.

CHITTORGARH AND UDAIPUR, THE COURTS OF THE MAHARANA OF MEWAR

The ancient capital of Mewar, Chittorgarh, was founded in the 7th century by Chitrangada of the Mori clan. It was conquered a century later by the Guhila (or Guhilot) clan which was in turn dethroned by the Pratihara in the 9th century. The city then passed through the hands of the Rashtrakutas and Paramaras in the 11th century before once again being occupied by the Guhilas.

A, B, D – The Shivite temple of Samidheswar was built in the 15th century in the fort of Chittor, the ancient capital of Mewar. Before it stands the pavilion of Nandi, the bull ridden by Shiva. The hypostyle interior (B) houses the linga and a three part image of the god (D).

C

A

B

PLAN OF CHITTORGARH
A-E INTERMEDIATE GATES
F RAM GATE
G SALINDHESWAR TEMPLE
H TOWER OF GLORY
I PALACE OF KUMBHA
J TEMPLE OF KUMBHASYAMA
K VICTORY TOWER
L THE TEMPLE OF SAMIDHESWAR
M GOMUKHA KUND
N HOUSE OF JAY MALL
O THE TEMPLE OF KALIKA MATA
P PALACE OF RATAN SINGH

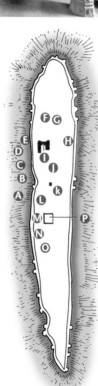

N

Chittorgarh is a city with one of the richest histories in Rajasthan and, together with the fort of Ranthambor 113 miles from Jaipur, was the strongest bulwark against the Moslem invaders. It was destroyed in 1303 by the sultan of Dehlhi Ala-ud-Din then retaken by the Rajput prince Hamir Singh of the Sisodia branch of the Guhila clan in 1326. The Guhilas founded the state of Mewar and were always in conflict with the sultans of Malva, Gujarat and Delhi. Ruled by an iron code of honor, the inhabitants of Chittor frequently performed the rite of *jauhar* like when the castle was taken by the sultan of Gujarat, Bahadur Shah of Ahmadabad, in 1534. On this occasion, women and children led by queen Karmavati took their lives on the open expanse today called the Mahasati esplanade. The same thing happened in 1568 when Akbar destroyed the fort although the *maharana* (a Mewar title equivalent to *maharaja*) Udai Singh had saved himself to ensure the continuity of the dynasty. The ruler built a new capital, Udaipur, 72 miles from Chittor and fought strenuously against the Moslems. His successors were the only Rajput princes not to come to terms with the invaders.

The main fortifications at Chittorgarh were built by the most illustrious *maharana* of the dynasty, Kumbha, who reigned from 1433 to 1468. The approach to the fort is from the west with seven gates to block the passage, but there is also an entrance at the north end with one gate and another on the east side with four gates. Most portals are built in the oldest Hindu fashion with corbelled arches. The *jalis* between the Bhairava Pol and the Hanuman Pol were built by Jay Mall, the "Lion of Chittor," who was the ruler of Merta, commander of the fort, and Kalla, his equerry, who both died in 1568 in the attempt to halt Akbar's advance. The Ganesha Pol and Lakshmana Pol house two small temples dedicated respectively to Ganesha, the elephant

F

G

H

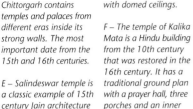

C – One of the oldest Rajput settlements, Chittorgarh contains temples and palaces from different eras inside its strong walls. The most important date from the 15th and 16th centuries.

E – Salindeswar temple is a classic example of 15th century Jain architecture

with its open hypostyle pavilions embellished with domed ceilings.

F – The temple of Kalika Mata is a Hindu building from the 10th century that was restored in the 16th century. It has a traditional ground plan with a prayer hall, three porches and an inner sanctum surrounded by an ambulatory and topped with a shikhara.

G, H – The 15th century palace of Kumbha was built on top of a 13th century construction and is one of the oldest parts of the rajput court. The porch used for public audiences and the two prasada (buildings with towers [H]) are the most outstanding elements of the complex. The latter were probably the private apartments of the ruler or his son.

Bhandar probably used to hold the treasury and the splendidly carved temple (1455-1456) dedicated to Shantinatha, the 16th Jain Tirthankara known as Salindeswar. Then come the ruins of the palace of *maharana* Kumbha, an adaptation of a 13th century building which makes it one of the oldest Palatine architectural ruins. A long, flat-roofed porch stands after the Tripolia Pol which was probably inspired by *talars* and used for public audiences. The private quarters follow where the division between the men's and women's quarters does not appear so very strict to judge by the layout of the rooms around the courtyards. Two *prasadas* can be distinguished in the area of the royal apartments and in the south-west perhaps reserved for the heir.

After leaving Kumbha's palace, the visitor comes to 27 Jain sanctuaries, the most splendid being the 11th century Sat Bis Deorhi temple, a small sculpted jewel. Equally attractive is the 11th century Kumbhashyama Vishnu temple restored by

MAP OF THE PALACE
OF KUMBHA
A TRIPOLIA GATE
B AUDIENCE PORCH
C INTERNAL COURT
  WITH THREE STORY
  STRUCTURE AND
  PRASADA
D COURT OF THE ROYAL
  APARTMENTS
E SOUTH WESTERN
  COMPLEX WITH A
  SECOND *PRASADA*

past the Jatashankara temple dedicated to Shiva. The tower was built to celebrate Kumbha's 1446 victory over Mahmud Khalji, sultan of Malva. The 120 foot high structure has 9 floors; it celebrates Vishnu but is adorned with many statues of other Hindu gods. It perpetuates the model established by the previous, 13th century, Tower of Glory erected by a Jain merchant near the Mahariva temple crowned with sculptures of Adinatha and other Tirthankara. Also interesting are the House of Jay Mall; the Samidheswar temple built in 1428 by Mokal in honor of Shiva which contains a *linga* and a triple image of the god as creator, conserver and destroyer; the 10th century temple of Kalika Mata was first consecrated to Surya, the sun god, seen on the architrave, but was restored in 1568 with the addition of sculptures and dedicated instead to Kali. The Gomukha Kund, a pool filled with water from a spout in the shape of a cow's head and overlooked from the north by the palace of *rana* Ratan Singh (1528-1532). The palace named after the romantic and tragic queen Padmini stands in the center of the pool; Padmini lived in the 13th century but the palace was built after her death; poorly restored in the 14th

god, and to Lakshmana, Rama's brother. This last gate is a splendid example of 15th century defensive architecture with solid octagonal towers, rich decoration and a hypostyle *mandapa* for the guard next to the temple of Rama. Crenellated bastions, buttresses and other defensive structures make the fort almost impregnable and it is perhaps the only intact example of medieval Hindu military architecture.

Next come the Tulaja Bhavani temple built from 1535 to 1540, the Naulakha

Kumbha in 1448. In front of it stands a kiosk with Garuda, Vishnu's part-man, part-vulture mount. The kiosk contains a porch, hypostyle room, ambulatory and inner sanctum topped by a *shikhara*. In the same wall, also built by Kumbha in honor of Krishna, stands the Mira Bai temple. Mira Bai was a 15th century princess of Jodhpur who married a *maharana* from Chittorgarh and was famous for her love songs addressed to Krishna.

The Victory Tower, 1448-58, stands

century, it may have been used as the *zanana* of *rana* Ratan Singh. The story of the queen beloved of Ala-ud-Din who saw her reflection in a mirror is still the subject of many local ballads. When Padmini's husband was taken prisoner, Ala-ud-Din wanted to exchange him for Padmini but the queen tricked him: she asked the Moslem ruler if she could bring with her the retinue of ladies-in-waiting that befitted her rank to which he consented. Once in the palanquins, the ladies were replaced by Rajput warriors in disguise who managed to free their *maharana*. Unfortunately, Padmini's husband was killed during Ala-ud-Din's siege of the fort, leading not only Padmini but all the women of Chittorgarh to commit *jauhar*.

A

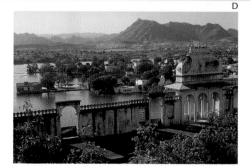

B

A, B, C, D – Founded in the 16th century, Udaipur stretches between two artificial lakes (A and D). The city is dominated by the largest palace in Rajasthan, the City Palace (C). Claiming to be the descendants of the sun, the rulers' favorite symbol was the peacock, depicted in the Courtyard of the Peacocks (B).

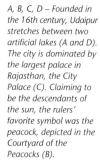

C

D

E – Built in granite and marble, the City Palace overlooks courtyards and gardens filled with fountains and open pavilions. Over the centuries, many buildings were added to the oldest part of the palace, built by Udai Singh in 1568.

F – The apartments are shaded by verandahs with wide overhangs on the ground floor and which on the upper floor are topped by chattris (kiosks on columns). There are also terraces screened by jali, fretted panels which hide the interior from sight but which allow cool air to pass through.

of the entire site. Other superb palaces are built on Lake Pichola besides the City Palace. There is the Jag Nivas, made from white marble and built in 1746 by *maharana* Jagat Singh II, now a hotel, and the Jag Mandir, a sandstone tower with the interior decorated with arabesques, built from 1615 to 1622. Udaipur has another artificial lake, Fateh Sagar, where various gardens have been created. The most famous is the Sahelion ki Bari of *maharana* Sangram Singh (1710-1734) with a lotus pool guarded by four marble elephants and pavilions surrounded by the flowers. In the nearby city of Ahar, once capital of the Guhila clan in the 10th century, there is the Mahasati with cenotaphs and Jain temples, like the 10th century Kesariyaji temple dedicated to Mahariva.

After the last tragic defeat in 1568, Udai Singh (1540-1572) established the "city where the sun rises" on the shore of the artificial lake Pichola Udaipur. It had perimeter walls but no citadel and the *maharana* reigned there until 1947. The ancient nucleus of the "City Palace," the largest in Rajasthan at almost 1500 feet long, is composed of the flat-roofed public audience hall which faces east, the direction of the main entrance, the colonnaded armory and the Raja Angan Chouk, with the palatine temple and treasury to the north, and private apartments entered from the Toran Pol to the south of the audience hall. The apartments were divided into the *mardana* to the north and the *zanana*, the Badal Mahal, to the south. Later, the Lakshmi Chouk was added to the *zanana*.

Some of the most famous parts of the site are: the Mor Chouk (Courtyard of the Peacocks) with colored mosaics, the Bari Mohul (Palace of the Marvels of China) in the Mogul style, the Dilkhush Mahal from the era of Karan Singh (1620-1628) with colored murals, the Moti Mahal glowing with colored glass and the marble Karan Mahal built at the top of the palace containing the most important apartments

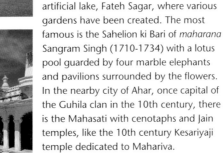

G – The lobed-arch interiors are often cooled by channels of water in imitation of those in the palaces of the Moguls. Decorations include niches, pictures and glass and mirror tiled mosaics.

H – Unlike the Mogul palaces which were built on no more than two floors, the courts of the Rajput had many levels, the legacy of the ancient prasada, the building with towers which was where the royal apartments were situated.

I – One of the most attractive elements of the City Palace is the fretted screens decorated with people and animals against intricate floral backgrounds. The loveliest example is at the Mor Chouk, the Courtyard of the Peacocks, decorated in the mid-19th century.

J – The figures shown in minute detail carved in the fretted screens give a good idea of the clothing of the period. Men wore the jama, a wide tunic, over tight trousers which were tied at the waist by a high sash.

K – One of the means of transport for nobles and the ruler was the elephant on which the houda - the large, open seat shown in the picture - was fixed over the caparison, or a closed palanquin if women were carried.

JODHPUR AND BIKANER, THE FORTS OF MARWAR

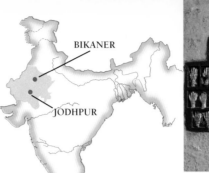

A, B - Meherangarh, the fort at Jodhpur was built in 1459 but underwent considerable rebuilding after occupation by the Mogul emperor Aurangzeb in 1678.

C

Jodhpur was founded by Rao Jodhaji Rathor in 1459 when it inherited the role of capital of Marwar from the city of Mandor. The ancient city of Mandor, capital from 1211, was founded in the 6th century; it was the site of the cenotaphs of the Rathor clan, the most important of which was Ajit Singh's from the 8th century. The fortunes of Marwar improved in 1581 when one of the princesses, Jodh Bai, married Akbar.

The red sandstone fort in Jodhpur was an unassailable bastion as well as being a luxurious palace. It was well-defended by a winding approach road closed by a series of gateways of which

A

the first, Fateh Pol, obliged aggressors to make a sharp turn to the left. The final gate, Suraj Pol, dedicated to the sun, led into Singar Choki Chouk, the courtyard used for public audiences with a marble dais for the throne. Among the palaces which face onto the courtyards, the most outstanding are the Moti Mahal, built by Jasvant Singh (1638-1678), with a sumptuous audience hall decorated with a glass tiled ceiling; the Phul Mahal of Abhai Singh (1724-1748) with *diwan-i-khas*; the *daulat khana* (royal apartments) with a complex of decorated rooms; the Khabka Mahal with external walls decorated with floral inlays; the *shish mahal* with large mirror panels inserted in the overall pattern of colored glass tiles; and the older *zanana* with balconies created by a series of *jalis* and topped by *bangaldar* overhangs to shelter the interiors from the desert heat.

C - A dramatic example of life in the Rajput court is given by the sculptures of the hands of the *satis*, wives that climbed onto the funeral pyre of their dead ruler.

D

E

E – On the north side of the court of the *daulat khana*, the private apartments of the ruler, stands the Phul Mahal (Palace of Flowers) with the 18th century *diwan-i-khas*, the private audience room.

F - Bikaner, founded in 1488, soon became a prosperous caravan center. Its wealth is shown by the fort of Junagarh in which the small courtyards on different levels are lined with fine mosaics.

G – Junagarh fort is enclosed by a red sandstone wall. It was enlarged in the 16th century and continually rebuilt over the centuries that followed. The result is that the various sections of the fort attest to the evolution of Rajput taste.

H – There is a considerable difference in style between the various levels of the Junagarh palaces: the ground and first floors are elaborately designed with spacious, airy rooms but the upper floors are square and severe with small, dark bedrooms.

I – The decoration of the interiors is enlivened by arcades and jali. There are traditional Rajput motifs, Mogul elements and, from more recent times, an English influence. The overall mix is typical of the last phase of Rajasthani courts.

F

G

H

I

D – Much of the Fort of Jodhpur has been transformed into a museum that collects objects of all kinds, from clothes to musical instruments, in an interesting insight into life during the rajput era.

The other large city in Marwar, Bikaner, was founded by the son of Jodha Rao Bikaji in 1488. It is dominated by the massive citadel of Junagarh with its labyrinthine palace decorated with 17th and 18th century pictures. Rao Bikaji's original construction was altered a century later by Rai Singh and then by his successors. The Karan Mahal is one of the site's most prominent buildings with its wonderful 17th and 18th century pictures. The private audience hall in the Anup Mahal, built by Surat Singh (1787-1828) with opulent red and gold mirrors and mosaics and the Chattra Nivas Hava Mahal, built by Dungar Singh (1828-1887), its ceiling lined with blue and white English porcelain tiles, are two examples of the "Baroque" taste of the *rajas*.

The royal cenotaphs with *chattris* and painted domes are situated near to Bikaner at Devi Kund. The white marble monument to Surat Singh has some of the loveliest examples of Rajput painting.

Bikaner was also home to a famous school of miniature painting as was Kishangarh, founded by Kishan Singh, eighth son of Udai Singh of Jodhpur. Kishangarh attained great splendor under Samant Singh (1748-64), a poet as well as ruler who wrote under the pseudonym of Nagari Das. He fell in love with the famous and cultured singer Bani Thani with whom he shut himself up in a hermit-like existence towards the end of his life.

THE SOLAR DYNASTIES OF AMBER AND JAIPUR

Amber was founded in the 10th century by a prince of the Kachhavaha clan in a strategic position on the caravan route between Delhi and Rajasthan. It became the

A

capital of a powerful state thanks to the alliance of its rulers with the Moguls. This link was further strengthened by the marriage of Maryam Zamani, sister of Bhagvan Das, to the emperor Akbar in 1562. It was to Maryam that Akbar's heir, Jahangir, was born. It was in Jahangir's name that Man Singh I (1589-1614) governed the huge area of Kabul, Bihar

B

and Bengal. Jay Singh I (1614-1667) was a governor of the province of Deccan on behalf of Shah Jahan, receiving the title Mirza Raja (noble sovereign).

The relationship between the Kachhavaha and the Islamic court gave rise to an interesting synthesis of architectural styles. Once Jay Singh II (1699-1743) had consolidateed his power, he built the city of Jaipur in 1727 and transferred his capital there. Able politician that he was, he succeeded in keeping his state independent during the difficult period that followed the collapse of the Mogul empire. Jay Singh's successors placed Jaipur under the British protectorate in 1818 and by always remaining faithful to Great Britain, even during the mutiny of the colored troops in 1857, they enjoyed

great privileges.

The city of Amber is set within strong city walls around an artificial lake. The lake has an island called the Garden of Dalaram (Dalaram being the architect of Jaipur) and is dominated by the Jaygarh (Victory Fort). Passing through Suraj Pol (Gate of the Sun), the visitor enters Jaleb Chouk, the service courtyard added by Jay Singh II. From here one passes through the Chandra Pol (Gate of the Moon) that leads to the temple dedicated to Narasimha, the leonine manifestation of Vishnu, and to the Jagat Shiromani (Gem of the World), a temple with an enormous prayer hall to accommodate the communal *bhakti* (devotion) of the Vishnu congregation. Passing through Lion Gate, next to which the palatine temple dedicated to Kali

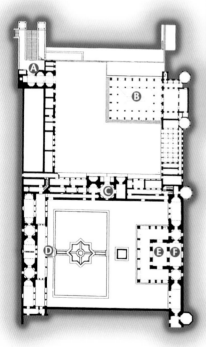

MAP OF VICTORY
FORT
A LION GATE
B *DIWAN-I-AM*
C GANESH GATE

D SUKHA NIVAS
E JAY MANDIR
F SHISH MAHAL AND
    JASH MANDIR

A – The origins of Jaygarh (Victory Fort), which dominates the residential area of Amber, date from the 10th century but the oldest surviving parts were built in the 16th century.

D

E

F

G

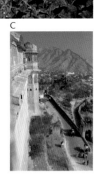

C

B, C - Jaygarh, with its bastions, buttresses and defensive walls in which the entrances (pol) to the fort are found, is very representative of Rajput forts. The access ramp below the massive walls could be easily guarded.

D - As in the past, the visitors that arrive at the fort at Amber by elephant dismount by the Lion Gate, the palace's main entrance.

E - The women of the zanana used the internal gardens for their amusement as they rarely left the palace grounds; little is left of the gardens' original beauty.

F - Ganesh Gate is a well-proportioned building with an arched facade and bangaldar roof. It allowed the women to watch public audiences from the top floor through a grille.

G - The diwan-i-am from the first half of the 16th century has a central hall supported by grey marble columns and is surrounded by a double series of red sandstone pillars; its design was inspired by the public audience rooms of the Moguls.

H

H - Mirror mosaics were one of the decorative elements in Rajput courts: this vase shines in a niche of the Jash Mandir.

I - The relationship with the Mogul court is evident in the Jay Mandir.

J - The shish mahal (Palace of Mirrors), receives light from a verandah decorated with stone squares.

K - The various wings of the palace are joined by columned galleries open on one side and screened by jali on the other. The combination creates a pleasing play of light.

the right. Here, the main hall with beautiful doors and sandalwood and ivory knockers is cooled by a water channel in the floor decorated with white and black zigzag marble strips. The channel is fed by hydraulic means and flows into a small waterfall in the char bagh, the traditional garden designed in four parts. The Jay Mandir stands on the left with a lovely diwan-i-khas and shish mahal. Above there is the Yash Mandir (Palace of Glory), magnificently decorated with glass, mirror and golden tiles and inlaid with semi-precious stones. Above there is a terrace with bangalar roof. In the same courtyard there is the zanana built on the orders of Man Singh I (1589-1614). It is a maze of bedrooms, stores, service rooms, bathrooms, kitchens and screened terraces.

I

J

K

stands, one enters the courtyard of the diwan-i-am, an imposing hypostyle building constructed by Jay Singh I with a central hall supported by marble columns and surrounded by a double series of red sandstone pillars.

The entrance to the private quarters of the fort, Ganesha Pol, has an attractive facade with arches screened by jali and a bangaldar roof. From the Sohag Mandir on the top floor, delicate fretwork allowed the women to follow the events in the public audiences unseen. The Bhojan Shala (Banquet Room) decorated by Hindu paintings is situated on the same floor.

The garden courtyard of the diwan-i-khas opens on the other side of the gate, with the elegant Sukha Nivas or Sukha Mandir, Jay Singh's "place of delight," on

Jaipur is called the "red city" for the color of its sandstone. It was built by Jay Singh II in 1727 about 5 miles from Amber following the rules of the *Shastra*, the Hindu treatises on architecture, which divide the site into a chessboard so as to facilitate the distribution of land to each caste and guild in precise and codified functional spaces. Wanting to incorporate the hills for purposes of fortification and having to take the lie of the land into account, the orientation of the city was slightly altered from the *Shastra*

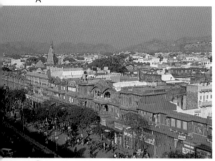
A

B

white sandstone to which the *jalis* and *bangaldar* bay windows give an almost rarefied air. Extensions have since complicated the original layout.

One passes through the main entrance to the palace, the Ser Deorhi ka Darvaza, and crosses the Nakkar Khana ki Darvaza courtyard with *chattri* galleries for the musicians before reaching the Jaleb Chouk; this is the enormous service courtyard that was also used for drilling the troops.

On the left stands the famous Jantar Mantar, the astronomical observatory built by Jay Singh II between 1728-33, the better to practise his passion for this science. The site of the observatory was filled with huge structures made from plastered brick - like other observatories in Delhi, Ujjain and Benares (all existing) and the one in Mathura (no longer standing) – these were for the gnomon, sextant, meridian and other instruments used to identify the co-ordinates of the planets such as their altitude, distance from earth, azimuth and so on.

The Gainda ki Deorhi (Gate of the Rhinoceros) is the entrance to the palace proper. First there is a courtyard overlooked by an elegant 19th century pavilion, the Mubarak Mahal. Passing through the Sarhad ki Deorhi with knockers made from copper, one reaches the private area of the palace with the *diwan-i-khas* in pink sandstone and decorated with white and black marble, and an enormous silver container used to carry water from the

C

D

A - Jaipur was built in 1727 on the traditional checker-board layout in which each caste, guild and functional area occupied a particular space.

B - It was called the "red city" for the color of its sandstone and has many palaces in Indo-Mogul style.

C - Of the nine sectors into which the city is divided, two are occupied by the City Palace, part of which is the Chandra Mahal shown here.

D - A wing of the court of the diwan-i-am embellished by inserts of white marble.

E, F - From behind the screen (E) of the Hava Mahal (Palace of the Winds) built in 1799, the women of the zanana could watch public functions unseen, protected by jali bow windows (F).

recommendations but, nonetheless, the city was still divided into nine *padas* (parts) by a road that runs east-west and two others that run north-south. All smaller roads run off these at right angles.

The residential area is protected by a city wall 20 feet high and 9 feet thick. It has seven gates of which the largest is dedicated to Shiva. In the center of the city, the City Palace occupies almost two *padas*. It was built following the traditional recommendations with an external courtyard and buildings of the *rajabhavana* (public structure) and a series of internal courtyards around which the *rajaniveshana* is distributed with a *prasada* occupying several floors. The seventh floor, Chandra Mahal, was the location of the *zanana* until 1799 when *maharaja* Pratap Singh had the Hava Mahal (Palace of the Winds) built especially for the women. This was made from red and

MAP OF JAIPUR
A Lake
B Artificial lake
C Gardens
D Previous *diwan-i-am*
E Chandra Mahal
F Jantar Mantar
G Hava Mahal
H Fort of Nahagarh
I-M City gates

E   F

sacred river Ganges that the *maharaja* took with them on their journeys.

The Chandra Mahal faces onto the same courtyard with its seven floors built in white marble. Inside, the ground floor is decorated with paintings celebrating the glory of the Kachhavaha; upstairs, there are the Shoba Nivas (Residence of splendor), shining with glass and mirror mosaics, the Silah Khana, one of the most beautiful "armories" in India, and the Mukut Mandir on the top floor with fine *chattris* and a marvellous view over the whole site.

On the other side of the garden, opposite the Chandra Mahal, stands the temple of Govinda Deva built by Jay Singh II for private prayer. In the courtyard alongside, the *diwan-i-am* was built with marble columns and *jali* naves for the women. It contains a private collection of the *maharaja* of Jaipur. Next to the Tripolia Gate, a private entrance for the rulers and their dignitaries, stands the Ishvari Lath, a seven-floor octagonal tower built to commemorate the ascent to the throne of the ruler of the same name.

The Albert Hall standing in the Ram Nivas gardens is a worthy example of late 19th century architecture. It currently houses a museum famous for its carpets.

The many 18th and 19th century palaces around Jaipur are evidence of the rich princely life of the city. The best preserved are those of Rao Bohra, Rupnivas and the exquisite small palace of the *maharani* Shishodia with beautiful pictures and a romantic garden. Funerary architecture can be admired in the cenotaphs in Gathor where the rulers were cremated while their queens are remembered in the *chattris* several miles from Dhruva Gate. The 9th century temple of Nakti Mata at Bhavanipura is a fine example of *nagara* architecture while the 17th century Hindu temples at Galta, dedicated to Shiva and Vishnu, and the Jain temple of the same period at Sanganer demonstrate the religious vitality and devotion of the population.

THE HAVELI OF JAISALMER

JAISALMER

A - Jaisalmer was a city built from yellow sandstone in the 12th century on caravan routes.

The walls and towers of the city rise mirage-like from the sands of the Thar desert.

C

D

B

Jaisalmer was founded in 1156 by the *maharaval* Jaisal Singh (*maharaval* is a synonym for *maharaja*). It soon became the largest caravan city in the Thar desert and attained a degree of magnificence under *raval* Amar Singh (1661-1702). With over 3 miles of turretted walls built in yellow sandstone, it seems to be part of the desert itself. The fort dominating the city contains the royal apartments, various Hindu and Jain temples built between the 12th and 15th centuries as well as an interesting library, the Jnana Bhandar (Repository of Knowledge), that includes manuscripts from as early as the 12th century.

The most important architectural aspect of Jaisalmer are the *havelis*, mansions built mostly in the 18th century by the *marwari*, a subcaste of the *banya*, the merchants of Rajasthan connected with the third largest Hindu caste, the *vaishya*. The *havelis* are reproductions of *prasada* with an austere ground floor enlivened only by the designs of the entrance and shop windows. Hypostyle verandahs, bay windows with *jalis* and *bangaldars*, beautifully engraved overhangs, inlaid decorations and screened terraces for living outdoors in the summer months are all found on the upper floors. One of the most beautiful examples is the Patron Ki.

B - The artificial lake, Garhisar, was created near Jaisalme. Its banks are dotted with temples and chattri, some of which were built to commemorate cremations.

C - This is one of the seven Jain temples built between the 12th and 15th centuries in the fort of Jaisalmer by the Jain community that emigrated from Gujarat to escape Moslem persecution.

D - The havelis were palatial residences built in the 18th century by the marwari, the most powerful subcaste of Rajasthan merchants. In the picture is the Nathmal ki Haveli.

E - Patuon ki Haveli faces onto an internal courtyard. Its topmost floors are where the most important and private rooms of the household are situated.

E

THE MINIATURES OF RAJASTHAN

One of the special features of the palaces of Rajasthan that further distinguish them from Mogul courts are mural paintings inspired by the Hindu religious tradition which also celebrate court life and the achievements of the rulers.

Bundi was the capital of a small kingdom 100 miles from Ajmer, built on the banks of Lake Naval by the head of the Hari Chahuan clan. The lively murals in the 17th century palace attest to the ability of the local artists: court, hunting and festival scenes alternate with conventional themes such as the furtive meetings of lovers or the wait for a loved one. Representations of particular ritual moments refer to ancient religious themes, as in the example of the game of the *hindola* or *dola* (swing) played to encourage the course of the sun and so increase the size of the harvests.

Bundi was also a famous center of miniature painting, a form of art that was greatly favored by the various courts of Rajasthan, Kotah (23 miles from Bundi), Udaipur, Jaipur, Jodhpur, Bikaner and, above all, at Kishangarh where the famous and refined 18th century painter Nihal Chand practised. These schools were in part influenced by the more realistic Mogul style particularly in portraiture and scenes of everyday life. The Rajput kings used to collect miniatures in their *citrashalas* (art galleries) and to patronize

G

H

F

F - The area of Shekavati is famous for the wall paintings on its houses. Men and women from the 19th century look out from wall panels, niches or ceilings in the Girdarilal Sigtia Haveli.

G - A famous school of miniature painting was established in the 17th century in the small principality of Bundi.

Krishna and the shepherdesses was one of its main themes.

H - Krishna is once again the main character on the walls of the Sultan Mahal of Samode; here he is in a pastoral setting as Gopala (protector of cows) playing his flute, the symbol of the attraction souls feel for God.

painters from the different parts of India, especially from the courts of Delhi and Agra.

The Rajasthan miniatures were inspired by religious themes, principally the mythology surrounding Krishna, his heroic exploits and his love affairs with the *gopis* (shepherdesses) with whom the dark-skinned god had lived as a young man. His passion for Radha, his favorite, was one of the main sources of inspiration for the Rajput painters who depicted the alternating episodes of betrayal, separation and reconciliation. Love was therefore the dominant theme, particularly in representations of the *nayaka* and *nayika* (hero and heroine) shown in all the nuances of their various situations.

There were also many court, hunting and ritual scenes that give an idea of the daily life of the era.

A typical miniature subject in Rajasthan

was the "Ragmala" (garland of *raga*), inspired by the *raga* (precise musical intonations) designed to awaken certain sentiments. These would be linked with seasons and moments of the day. In all fields, musical, literary or pictorial, the apogee is reached when the artist achieves the *rasa* (quintessence) of the aesthetic emotion that unites the artist and the viewer in spiritual accordance. This is accomplished by evoking a perception in the human soul that is not personal but universal. Love, heroism, joy, sorrow, anger, fear, disgust, amazement and peace are the 9 principal sentiments that "move" the heart and are linked to precise situations, colors, tones, rhythms and so on. To create this effect, the background, coloring and inclusion of certain animals or objects are used to create the right context to represent the feelings of the characters.

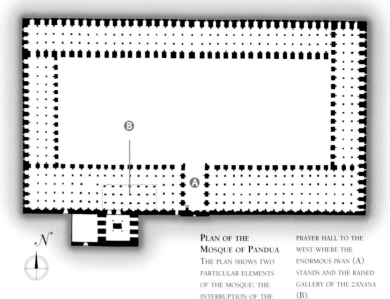

N

OTHER SITES OF MOSLEM ART

PLAN OF THE MOSQUE OF PANDUA THE PLAN SHOWS TWO PARTICULAR ELEMENTS OF THE MOSQUE: THE INTERRUPTION OF THE PRAYER HALL TO THE WEST WHERE THE ENORMOUS *IWAN* (A) STANDS AND THE RAISED GALLERY OF THE *ZANANA* (B).

A

A - The Bengali style reached maturity at Gaur in the 17th century with the Bara Sona Masjid (Great Gold Mosque) opening onto a vast courtyard. Its prayer hall is crowned with forty-four cupolas.

B - Ahmadabad experienced an age of great splendor from the 15th to the 17th centuries. It was based on a regular layout with a central street

that started at the triumphal Tin Darvaza (Triple Gate) in the illustration and connected all the most important buildings.

C - There are very many mosques in Ahmadabad; the Sidi Sayyid Masjid from 1572 has splendid inlaid marble windows with the attractive design of the tree of life.

GAUR AND PANDUA IN BENGAL

The only remnants of the Moslem presence in Bengal are the two empty cities of Gaur and Pandua. Their mosques were one of the first attempts to synthesise the flat-roofed structure of Hindu architecture with the arched architecture of Islam.

Construction of the huge Adina Masjid built in Pandua in 1374, with the *zanana* gallery raised on thick pillars, was very much influenced by Hindu and Buddhist styles. Full maturity of the individual Bengalese style was reached a century later with the five-story Firoza Minar and the Tantipara Masjid in Gaur. The latter was built in 1480 with five terracotta arches and decorative minarets at the corners. Civil architecture is represented by the terracotta Dakhil Darvaza, a triumphal arch, at Gaur.

The design of local huts made from clay and bamboo with the *bangaldar* (typical curved roof) provided the model for the design of mausoleums, as is shown by the tomb of Fateh Khan in Gaur and the mausoleum of Eklakhi at Pandua which had the addition of a cupola.

AHMADABAD AND JUNAGADH IN GUJARAT

B

C

Ahmadabad was founded in 1411 by the Moslem governor Ahmad Shah who had made himself independent of the sultanate of Delhi. The city flourished in the 15th-17th centuries and was known in the West for its textiles (see the Calico Museum with its splendid 17th century wooden facade) which were exported from the nearby port of Surat. The city was based around a central street that led from the triumphal arch to the main square and enjoyed its period of greatest splendor under Mahmud Begartha (1459-1511). When the sultans of Gujarat were defeated by the Moguls, the city was comprehensively sacked in 1755 by the Maratis, a Hindu people from Maharashtra, and only recovered with the arrival of the British fifty years later.

The following are among the most

D - The prayer hall of the Great Mosque has 260 pillars, 15 cupolas, raised zanana *galleries and fretted screens in traditional Hindu and Gujurati Jain style.*

PLAN OF THE JAMI MASJID
THE GREAT MOSQUE OR
JAMI MASJID IN
AHMADABAD WITH THE
15 DOME PRAYER HALL ON
THE WESTERN SIDE OF THE
COURTYARD.

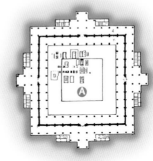

A TOMB OF THE
   WIFE OF
   AHMAD SHAH
B TOMB OF
   AHMAD SHAH
C GREAT MOSQUE

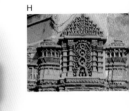

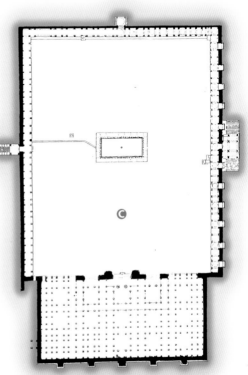

E - The Great Mosque is covered with fine domed ceilings. The photograph shows the splays that are the means by which the square is turned into a circle, passing through the shape of an octagon.

F - The Great Mosque of 1423, also known as Jama Masjid, faces onto a vast courtyard with its washing pool enclosed by a colonnade.

G - One of the most decorated mosques in India, the Jama Masjid fuses Hindu images

with elements of Islamic ornamentation: the flower, shown from two points of view, is a radiant corolla and a symmetrical cross of petals.

H - Details of the marble decorations of the Mihrab courtyard of the Jama Masjid.

A - The walls of the Rani Sipri Mosque have been lightened with large jali panels which were widely used in civil architecture; fretted screen windows also became a major ornamental feature.

B - The hypostyle interior of the prayer hall of the Rani Rupmati Mosque with its domed ceilings resembles Jain temples. This is a good example of the fertile union of the two cultures.

C - "Profane" themes have been included in the design of the mausoleum and the Rani Rupmati mosque: a jharokha (a small elegant balcony) has been added to make the building dedicated to the queen, Rani Rupmati, more elegant.

D - Local Hindu art affected Islamic architecture in Gujarat: the moldings, the niches in the shape of a holy building and the profuse decoration all make the building closer to a temple than a mosque. The photo shows an element of the Rani Rupmati Mosque.

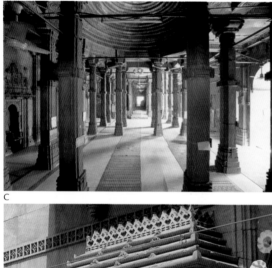

important mosques, having either a hypostyle prayer hall that opens onto the courtyard or a decorated facade with *iwan*: Ahmad Shah, built 1414 and thus the oldest, Sidi Sayyd, 1572, featuring arches with double coverings with splays and crosspieces, and windows with marble inlays suggesting the tree of life, Sidi Bashir mosque with its airy twin minarets and the Great Mosque of 1423 with its wonderful prayer hall supported by 260 pillars, 15 highly decorated cupolas with Jain influenced ceilings and raised *zanana* galleries screened by marvellous fretwork.

The most significant *rauza* (mausoleums annexed to a small mosque) are those of Rani Rupmati, from circa 1440, and Rani Sipri, 1514, both tombs of queens.

E - The extraordinary stone-carving ability of the local artists had its roots in the past when buildings were made of wood; this tangle of plants in a niche on the Rani Rupmati mosque is a perfect example.

F - Rauza (burial sites comprising a mausoleum and a small, annexed mosque) are typical of Ahmadabad: one of the most interesting is Rani Rupmati which was possibly built in 1440.

G

H

I

G - This rauza *dedicated to a queen, Rani Sipri, was built in 1514. The mosque has transformed the minarets into delicate ornamental turrets that surround the prayer hall. The mausoleum stands beside it.*

H - Designed as a pavilion with screened jali *verandahs, the mausoleum of Rani Sipri is topped by another small, domed pavilion with four small, depressed cupolas at the corners.*

I - There are two types of mosque in Ahmadabad, those with the hypostyle prayer hall open towards the courtyard and those with a decorated iwan *facade. The mosque of Rani Sipri is one of the first type.*

A - *The* baoli *(underground civil constructions) were provided by every good Hindu ruler. The Moslems inherited the tradition and built the* baoli *of Dada Hari near the mosque of the same name between 1499-1501.*

A

B

C

B, C - *The* baoli *of Dada Hari has four floors, one above ground and three hypostyle floors below. The construction is* embellished with niches, balconies, Hindu symbols and Moslem writings. At the bottom there is an octagonal cavity.

D - *Perhaps once used for ritual washing, the* baolis *evenetually become postal centers and rest points for pilgrims and caravans. The decoration is worthy of a palace.*

E - *The mosque of Dada Hari with its mausoleum annex was built at the start of the 16th century. Its severe design was meant to express both power and sobriety.*

150

F - The mausoleum of Dada Hari is a simple cubic construction topped by a flatened cupola and surrounded by a hypostyle verandah with wide overhangs and four small cupolas at the corners. D

In the case of the Mosques, minarets were transformed into delicate ornamental turrets with "profane" additions such as balconies, projections and overhangs while the mausoleum walls were "lightened" by wide *jali*-style panels, a local tradition dating back to when the buildings were made of wood. The last of the mausoleums is that of Shah Alam of 1475 featuring a dome decorated with gold and semi-precious stones by Asaf Khan, the father of Mumtaz Mahal, in the 17th century.

With regard to civil constructions, the *baoli* (underground constructions) from the district of Asarva deserve mention; the oldest is that of Mata Bhavani from the 11th century, of Hindu origin, but the most famous is that of Dada Hari near the

G

H

E

F

I

G - The citadel of Uparkot in Junagarh was conquered by the Moslems in the 15th century. It comprises a mosque built with materials taken from Hindu temples.

H - The large underground wells like this one at Uparkot were the first elements to be dug in a fort.

I - The citadel at Uparkot was fortified with a triple wall after the Moslems had taken it from the Hindu raja. The remains of monastic settlements from the 3rd century BC are found here.

mosque and mausoleum of the same name, built between 1499-1501. Of the four floors three are underground; they are supported by pillars and decorated with niches, balconies, Hindu symbols and Moslem writings. An octagonal cavity at the bottom was perhaps once used for ritual washing but was eventually used to house pilgrims and tradesmen.

Other Indo-Islamic artistic remains can be seen at Junagadh, the ancient Rajput kingdom, where the oldest part of the Uparkot citadel has a series of caves dug out by ascetics in the 3rd-2nd century BC. Junagadh was conquered by the Moslems in the 15th century and after the fall of the Mogul empire became the capital of the Moslem kingdom of Saurashtra until 1947. The mausoleum of Sahib Baba-ud-Din Bhar is a rococo construction with minarets with external spiral staircases.

J

J - The most unusual building at Junagarh is the mausoleum of Sahib Baba-ud-Din Bhar, an extravagant rococo building with minarets featuring external spiral stairways.

A

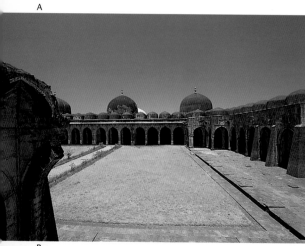

MANDU

A - Mandu, the
splendid Moslem
capital in the 15th-
16th centuries, was
fortified with 25 miles
of walls by Hushang
Shah. The religious
center of Mandu is the
Jama Masjid built in
1454 by Hushang
Shah. Its prayer hall
has no iwan and
opens onto a huge
courtyard enclosed by
a triple colonnade.

B

C

MANDU IN MADHYA PRADESH

ow a ghost town on a plain
dotted with wells and
overgrown by vegetation,
Mandu used to be known as Shadyabad
(City of Joy) and belong to munificent
Moslem princes in the 15th and 16th
centuries. It was previously inhabited by
Rajput clans from Paramara that had
made Dhar their capital and the state of
Malwa their center of operations. Mandu
was then conquered by the ruler of
Delhi, Ala-ud-Din, and entrusted to a
governor. It became independent in

PLAN OF MANDU
A DELHI GATE
B PALACE AREA
    (HINDOLA MAHAL,
    JAHAZ MAHAL)
C MAUSOLEUM OF
    HUSHANG SHAH
D JAMI MASJID
E ASHRAFI MAHAL
F THE MAUSOLEUM
    OF DARYA KHAN
G REVA KUND AND
    OTHER PALACES (BAZ
    BAHADUR, RUPMATI)

N

B - Austere and solid with
its three low cupolas, the
mosque is reached by a
wide flight of steps and
is built on a tall plinth in
which shops were once
housed.

C - The interior of the
mosque is decorated in
a sober manner. A
Greek fret design in blue
enamelled tiles can be
seen on the mihrab
surrounded by
polychrome inserts.
This is a typical Mandu
decoration.

D - The Ashrafi Mahal opposite the mosque is where the old madrasa (Koranic school) once stood. It was later remodelled to make room for the mausoleum of Mahmud Shah (1436-1462).

E - The 1540 mausoleum of Hushang Shah stands beside the mosque in a porticoed courtyard. It was one of the first mausoleums to be completely lined in marble.

F - In the image can be seen a decorative element of the mirhab of the Jami Masjid.

G - Raised on a platform and crowned by a well-proportioned cupola with four corner towers, the mausoleum is a solid cubic structure given a degree of gracefulness by the iwan and jali windows.

H - Inside the mausoleum, the burial chamber is covered by a vaulted ceiling which reveals an Afghan influence. It contains stepped cenotaphs of the king and the members of his family.

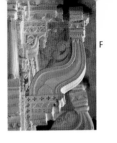

F

D

E

1402 and was fortified by 25 miles of walls by Hushang Shah. It then evolved into the center of a Moslem kingdom which was famous not only for its buildings but also for its school of miniatures. The Mandu declined during the reign of Baz Bahadur (1555-62 and noted in popular ballads for his love for the beautiful singer Rupmati) who was defeated by the Mogul emperor Akbar.

The city was surrounded by fortifications and the palaces inside were further protected by their own walls. Ten red sandstone gates with crenellations decorated by ceramic tiles gave access to the citadel in which the religious center was represented by Jama Masjid, built on the orders of Hushang Shah in 1454. This austere and solid building has three low domes and a triple row of columns around the iwan-less prayer hall. The madrasa (Koranic school) stood opposite in the Ashrafi Mahal but this was later rebuilt to make room for the tomb of Mahmud Shah (1436-62).

Not far from the mosque stands the mausoleum of Hushang Shah, completed in 1540, which was one of the first to be entirely lined with marble. Placed on a platform in the center of a courtyard with portico, the tomb is a heavy cubic structure hardly enlivened by the iwan and jali windows. It has a well-proportioned dome surrounded by four corner towers.

G

H

A - One of Mandu's most romantic constructions is the Jahaz Mahal (Boat Palace) which was wedged like a boat between two pools and used as a zanana, the area reserved for the women.

B - When Mandu was conquered by the Moguls, the Jahaz Mahal became a favorite place for relaxation of Nur Jahan and Jahangir. In his memoirs, Jahangir described the attraction of the palace reflected in the waters of the pool.

C - The complex of royal palaces is sited between two lakes, the Munja Talao in the photograph and the Kapur Talao connected by an underground canal. The water of the Munja Talao was raised to the palace by a Persian water wheel.

D

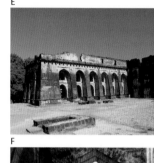

E

D - Several small pavilions covered with a high drum and dome stand on the terrace. Fragments of colored tiles and traces of paintings still remain on the plaster-lined walls.

E - Despite its attractive name, the Hindola Mahal (Oscillating Palace) is a massive T-shaped construction with heavy arches that was used for official audiences.

G

A

B

C

F

The palaces at Mandu are split into buildings used for the public and private lives of the rulers: there is the Hindola Mahal (the Oscillating Palace) which, despite its name, is a solid 15th century tapered building housing a vast room with an ogival arched ceiling on the long side (the hall of official audiences), and two floors of public rooms along the short side. In front, the Champa Baoli (a massive underground construction with vaulted rooms) ensured coolness in the hot months.

The nearby *daulat khana* is nothing but ruins.

The romantic Jahaz Mahal (the Boat Palace) was built during the same era. This building was wedged between two pools. It had two floors topped by a terrace with domed pavilions which could be reached via a long external flight of steps. The ground floor contained three large hypostyle rooms with a cloister dominated by a lovely lotus flower vase; the first floor was for a number of smaller rooms, some of which had a bathroom. The plaster coating still has traces of paintings and fragments of multi-colored tiles.

H

F - Built at the end of the 15th century, the Hindola Mahal contains an enormous room with arched ceiling along the long side and two floors of small rooms along the short side.

G - The Jahaz Mahal is built on two floors and topped by a terrace with domed pavilions. The terrace can also be reached from the outside up a long flight of steps.

PLAN OF MANDU, AREA OF THE PALACES
A JAHAZ MAHAL
B INDOLA MAHAL
C CHAMPA BAALI
D DAULAT KHANA
E DILAWAR KHAN MOSQUE

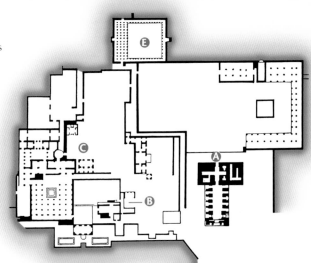

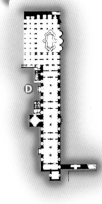

H - An arch of Champa Baali frames the buildings of Jahaz Mahal.

I - A lovely lotus flower tank opens onto a cloister on the ground floor. Fountains and small waterfalls were a permanent feature of the zanana as shown in many miniatures of Mandu.

J - Three large rooms with pointed arches topped by vaulted ceilings occupy the ground floor; a series of smaller rooms, including a bathroom, take up the first floor.

I

J

A

D

A, H - The Darya Khan mausoleum was decorated with enamelled tiles some of which can still be seen today. The blind openings reproduce the design of wooden screens of the period.

B, C - The Dilawar Khan palatine mosque built in 1405 stands next to the enclosure walls of the royal palaces. This is the oldest mosque in Mandu and was built with materials plundered from Hindu temples as can be seen in the columns of the prayer hall (B).

B

E

F

G

C

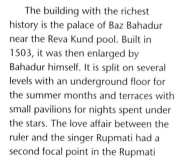

The building with the richest history is the palace of Baz Bahadur near the Reva Kund pool. Built in 1503, it was then enlarged by Bahadur himself. It is split on several levels with an underground floor for the summer months and terraces with small pavilions for nights spent under the stars. The love affair between the ruler and the singer Rupmati had a second focal point in the Rupmati

D - The Rupmati palace was built over the foundations of the ancient fort of the Hindu king, Paramara, from the 11th century. It is split into a series of hypostyle rooms of which we see the vaulted ceiling divided into 16 sections topped by a terrace.

E - *The palace is split on several levels, including an underground floor for the hot season. It is set around two courtyards, the larger having a pool at its center. The chattris on the terrace roof stand on slender columns.*

F - *The palace of Baz Bahadur was built in 1503 near the Reva Kund. It was later enlarged and remodelled by the ruler whose name it bears.*

G - *A detail of the octagonal tower of the Baz Bahadur palace. The name of the ruler is linked to the beautiful singer Rupmati for whom he built a palace on the highest site in Mandu.*

H

I

Palace which stands in the highest part of Mandu over the 11th century Paramara fortress. It features a large hypostyle room crowned by a terrace with two elegant *chattri*.

The Nilakantha Mahal (Palace of the Blue Throat) is associated with the Hindu god, Shiva. It was built in red sandstone and was loved by Akbar and Jahangir as a holiday residence.

I - *The early 16th century mausoleum of Darya Khan is reflected in the Sagar Talab tank. It is a classic example of a qubba, a cubic structure topped by a cupola.*

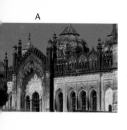

LUCKNOW

JAUNPUR

LUCKNOW AND JAUNPUR IN UTTAR PRADESH

apital of the heavily populated state of Uttar Pradesh, Lucknow reached its peak with the local Moslem dynasty of the *nawab* of Oudh during the 18th –19th centuries. Although it is little known, Lucknow is one of the most interesting examples of late Indo-Moslem art. The city is located on an ancient Hindu site where the Moslems built a fort in the 13th century but it only began to develop under the Mogul emperors. By the end of their reign, Lucknow had become the capital of the independent state of Oudh but the state experienced varying circumstances and was eventually abolished by the British in 1857.

One of the most interesting buildings

A - When the Mogul empire collapsed, Lucknow became the capital of the prosperous independent state of Oudh. It opened itself to western influences as is shown by the vaguely Gothic facade of the Great Mosque of 1840.

B - The La Martinière College in Lucknow, known as the Constantia Palace, is named after the French adventurer Claude Martin who organized the local ruler's artillery corps in the second half of the 18th century.

C - The Rumi Darwaza (Turkish Gate) with the enormous iwan flanked by slender minarets decorated with chattris was inspired by Persian architecture. The chattri motif is repeated on the pediment.

is the Chatar Manzil and its pleasure pavilions standing in lovely gardens. The Qaisar Bagh is a park where the local rulers and their wives are buried; there are many palaces in the park, the most curious of which is the Constantia, the residence of the French adventurer, Claude Martin, who organized the *nawab*'s artillery corps during the second half of the 17th century. The Machli Bhavan (Fish Palace) is a local military quarter and includes the Imambara complex. The Imambara contains an enormous vaulted room with a double series of *chattri* pediments which gives the site its name. The mausoleums of Asaf-ud-Daula (1775-95) and the building's architect are included along with a mosque and the tomb of a holy man. Outside the Rumi

D - The mausoleums of Khurshidzada (in the picture) and his consort Sadat Ali Khan from the early 19th century are the most important in Lucknow. Although many classical architectural features remain (verandahs, cupolas and chattris), the composition has a strong colonial feel.

E - The most unusual building on the site is the Bara Imambara built by Asaf-ud-Daula to accommodate the communal ceremonies of the muharram, the Shiite celebration of the martyrdom of Hussain.

F - The Bara Imambara includes one of the largest vaulted rooms in the world which stands between two wings that help to support the forces created by the ceiling. A maze of corridors and galleries fills the upper floor.

I - Inspired by the Taj Mahal but falling way short of the original, the mausoleum of Zenab Asya, daughter of Muhammad Ali Shah, is an illuminating example of the questionable aesthetic concepts of the period.

J - The interior of the Chota Imambara further underlines the indiscriminate and decidedly kitsch taste of the 19th century Indian rulers. The large, silver and clearly Asian throne is illuminated by glass lamps of all shapes that are of western manufacture.

PLAN OF THE ATALA MASJID, 1408

A ENTRANCE DOORWAYS
B COURTYARD
C PORCHES
D PRINCIPAL PRAYER HALL
E AUXILIARY PRAYER HALL

Darwaza (Turkish Gate) stand the palace of Asaf-ud-Daula and the Imambara of Hussain: the latter is a curtain wall containing mausoleums decorated with stuccowork, gold paint and mirror glass.

Faizabad, 78 miles from Lucknow, is noted for the white marble mausoleum of Bahu Begum, the favorite wife of Shuja-ud-Daula (1753-1775), buried next to her.

Also in Uttar Pradesh and 140 miles from Lucknow, Jaunpur was founded by the sultan of Delhi, Firuz Shah, in 1358. It has numerous noteworthy mosques characterized by unusual iwans flanked by tall and solid square towers. The most attractive is the Atala Masjid, 1408, built over a Hindu temple in grey sandstone and granite with black marble inserts.

G - The Imambara site, begun in 1784, comprises a series of buildings including the Asafi Masjid, an impressive mosque with many minarets standing on a wide flat area with an elaborate flight of steps.

H - The Chota Imambara (Little Gate) is a magnificent construction with verandahs built in 1939. It is also known by the name of Hussainabad Imambara and houses the mausoleum of Muhammad Ali Shah.

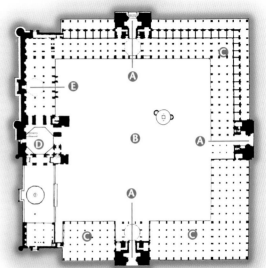

KASHMIR — SRINAGAR

AMRITSAR

THE GARDENS OF KASHMIR

The Moguls' love for nature went back to Babur who dreamed of the gardens of Samarkand and the orchards of Kabul. His successors paid great attention to creating natural settings around their buildings which evolved into projects creating gardens surrounded by tombs and palaces. The capital of Kashmir, Srinagar, is often called a "paradise on earth." It has pre-Christian origins and its name derives

D

E

A

B

C

from the goddess Sri, companion of Vishnu and Lady of beauty and abundance, also known as Lakshmi. When Kashmir was influenced by Islam in the 14th century, Srinagar became one of the Mogul emperors' cities, especially Jahangir who built beautiful gardens there. These became the city's main artistic attraction even if its mosques, for example, Shah Hamadan Masjid and Jami Masjid, both featuring pyramidal roofs topped by a spire are also noteworthy.

The Mogul gardens on and nearby Lake Dal are places of idyllic beauty. The oldest are the Nasim Bagh (Sapphire Gardens) created by Akbar in the 16th century though the most beautiful are the Shalimar Bagh (Gardens of Love) built by Jahangir in 1619 for his wife Nur Jahan. These have marble pavilions built on three sloping terraces, the first accessible to the public, the second reserved for guests of the emperor, and the third for the women of the harem. They are decorated with marble pavilions, canals and fountains. The Chashma Shahi (Royal Spring) built by Shah Jahan in 1632 and the Nishat Bagh (Garden of Joy) created by Asaf Khan, brother of Nur Jahan and split into twelve terraces linked to the signs of the zodiac are also beautiful.

A - A love for gardens was a communal passion of all Mogul emperors. Besides those created in tombs and palaces, they also had others created purely for pleasure, such as the Nishat Bagh in Srinagar.

B - Numerous pavilions are dispersed around the Garden of Love which were used for the public and private functions of the court. Most of the present pavilions have unfortunately been rebuilt.

C - Built on three levels of terraces, the Shalimar Bagh is laced by a series of canals that feed small pools, waterfalls and fountains that are an integral part of the garden.

D - The Nishat Bagh (Garden of Joy) was built in 1634 by Asaf Khan, brother of Nur Jahan. It is spread over twelve terraces associated with the signs of the zodiac.

E - Srinagar, the capital of Kashmir, was one of the Moguls' favorite places to relax: the Shalimar Bagh (Garden of Love) was built by Jahangir in 1619 for his wife Nur Jahan.

F - The Harmandir (Divine Temple) in Amritsar, also known as the Golden Temple, is not only the holiest site of the Sikh religion but also a splendid example of Indo-Moslem art.

THE GOLDEN TEMPLE AT AMRITSAR, HEART OF SIKHISM

Called Darbar Sahib (Court of the Lord) or Harmandir (Divine Temple), the Golden Temple at Amritsar in the Punjab is a splendid example of Indo-Moslem art. It was begun in 1574 and continually restored and embellished. It stands in the center of a pool circled by marble steps and wings of buildings. The pavilion on the water is connected to the enclosure wall by a narrow marble bridge, a symbol of what souls are required to pass through after death: the footbridge is as narrow as a razor-edge and slender as a hair, it will support the weight of the pious but wrongdoers will fall to hell below.

The temple is built from white marble and crowned by a terrace with a gold *bangaldar* pavilion flanked by four *chattris*. The Harmandir is further decorated on the outside and inside by floral patterns composed of precious stones and verses from the Granth Sahib, the holy book of hymns for prayer and meditation kept in the central chamber. Despite the splendor, an atmosphere of deep religiousness envelops the temple.

Sikhism was founded by Nanak who was born in a village near Lahore in the Punjab in 1469. While on

H

F

I

continual wanderings, Nanak collected a growing number of *sikhs* (disciples) around him who shared his monotheistic vision mixed with mystical notions.

After Nanak's death in 1539, the community was directed by a succession of nine *gurus*, enlightened masters, some of whom were martyrised by the Moslems. The tenth guru, Gobind, transformed the *sikhs* into a warrior community by introducing the *Khalsa* ("All that belongs to God and that is pure") in 1699. The members of the *Khalsa* were initiated with a special ceremony and committed themselves to defending faith with force.

J

G - The temple was begun in 1574 and has been continually restored. It is built in white marble topped by a terrace with gold bangaldar pavilions flanked by four chattris. The "Adi Granth" (the Sikh holy book) is kept in the central chamber.

H - The symbolism underlying the golden building refers to the origin of life when the spark of existence and the two elements – water/female and fire/ male of which the temple is the manifestation - freed themselves from the womb of the cosmic waters.

I - The name Golden Temple comes from the gold-colored lining of the building from the copper cupolas down to the marble walls. The temple has always been celebrated for its riches and has been plundered several times over the centuries.

J - Although the Sikhs are monotheistic and do not believe in the theory of the avatars, some of the Hindu pantheon is still part of their iconography: the serpent in the hand of the ascetic and the tiger skin he sits on are attributes of the god Shiva.

A - The Harmandir is the heart of Sikhism, the religion founded by Nanak. He gathered a number of disciples (sikh) around him who were united by a religious vision that combined monotheism with a degree of mysticism.

B, C, D - The decoration of the Harmandir was strongly affected by the Islamic influence. Examples are the niches in the golden lining and the marble panels with floral inlays.

E - The monument to guru Govind Singh, last spiritual master of the Sikh religion, stands near the Golden Temple. After his death, the supreme Sikh authority was no longer exercised by a guru but represented by the "Adi Granth" (Voice of God).

A

B

F - The Harmandir is connected to the land by a marble bridge of which the entrance pavilion is shown. The bridge is symbolic of what the soul has to overcome after death.

The sikh could be identified by five elements: the hair and beard that were never cut, a comb carried under the turban, knee-length trousers to facilitate fighting, an iron bracelet and a sword. Gobind also decreed that after his death there would be no more gurus but all authority would be held by the Granth Sahib, the holy book and voice of God.

The religious history of the Sikh community ended with the death of Govind who died at the hands of an Afghan fanatic in 1708. Instead, their political history started which took them

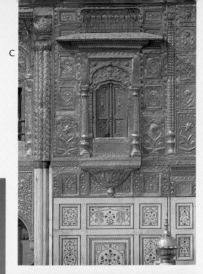

C

D

E

F

G

personified among men – Sikhs refute the Hindu theory of *avatars* (descent of the gods) – God is the father and present in kindred souls as the Voice that guides and that waits only to be listened to so that the believer can be helped to reach enlightenment.

The way to the Lord is open to all men and women, without distinction of caste or race, and implies living in the phenomenal world in the bosom of the family, earning one's living, abandoning oneself completely to God and shunning all empty ritualism. Nothing is more important than the purity of one's heart and *seva* (service), the realization of brotherhood. This finds its greatest expression at the *gurudvaras* (the major places of worship) where free food is distributed in the *langar* (public kitchens).

Ritual practices are almost non-existent. Sikhs gather in communities open to anyone and exist in a relationship of total equality. They meet at the *gurudvara* in the mornings for ablutions and the recital of special hymns, and in the evening for chanting, prayers and communal eating to cement their relationships with other believers and God.

G - The Akhal Takht in front of the Golden Temple was built in 1609 and remodelled several times. It is the place where the high exponents of Sikhism meet and where the "Adi Granth" is guarded in certain hours of the day.

to the peak of their power in Punjab in the 18th-19th centuries.

Inspired by Islamic dogma, such as monotheism and aniconism, and by Hindu beliefs, like the law of the *karman* and the path to liberation from the cycle of rebirths, Nanak elaborated a mystical theology in which God is both transcendent and immanent, endowed with infinite attributes and completely free of qualifications, without form of any kind and with the triple role of creator, preserver and destroyer. God is the First Cause that contains matter and all its potential, to him are given the epithets "He that is" and "He whose name is Truth." With this, Nanak wanted to emphasize that God is the only perfect Being and the only personification of the Truth. All phenomena is drawn from him and is periodically reabsorbed by him in the infinite cosmic cycle of evolution and involution of the universe.

Although the Sikh God is never

GLOSSARY

ABHAYAMUDRA: "gesture without fear;" a position of the hands indicating "do not fear, approach with trust."

ADHISTHANA: plinth, base, platform.

AGNIKULA: "family of the fire," a lineage to which four Rajput dynasties belonged.

AHAVANIYA: sacrificial fire of the east.

ALAMKARA: decoration.

ALASAKANYA: "reclining girl;" an erotic female figure used in temple decoration.

AMALAKA: a type of segmented cushion like a myrobalan fruit crowning the ogival structure over the *inner sanctum* of north Indian temples.

AMLA: see *amalaka*.

AMRITA: nectar of immortality, symbol of consciousness.

ANDA: central body of a domed *stupa*.

ANGASHIKHARA: a small *shikhara* built around the central one.

ANTARALA: hall between the *mandapa* and the temple sanctum.

APADANA: hypostyle reception room used by Persian kings.

APSARAS: heavenly nymph.

ARASA: type of marble from Gujarat.

ARDHAMANDAPA: hypostyle entrance porch to the temple.

ARHAT: "venerable saint;" Buddhist monk who has achieved detachment.

ASURA: demon, force from the darkness.

AVATARA: descent of the Divinity to earth in animal or human form.

BANGALDAR: Bengalese roof with arched overhangs.

BANYA: merchants.

BAOLI: underground constructions with several floors used as a rest place in Gujarat.

BARA DEUL: "large temple;" term that refers to the sanctuary.

BARA: part of the temple in Orissa that corresponds to the walls.

BARADARI: pavilion with twelve openings.

BEKI: small neck of a column on which the *amalaka* rests.

BHADRA DEUL: "auspicious temple" or a *mandapa* or *jagamohana* in temples in Orissa.

BHOGAMANDAPA: "hall of offerings."

BHUMI: floor of the *rekha*.

BHUMIJA: type of *shikhara*.

BINDU: point or instant from which All originates.

BODHI: enlightenment.

BODHISATTVA: highly venerated Buddhist figure who foregoes enjoyment of *nirvana* and remains in the world to help suffering mankind achieve liberation.

BRAHMAN: member of the highest Hindu caste, the priest caste.

CHAITYA: place of worship, usually Buddhist, constructed with apsidal naves.

CHAM: buddhist ritual dances.

CHANDRASHILA: half-moon step on the threshold of an inner sanctum.

CHAR BAGH: Islamic garden divided in four parts.

CHATTRAVALI: end pillar of a *stupa* that supports one or more parasols.

CHATTRI: kiosk supported by columns.

CHATURMUKHA: temple with inner sanctum open on four sides.

CHORTEN: "receptacle of offerings;" a particular form of *stupa* in Ladakh.

DAKINIS: female figures in the Tantric Buddhist pantheon, ascetics endowed with initiatory powers.

DAKSHINAGNI: sacrificial fire of the south.

DARBAR: room where the king held court.

DARGAH: tomb of a Moslem holy man.

DARSHANA: vision of the Holy and, by extension, a philosophical system.

DAULAT KHANA: "abode of the king;" the ruler's apartments.

DEUL: temple in Orissa.

DEVA: force from the light, deity.

DEVADASI: "handmaiden of the god;" or sacred dancing girl.

DHARMA: cosmic order in the Hindu world that governs the phenomena in the universe and the moral law that inspires mankind; in the Buddhist world, the doctrine preached by the Buddha.

DHARMACHAKRAMUDRA: "gesture of the Dharma wheel;" a position of the hands that relates to the first of the Buddha's noble truths.

DHARMAPALA: buddhist divinities, guardian of the faith.

DHYANIBUDDHA: the five figures of Buddha used for purposes of meditation.

DIGAMBARA: "clothes of heaven;" Jain ascetic who wears no clothes.

DIKPALA: guardian deity of the eight regions of the universe.

DIWAN-I-AM: pavilion used for public audiences.

DIWAN-I-KHAS: pavilion used for private audiences.

DIWAN: hypostyle pavilion in Indo-Islamic palaces.

DO CHALA: Bengalese temple with a twin structure.

DOLA: swing.

DRAVIDA: architectural style from south India.

DVAJASTAMBHA: temple flagpole.

DVARAPALA: armed figure that guards entrances of temples.

FANSIGHAR: labyrinthine set of underground rooms in Mogul palaces.

GANA: pot-bellied genie in Shiva's retinue.

GANDHARVA: genie of the air and attendant of the gods.

GANDI: part of a temple in Orissa corresponding to the roof.

GARBHAGRIHA: "room of the embryo;" womb, inner sanctum of the temple.

GARBHAMUDA: inner sanctum in temples in Orissa.

GARHAPATYA: sacrificial fire of the west.

GAYATRI: *mantra* in honor of Surya, the sun god.

GHANTA: bell-shaped decorative element.

GHAZI: soldier of the Islamic faith.

GÖNPA: Buddhist monastery in Ladakh.

GOPI: shepherd girl companion for games and love with the god Krishna.

GOPURA: massive structure over the entrances in temple enclosure walls in south India.

GUDHA: cover over a *mandapa*.

GUNA: three qualities that make up the operating methods of the *prakriti*: *sattva*, the creator of what is stable, luminous, pure and joyous; *rajas*, the cause of what is dynamic, passionate or sorrowful; *tamas*, the root of what is inert, slow or dim.

GURU: spiritual master.

GURUDVARA: Sikh place of worship.

HAMMAM: bath.

HARAM SARAY: part of a Moslem palace reserved for women.

HAREM: part of a Moslem palace reserved for women.

HARMIKA: square balustrade on the top of a *stupa* from which the pillar with parasols emerges.

HAVELI: mansions of Rajasthan.

HERUKA: category of terrifying deities in Tantric Buddhism or Vajrayana.

HINDOLA: swing.

IWAN: monumental facade with entrance framed by an arch.

JAGAMOHANA: the *mandapa* in the temples in Orissa.

JALI: fretted screen.

JAUHAR: voluntary immolation of *rajput* women so as not to fall prisoners to the Moslems.

JIVA: souls.

KALASHA: water vase on top of Hindu temples.

KALPAVALLI: mythical climbing plant that grants all wishes.

KANYA: "divine girl;" ornamental seductive figure.

KARMAN: deed, cause and effect of action that links beings to *samsara*, the return to existence.

KARUNA: "compassion;" cardinal Buddhist virtue.

KHAKHARA: oblong cover of temples in Orissa that looks like half a coconut.

KHAPURI: spherical cover that supports the *kalasha*.

KINNARA: part-animal, heavenly musician.

KONA: corner.

KUDU: small, horseshoe arches.

KUMBHA: element in the shape of a vase - see *kalasha*.

LAMA: "venerable master" of the ladakhi buddhism.

LATA: climbing plant, liana, vine.

LATINA: type of *shikhara*.

LILA: inscrutable game of the gods of emanation and reabsorption of the universe.

LINGA: phallic stone symbolising the god Shiva.

LINGAYONI: union of *linga* and *yoni*, symbol of Unity as shown by male and female, god and goddess.

LOKAPALA: see *dikpala*.

MADRASA: school for teaching the Koran, annexed to a mosque.

MAHAL: palace.

MAHAMANDAPA: large *mandapa*.

MAHARAJA: "great king."

MAHARANA: "great king."

MAHARAVAL: "great king."

MAHARI: holy dancer at Orissa.

MAITHUNA: ritual sexual union.

MAKARA: mythical aquatic monster.

MANDALA: symbolic design reflecting the ordering of the psyche and cosmos.

MANDAPA: hypostyle room or pavilion.

MANDIR: temple and palace.

MANDUKA: plan of a temple based on 4 squares divided into a 64 cell grid.

MANI: "jewel;" in Ladakh the term is used to define walls made of stone that have *mantra* engraved in them.

MANTRA: holy formula.

MAQBARAH: Islamic mausoleum.

MARDANA: palace area reserved for men.

MARMAN: vital point of a construction that is not incorporated in the walls.

MARVARI: subcaste of merchants in Rajasthan.

MASJID: mosque.

MASTAKA: apex of temples in Orissa.

MEDHI: base of a *stupa*.

MIHRAB: niche in the prayer hall that indicates the direction of Mecca.

MINBAR: sort of pulpit the Koran is read from in the prayer hall of a mosque.

MITHUNA: a pair of lovers depicted on temple walls as a sign of fertility and good auspices.

MUDRA: gesture of the hands that refers to the salient moments of spiritual experience.

MUEZZIN: the man who makes the call to prayer from the minaret of a mosque.

MUKHAMANDAPA: inner sanctum open on the sides of the four compass points.

MUKHASHALA: see *jagamohana*.

MUQARNAS: decorative weft that creates a honeycomb effect on Islamic constructions.

MURTI: image of the deity enclosed in the inner sanctum of a temple.

NAGA: part-human, part-snake figure connected with water, fertility and awareness.

NAGARA: architectural style in north India.

NAGINI: companion of the *naga*.

NAKSHATRA: the 28 lunar houses.

NATAMANDIR: "dance hall."

NAUBAT KHANA: "building of the drum."

NAVARATNA: "nine jewels."

NAWAB: honorary Moslem title.

NIGODA: vegetable micro-organism.

NIRVANA: ineffable state of extinction of the continuous and sorrowful return to existence.

PACHISI: game with chessboard and pawns.

PAGA: projection of the temple also called *raha*.

PAIRI DAEZA: "place enclosed by a wall;" Persian paradise.

PANCHARATHA: temple with "five projecting elements."

PANCHAYATANA: temple with "five structures," one central structure and one at each of the four corners.

PARAMASHAYIN: ground plan of a temple based on 9 squares and divided into a grid of 81 cells.

PATTIKA: drum that links the *shikhara* and the *amalaka*

PIPAL: *Ficus religiosa*, sacred tree.

PIRHA DEUL: part of the temple of Orissa that includes the *jagamohana*.

PIRHA: pyramidal sheets over the *jagamohana*.

POL: entrance gates to the *rajput* and *moghul* cities.

PRADAKSHINA: ritual walking (deambulation) round the object of worship in a clockwise direction.

PRAJNA: perfect intuitive wisdom, deified as a goddess.

PRAKRITI: Natural, eternal primordial energy; non-spiritual, unconscious and dynamic energy from which the universe evolves.

PRANA: vital breath that animates the micro and macrocosms.

PRASADA: multi-floor construction; either the main structure of a temple or of a palace.

PUR: citadel/city.

PURUSHA: a cosmic giant that was sacrificed to generate the universe in the earliest period; later, and above all in the Samkhya philosophical school, an eternal, spiritual, conscious and static entity.

QIBLA: direction of Mecca; in India Mecca is to the west.

QILA: fortress.

QUBBA: cubic structure topped by a cupola.

RAGA: musical tone.

RAHA: central *paga* that becomes sizeable on the *shikhara* and often decorated with niches housing statues.

RAJA: ruler.

RAJABHAVANA: royal building, public part of the palace.

RAJANIVESHANA: royal residence, private part of the palace.

RAJAPUTRA: son of the king, Rajput.

RAJAS: see *guna*.

RANA: ruler.

RASA: quintessence of aesthetic emotion.

RASALILA: Krishna's dance with the *gopi*.

RATHA: wooden processional carriage that carries images of the gods when they are taken outside the temple.

RATNAMUDA: series of empty rooms with flat roofs whose purpose is to carry the weight of the *rekha*.

RAUZA: set of funerary buildings composed of a mosque and mausoleum, mostly in Gujarat.

RAVAL: ruler.

REKHA: the inner sanctum and the structure over it in Orissa – also *rekha deul*.

SABHAMANDAPA: open "assembly" pavilion.

SAMSARA: return to existence in different guises based on the sum of overall behavior in the previous life.

SAMVARANA: particular covering of the *mandapa* with bell-shaped elements on top of a pyramid.

SANGHA: monastic community.

SANGHARAMA: place that accommodates monks, see *vihara*.

SATI: "virtuous" bride that follows the husband in the fire.

SATTVA: see *guna*.

SAVITRI: *mantra* in honor of Surya, the sun god, also called *gayatri*.

SEKHARI: type of *shikhara*.

SERDAB: underground rooms in palaces for the hot season.

SEVA: brotherly service amongst Sikhs.

SHAKTI: female energy of deity, the Great Goddess.

SHALABHANJIKA: tree nymph.

SHARDULA: gryphon.

SHASTRA: traditional texts.

SHIKHARA: ogival structure over the inner sanctum in north Indian temples.

SHISH: mirror, glass.

SHUKANASA: projection jutting out of the *shikhara* towards the roof of the *mandapa*.

SHUNYA: empty.

SHUNYATA: emptiness.

SHVETAMBARA: "clothes of white;" Jain ascetic.

SIDDHA: "perfect souls;" freed.

SIKH: "disciple;" name of a religious congregation.

SPANDA: primordial vibration of the One that determines the emanation and expansion of the universe.

STHAPATI: "head of the workforce;" almost always a *Brahman*

STUPA: bell-shaped reliquary derived from tumuli erected on the cremation ashes of the Buddha, later a cosmic symbol.

SUFI: Islamic ascetics.

SURASUNDARI: divine girls, experts at love-making.

SVASTIKA: "swastika;" symbol of the expansion of the First Principle in time and space.

TALA: unit of measurement for statues.

TALAR: hypostyle room with throne wall.

TAMAS: see *guna*.

TANDAVA: Shiva's dance of cosmic dissolution.

TANKA: Buddhist painting on cloth popular in Ladakh.

TELI: caste of oil sellers.

TIRTHANKARA: "ford makers;" the 24 prophets that preached the Jain doctrine.

TORANA: access portal to enclosure of the *stupa*.

TRIBHANGA: triple 'S' curve of a figure.

TRIMURTI: "three part form" that the deity assumes as creator, conserver and destroyer of the cosmos in the figures of Brahma, Vishnu and Shiva.

TRIRATNA: "three part jewel;" the Buddha, his doctrine and the community of monks.

TUK: walls of Jain temples.

UPAYA: the right "means;" i.e. compassion, that permits *prajna* to be attained.

URUSHRINGA: small *shikhara*.

USTAD: "master;" honorary Persian term.

VAHANA: vehicles and mounts of the gods.

VAISHYA: third caste in the hierarchic-sacred Hindu system, merchants.

VAJRA: diamond sceper, symbol of the immutable consciousness of the truth.

VASTUPURUSHA: giant of existence, ideal archetype of construction.

VASTUPURUSHAMANDALA: square grid that forms the ground plan of a temple.

VASTUVIDYA: "science of architecture."

VEDIKA: enclosure of holy buildings.

VESARA: mixed architectural style.

VIHARA: monastery.

VYALA: gryphon.

YAB-YUM: "Father and Mother," divine couple embracing that symbolizes primigenial Unity in Vajrayana Buddhism.

YAKSHA: pot-bellied genie of the trees.

YAKSHI or *YAKSHINI:* dryad.

YOGINI: ascetic expert in the practice of yoga.

YONI: matrix and symbol of the Great Goddess.

ZANANA: part of the palace reserved for women.

ZIGGURAT: Persian stepped pyramid.

INTRODUCTORY BIBLIOGRAPHY

Abbate: *Arte Indiana,* Milan 1966

Agrawala V.: *Gupta Art,* Varanasi 1977, ed. Prithivi Prakashan

Anand M.R.: *The Hindu View of Art,* London 1933, ed. George Allen & Unwin

Basham A.L.: *The Wonder that was India,* London 1956

Berinstain V.: *L'India dei Moghul: i fasti di un impero,* Trieste 1997, ed. Electa Gallimard

Brown P.: *Indian Architecture,* Bombay 1956, ed. Taraporevala, 2 vol.

Brunel F.: *The Splendour of Indian Miniatures,* Boulogne, Clarion Books

Burkhardt T.: *L'arte sacra in oriente e occidente,* Milan 1990, ed. Rusconi

Bussagli M.: *La miniatura indiana,* Milan 1966, ed. Fabbri

Bussagli M.: *Architettura orientale,* Milan 1981, ed. Electa

Chakrabarti J.: *Techniques in Indian Mural Painting,* Calcutta1980, ed. Bagchi & Company

Chakravarty K.K.: *Orchha,* Bhopal 1984, ed. Arnold Heinemann

Christopher Tadgell: *The History of Architecture in India,* Hong Kong 1990, ed. Viking

Coomaraswamy A.: *Introduzione all'arte e alla mitologia dell'India,* Milan 1984, ed. La Salamandra

Coomaraswamy A.: *La trasfigurazione della natura nell'arte,* Milan 1976, ed. Rusconi

Das Gupta S.N.: *L'intimo aspetto dell'arte indiana,* Rome 1940, ed. Is.M.E.O.

Debala Mitra: *Udayagiri & Khandagiri,* Archaeological Survey of India, New Delhi 1975

Debala Mitra: *Sanchi,* Archaeological Survey of India, New Delhi 1978

Debala Mitra: *Ajanta,* Archaeological Survey of India, New Delhi 1983

Debala Mitra: *Konarak,* Archaeological Survey of India, New Delhi 1986

Delahoutre M.: *Lo spirito dell'arte indiana,* Milan 1994, ed. Jaka Book

De Mallmann M.T.: *Introduction à l'iconographie du Tantrisme Bouddhique,* Paris 1975, ed. Adrienne Maisonneuve

Deva Krishna: *Temples of India,* New Delhi 1975, ed. Motilal Banarsidass, 2 vol.

Diez E.: *L'Inde* in "La civilization de l'Indus," Paris, Petite Bibliothèque Payot

Goetz H.: *India, cinquemila anni di civiltà indiana,* Milan 1959, ed. Saggiatore

Goetz H.: *L'arte dell'India musulmana e correnti moderne* in "Le Civiltà dell'oriente" vol. IV, Rome 1962, ed. Casini

Hajek L.-Forman W.B.: *Miniature indiane,* Rome 1961, Editori Riuniti

Hallade M.: *L'arte dell'India e di Ceylon* in "Le Civiltà dell'oriente" vol. IV, Rome 1962, ed. Casini

Iyer B.: *Arte indiana,* Milan 1964, ed. Mondadori

Kramrisch S.: *The Hindu temple,* Delhi 1946,1980, Motilal Banarsidass, 2 vol.

Kramrisch S.: *L'arte indiana,* Florence 1967, ed. Sansoni

Mackenzie S.P.M. e Taeda M.: *Ajanta. I monasteri rupestri dell'India,* Milan 1982, ed. Arnoldo Mondadori

Manucci N.: *Usi e costumi dell'India dalla "Storia del Mogol" di Nicolò Manucci Veneziano,* Milan 1964

Miceli: *India Antica,* Milan

Michell G.: *The Hindu Temple. An Introduction to its Meaning and Forms,* London 1977, ed. Elek

Mishra L.P.: *Agra e Fatehpur Sikri* in "Documenti d'arte," Novara 1982, ed. De Agostini

Mookerjee A.: *L'arte rituale in India,* Milan 1986, ed. Garzanti

Munsterberg H.: *L'arte indiana,* Milan 1970, ed. Rizzoli

Omodeo Salè M.: *Breve storia dell'arte indiana,* Florence, ed. Giunti/Martello

Patil D.R.: *Mandu,* Archaeological Survey of India, New Delhi 1982

Rawson P.: *La pittura indiana,* Milan 1964, ed. Electa

Rowland B.: *The Art and Architecture of India,* Bungay, Suffolk 1953, ed. Penguin Books

Sivaramamurti C.: *India Ceylon Nepal Tibet,* Torino 1988, ed. Utet

Sivaramamurti C.: *The Art of India,* Paris 1974, ed. Mazenod

Taddei M.: *India antica,* Milan 1972, ed. Mondadori

Taddei M.: *India* in "Archaeologia Mundi, Enciclopedia Archeologica," Geneve 1976, ed. Nagel

Tillotson G.H.R.: *The Rajput Palace,* New Haven and London 1987

Varenne J.: *L'art de l'Inde,* Paris 1983, ed. Flammarion

Volwahsen A.: *Architettura indiana,* Milan 1968, ed. Parnaso

PHOTO CREDITS

*All the photos in this book are by **Massimo Borchi/Archivio White Star**, except for the following:*
Marcello Bertinetti/Archivio White Star: pages 10 A, 16, 17, 20 B, 24 A, 26 A, D, 27 F, 29 G, 38, 39, 56, 58, 65 E, 66 A, 67 G, 69 F, 80 C, 87 D, 94 D, 95 G; J. Allan Cash Ltd: pages 102 D, 114 B, D, E, F, G, 136 B, 138 A, 141 H, 146 A; B.A. Acharya/Dinodia Picture Agency: page 151 J; Tiziana and Gianni Baldizzone/Archivio White Star: pages 20 A, 131 H, I, 132 A, C, D, E, 133; Tiziana and Gianni Baldizzone: page 132 B; Diane Barker/Tibet Images: pages 98 C, 99 H; Benelux Press B.V.: page 138 B; Bildarchiv Hans Huber/Sime: page 140 B; Christophe Boisivieux: pages 74 C, 84 A, 85 C, E, 86 B, 87 C, 88 A, B, C, 90 A, D, E, F, 91 I, 92 A, F, 93 G, 95 E, 96 A, B, C, D, 97 F, G, H, 98 B, 100 C, 101 G, 108 B, 109 G, 114 A, 128 A, B, 129 D, E, 130 A, C, 131 E, F, 134 C, 136 C, D, 137 J, 143 E, F, 144 A, B, D, 151 H, 160 A, B, C, E; Massimo Borchi/Atlantide: pages 130 B, D, 131 G, 134 A, B, D, 135, 137 G, H, 138 C, 139, 141 K, 142 A, B, 144 C, E; Ian Cumming/Tibet Images: pages 84 B, 88 D, 90 B, C, 92 C, 97 I, 99 E, F, G, 168; Damm/Zefa: page 141 D; Viren Desai/Dinodia Picture Agency: pages 74 A, 151 G, I; Michel Dortes: pages 103 G, 107 G, 108 D, 137 F; Patrick Frilet/Hemispheres: pages 92 B, 95 F, 97 E; Index: pages 121 H, 122 B, C, 123 G; N.M. Jain/Dinodia Picture Agency: page 106 D; Roderick Johnson/Images of India: page 125 I; Earl Kowall: pages 85 D, 92 E, 93 H, I, 94 A, B, 95 H, 129 C, 137 E, K; M.M.N./Dinodia Picture Agency: page 120 C; Marco Mairani: pages 86 A, 91 J; Zefa/Marka: page 142 D; Roland Michaud/Rapho: page 136 A; C. Milind/A. Ketkap/Dinodia Picture Agency: pages 108 E, 160 D; Colin Monteath/Hedgehog House: page 98 A; Ernesto Noriega/Tibet Images: page 87 C, 94 C; Flavio Pagani: pages 108 A, 109 K, 120 D, 123 E, 124 E; Alain Petit/Agence Top: page 141 I; Luca Rinaldini: pages 89 F, 99 D; Gianluigi Sosio: page 119 G; Henri et Annie Stierlin: pages 109 I, J, 121 I, 122 A, 123 D, F, 124 B, D, 126 B, 127 C, D, 141 G, J; Stockshooter/Marka: page 142 C; Nick Tapsell/Ffotograff: page 89 E; N.C. Turner/Ffotograff: pages 89 G, 91 H, 92 D, 97 J, 101 F; Nico Tondini/Focus Team: page 141F; Alberto Zabert/Realy Easy Star: pages 137 I, 140 A.

Cover
*Northern gateway of
the great stupa of
Sanchi, Madhya
Pradesh.*
Photograph by
Marcello Bertinetti/
Archivio White Star

Back cover
*top left Govinda
Mahal at Datia,
about 25 miles from
Orchha.*
Photograph by
Massimo Borchi/
Archivio White Star

*top right The
courtyard of the daulat
khana at Fatehpur Sikri
with the Anup Talab
pool and the main
buildings arranged
around its sides.*
Photograph by
Massimo Borchi/ Archivio
White Star

*bottom Hypothetical
reconstruction of the
Temple of the Sun,
Modhera, Gujarat.*
Drawing by
Roberta Vigone/ Archivio
White Star

168 *This Maitreya,
Buddha of the future,
is at Tikse monastery,
Ladakh.*